IMAGES
of America
CLAYTON

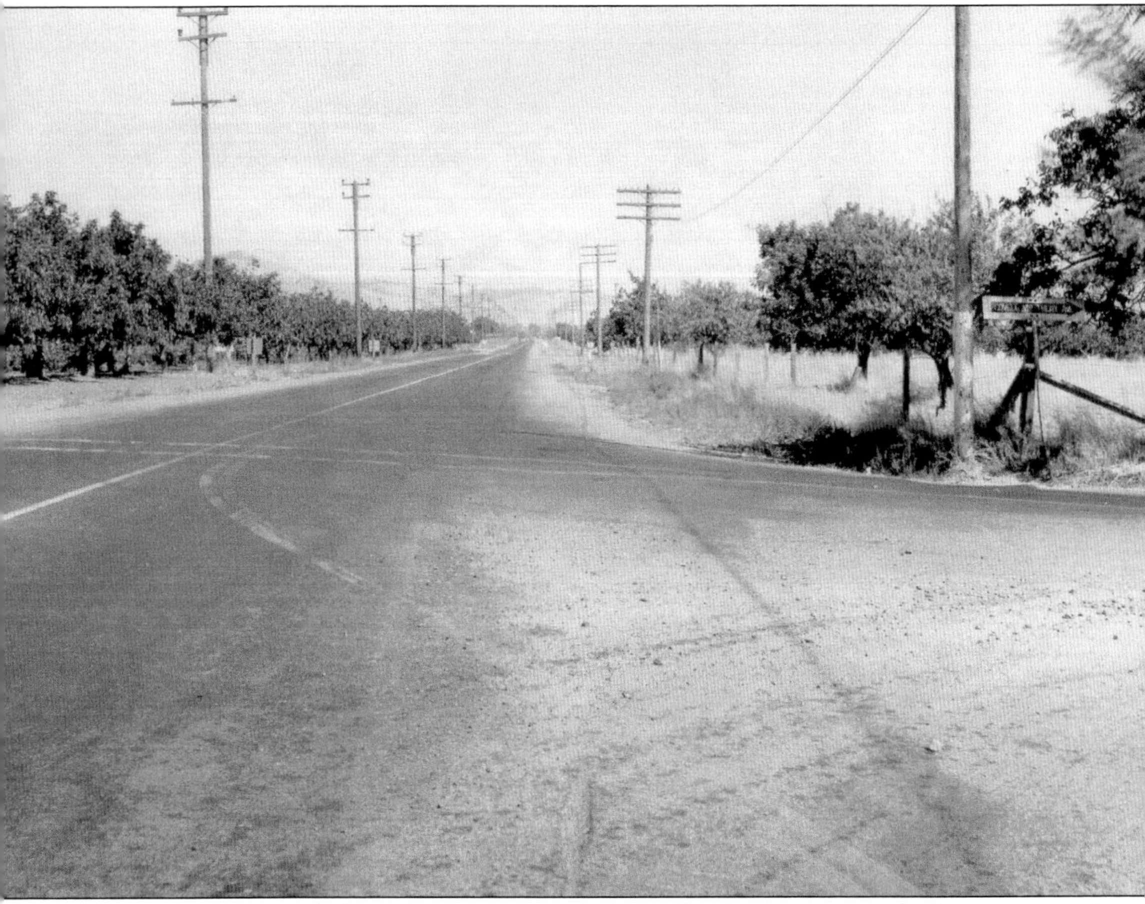

This 1940 photograph shows the intersection of Clayton Road and Treat Lane, looking east toward Clayton. At that time, there were orchards on both sides. Chances were that people recognized whomever they encountered on the road during the era.

ON THE COVER: This photograph, taken before 1900, shows the front of Jacob "Jake" Rhine's Hotel and Saloon on Main Street.

IMAGES
of America

CLAYTON

Clayton Historical Society

ARCADIA
PUBLISHING

ISBN 978-0-7385-3093-2

Published by Arcadia Publishing
Charleston, South Carolina

Printed in the United States of America

Library of Congress Catalog Card Number: 2005934846

For all general information contact Arcadia Publishing at:
Telephone 843-853-2070
Fax 843-853-0044
E-mail sales@arcadiapublishing.com
For customer service and orders:
Toll-Free 1-888-313-2665

Visit us on the Internet at www.arcadiapublishing.com

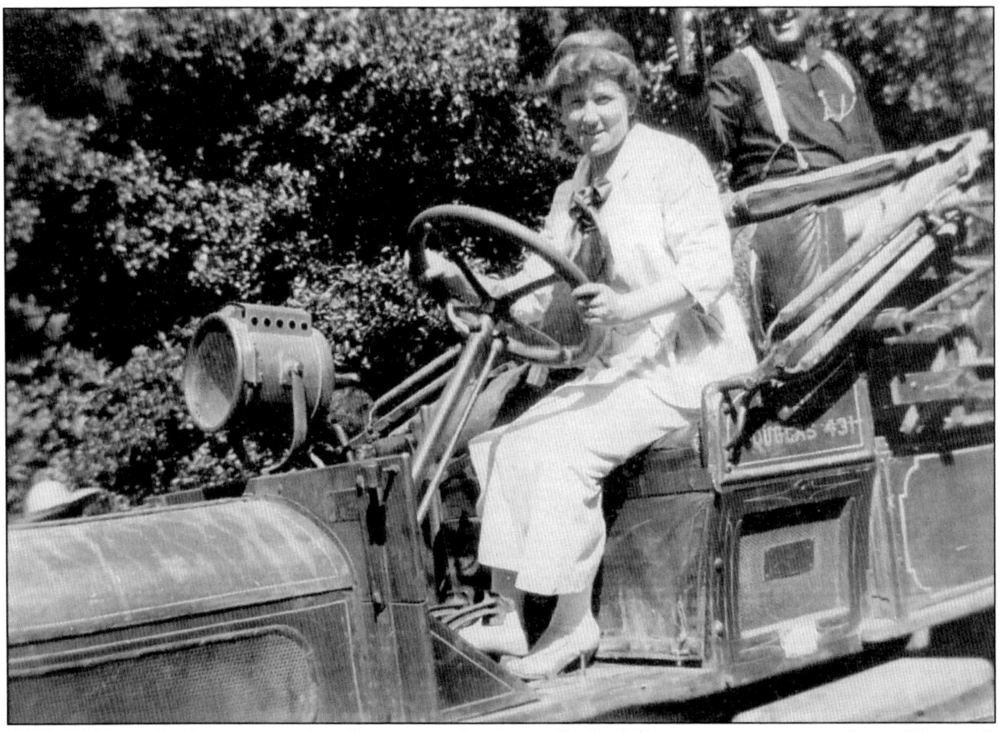

Hilda Rhine Atchinson, wife of stagecoach driver Jack Atchinson, is pictured in Clayton's first Ford automobile.

Contents

Acknowledgments 6

Introduction 7

1. Downtown 9
2. Community Activities 43
3. Agriculture and the Countryside 59
4. Everyday Life 77
5. Characters and Oddities 119

ACKNOWLEDGMENTS

The publication committee for this book included Janet Easton, a fifth-generation resident of Clayton; Richard Ellis, president of the Clayton Historical Society; and Mary Spryer, curator of the Clayton Historical Museum. The historical information was provided by materials in the museum and by speaking with members of old Clayton families.

This book would not have been possible without the photographs and information gathered from others, including the Contra Costa County History Center in Martinez, the Martinez Historical Society, Mary Viera Delamater, Tery McCade, Iola O'Grady, Earl Duncan, Enroy Gomez, Norma Bloching Dempsey, Carmen Frank, Charmetta Mann, Melvin Gomez, Jane Olsson Stockfleth, Willmetta Frank Mann, Harold Russell, Tony Galvin, Paul Larson, Mildred Mendivil, Sally Turner, and others.

We welcome any corrections, additions, or additional information. The address of the Clayton Historical Society is P.O. Box 94, Clayton, CA, 94517. The telephone number is (925) 672-0240. Our Internet address is www.claytonhs.com.

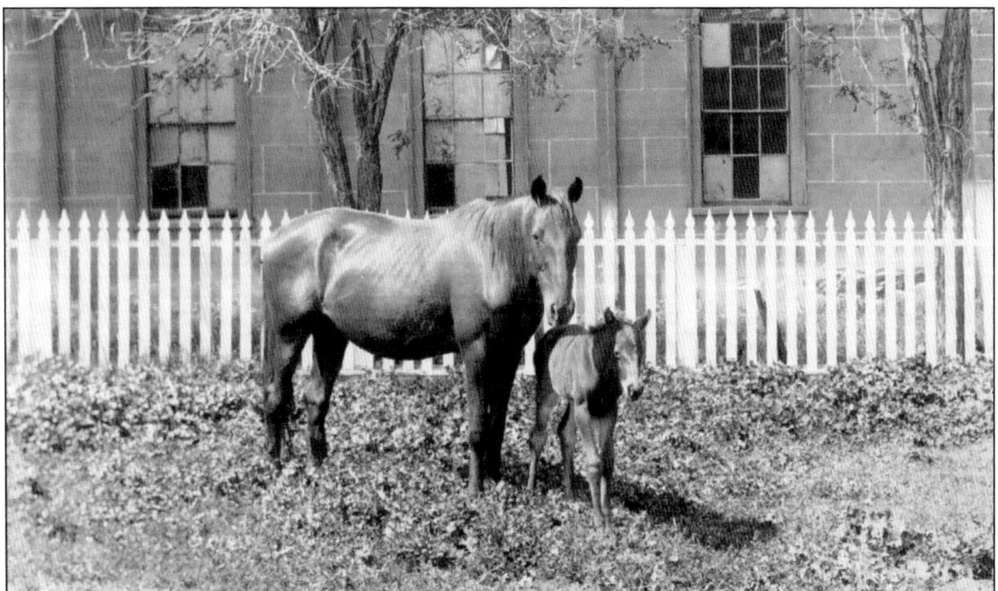

Livestock downtown was common. These horses are in a field next to the congregational church. Dairy cows were also kept on a lot on Center Street.

INTRODUCTION

The eldest of 11 children, Joel Clayton left the mining town of Bugsworth (now spelled Buxworth), England, in 1837 when he was 25 years old. He came to America to work for his uncle Peter Bate in Pittsburgh, Pennsylvania.

In 1840, Clayton's parents and several of his siblings joined him in the United States. He met and married Margaret Ellen McLay, a native of Scotland, in 1841 in Wisconsin.

In 1845, Joel and Margaret Clayton owned a general store and tavern in Wisconsin. In 1848, he purchased land along the Pecatonica River, and he owned a water powered flour and gristmill called Mifflin Mill. He laid out a town map there and proceeded to become the chairman of Mifflin Township and its first postmaster.

Obviously not one to stay in a place for too long, Joel Clayton became associated with the Hudson Bay Company, which had control over much of the Northwest Territory. Leaving wife, Margaret, in Wisconsin, Joel was the wagon master on several trips to the west coast of America. Joel moved permanently to California in 1850 to engage in mining and ranching.

Margaret McLay Clayton eventually followed her husband to California, arriving in San Diego via the Isthmus of Panama. During their marriage, Joel and Margaret had nine children, five of whom died of childhood diseases.

In 1857, Joel Clayton mapped out the town of Clayton. A coin toss between Joel and Charles Rhine, a former Nortonville coal miner and fellow entrepreneur, decided the town's name—either Clayton or Rhinesville. Early surveyors called the Clayton area "Deadfall," perhaps in reference to the large number of fallen trees.

Joel Clayton died in 1872 of "quick pneumonia" in Nortonville after having rescued a sick calf in the rain. Margaret moved to San Francisco shortly thereafter to live with their daughter Eliza Clayton Clark. Joel and Margaret and two of their children are buried in Live Oak Cemetery near Clayton.

Charles Rhine arrived in the area around the same time as Joel Clayton. He operated a general merchandise store in the coal mining town of Nortonville just east of Clayton. After he opened his general store on Main Street in Clayton, his brother Jacob joined him. Jacob Rhine opened a hotel and saloon on Main Street. Both Charles and Jacob Rhine and their families left Clayton in the 1910s and moved to the Oakland area.

The early inhabitants of Clayton came from all over the United States and some came directly from Europe. There were coal miners from Wales and Ireland, butchers from Pennsylvania, carpenters from England and Scotland, sailors from Maine, merchants from Massachusetts, vintners from Italy and brew meisters from Germany. A saddler came from New York, a blacksmith from Kentucky, teamsters from Ohio and ranchers from Portugal. The Heden family left Sweden because of a famine. There were a few American Indians in the area when the settlers arrived, but most had gone to the missions.

An unusual number of sea captains migrated to Clayton. Among them were Captains DeWolfe, Ploog, Russelmann, Hanson, Stockfleth, and Nichols. It is suspected that one captain visited and, liking what he found, spread the word among the other mariners, who thought Clayton might be a better place to raise a family than in a waterfront city in Bay Area ports.

In the 1870s, the Frank family, of German descent, arrived in Clayton, having first lived in Michigan and Oregon. Their first two children were named after their parents, Elizabeth and Frederick Jr. They had 10 more children, all of whom were raised in Clayton. Fred Sr. was a farmer. Fred Jr. went to the Yukon gold rush in the late 1890s with his sister Elizabeth's husband, Lars Olsen, and other Clayton men, including Percy Douglas. Fred Jr. was engaged to be married to Lillien Russelmann. Upon Fred Jr.'s return from Alaska in 1900, he died from a burst appendix. With the money earned in Alaska by Fred Jr., Fred Sr. was able to buy the property he was renting near the school at the top of the hill. The Frank family was relatively poor, but all of the 12 Frank children "married up" into local families. All remained in the Clayton area except Matthew and Annie Frank Schwendel, who moved to Oregon. The offspring of Fred and Elizabeth Frank's children married into local families too. Within one or two generations, there was a standard line: "If you weren't a Frank you were related to one."

The Portuguese who came to Clayton were mostly farmers and ranchers, hard working and fun loving. The terrain and climate in the Clayton area was similar to what they left behind in Europe. Portuguese women were known as good cooks. The Nunez family bought Charles Rhine's home on Main Street and built the Eagle Saloon.

By the 1950s, many of the property owners could no longer sustain their families with the profits of their labors. Taxes were rising and the prices fetched for the crops and livestock they produced were not increasing commensurately. They were land rich and cash poor. Simultaneously the general population of the bigger Bay Area cities was expanding. People were willing to commute to the cities in exchange for a more rural environment in which to raise their families.

Developers and builders offered what were then handsome prices to farmers and ranchers. Some of the natives sold their land and moved to more affordable areas of California. Some sold a portion of their property, kept part, and were able to retire comfortably. Others kept their land but obtained other work while supplementing their incomes by farming or ranching on the side. Subdivisions sprang up, slowly at first, then rapidly.

Today Clayton is an upscale incorporated city whose politicians and residents endeavor to maintain its rustic charm. Images of America: *Clayton* covers the 100-year time span from 1857 until 1957 in the town of Clayton and parts of the Clayton Valley, Morgan Territory, and Marsh Creek.

One

Downtown

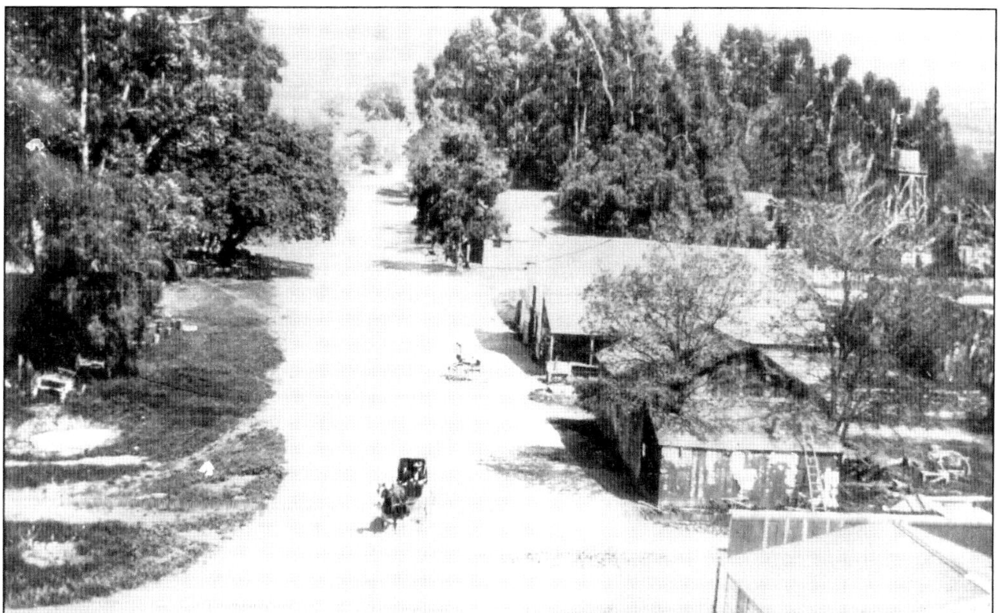

At one time, Main Street had four saloons. Businesses and some houses were also situated on Main Street. Center Street boasted churches and a slaughterhouse. The remaining areas in the downtown mapped by Joel Clayton were residential and agricultural. In 1903, when this photograph was taken, registered voters in the Clayton precinct numbered only 120.

A restored Map of Clayton (original: 20"X20") of Joel Clayton's, drawn in 1857. Joel (mining engineer, dairy farmer, trader, leader of four settlers' wagon trains to the west--the last one arriving in 1850 and founder of the town--Clayton) & Margaret owned 1400 acres. Officially mapped by County Surveyor W. K. Taylor in 1857.

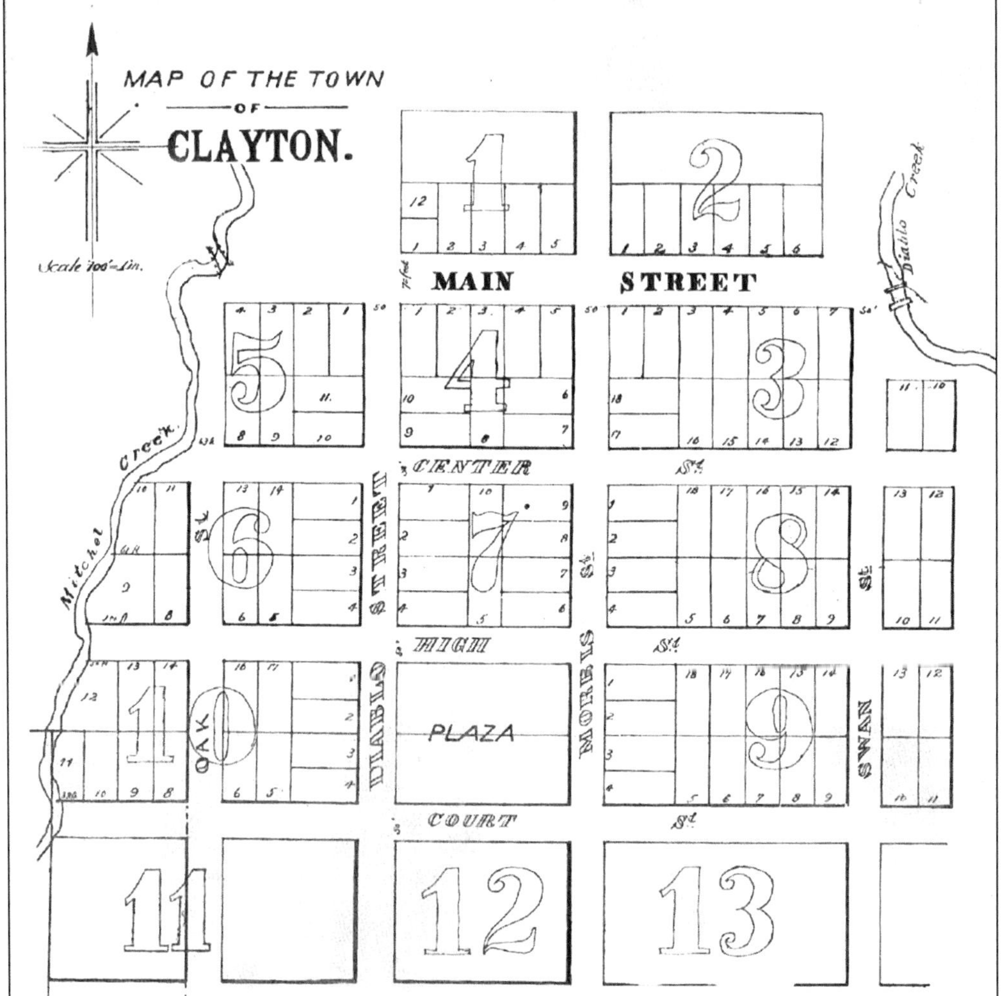

The map of Clayton's downtown was platted by Joel Clayton in 1857. What he named Swan Street in 1857 became Marsh Creek Road as it left town. The road to Nortonville started at the east end of Main Street, and Center Street was commonly called "the back street."

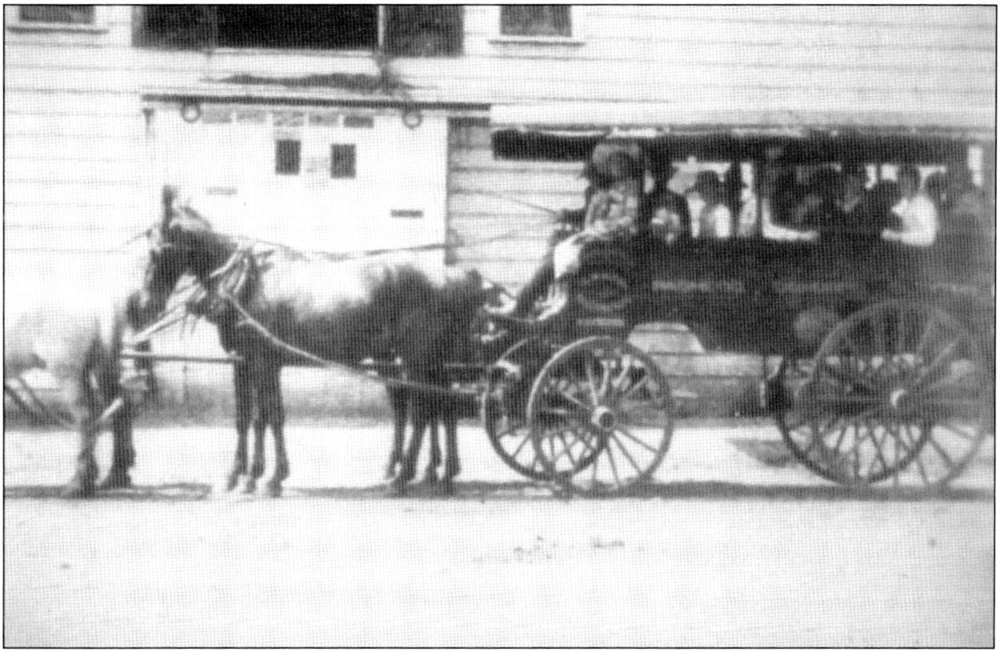

The Atchinson Stage Line, operated by brothers Jack and George, ran from 1898 until 1914 between Clayton, Martinez, Pacheco, Concord, Nortonville, Somersville, and Antioch. It carried money, mail, and passengers. One-way passenger fare was 75¢. The driver was required to carry a .45 revolver.

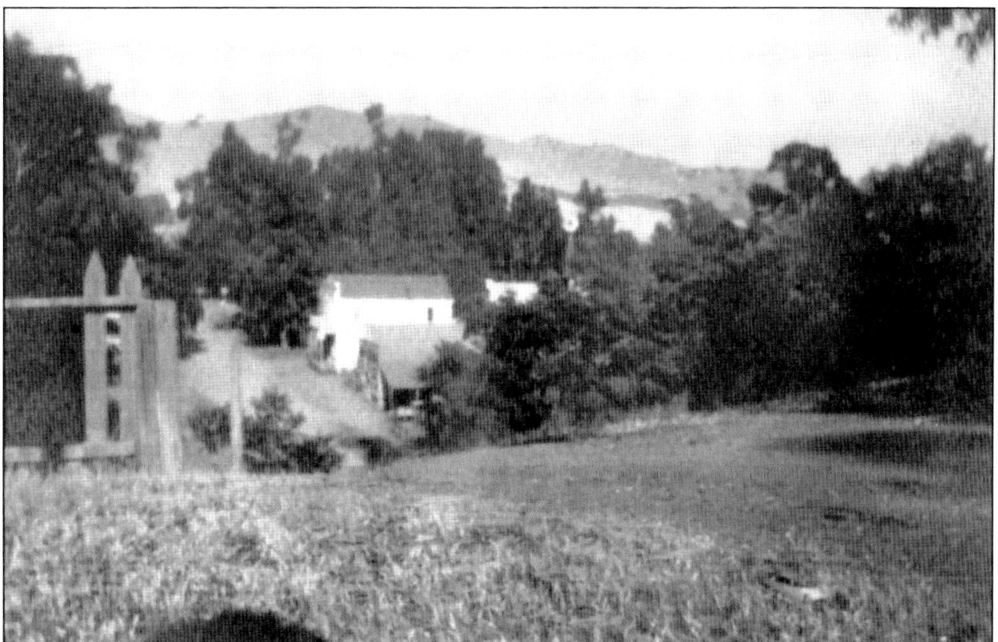

This view of Main Street was taken from the school hill and shows the store (the tall building) and the livery on the right. The wagon road pictured at the top of the hill proceeded down and entered Oak Street at High Street.

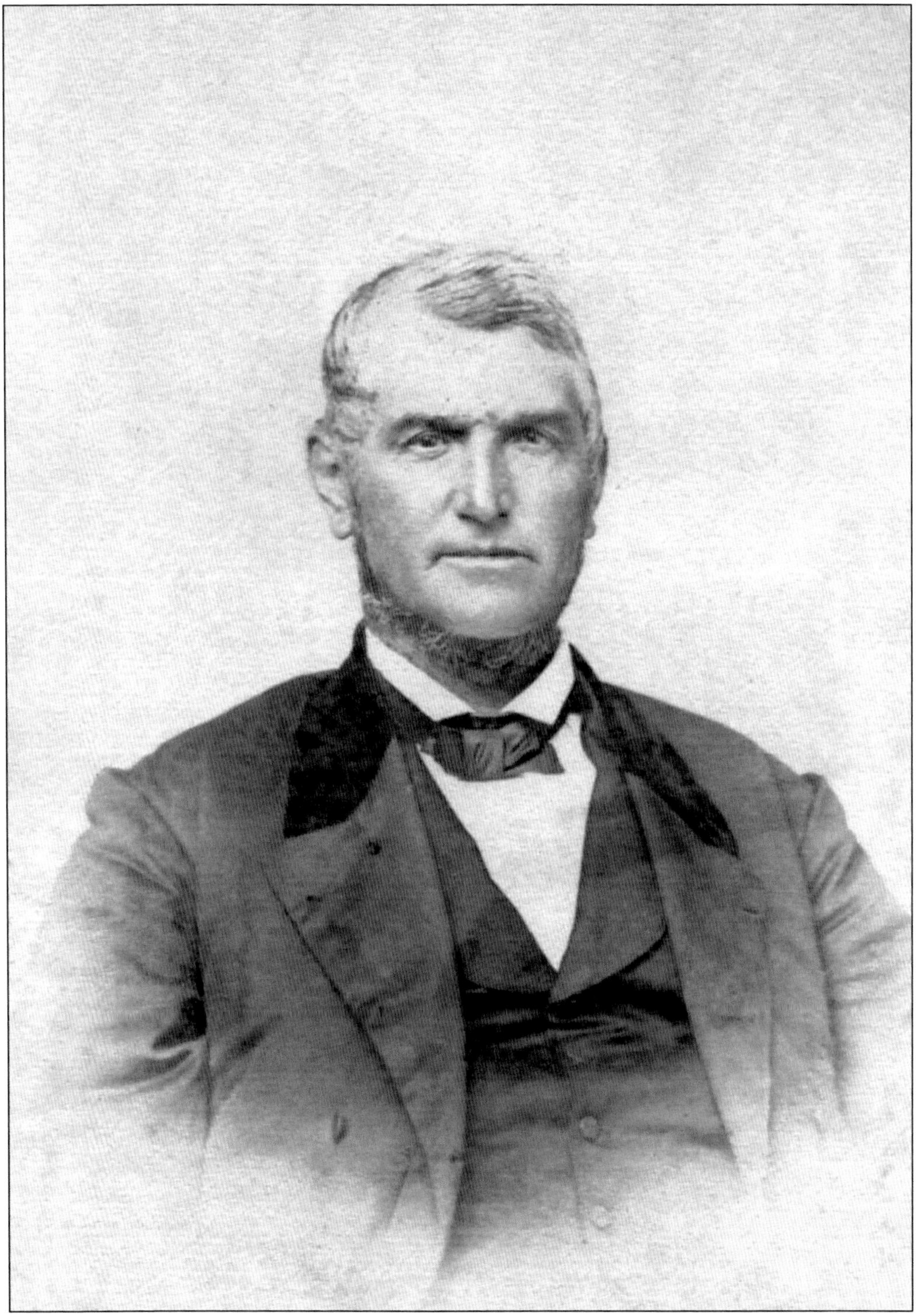

Town founder Joel Clayton was born in 1812 in Bugsworth, England. During his lifetime, he was a miner, farmer, dairyman, wagon master, and a trader. In 1872, he died in Nortonville of quick pneumonia.

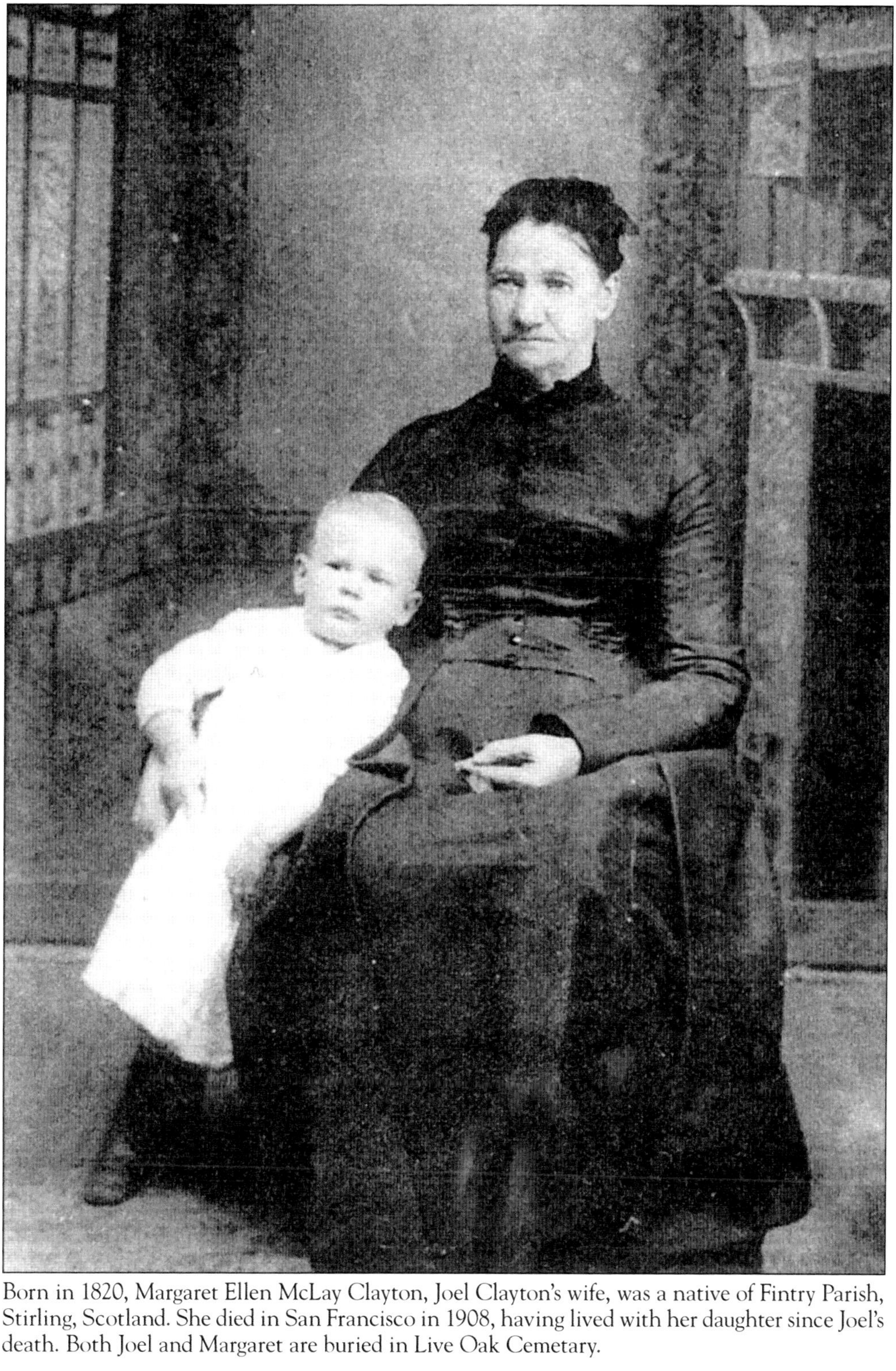

Born in 1820, Margaret Ellen McLay Clayton, Joel Clayton's wife, was a native of Fintry Parish, Stirling, Scotland. She died in San Francisco in 1908, having lived with her daughter since Joel's death. Both Joel and Margaret are buried in Live Oak Cemetary.

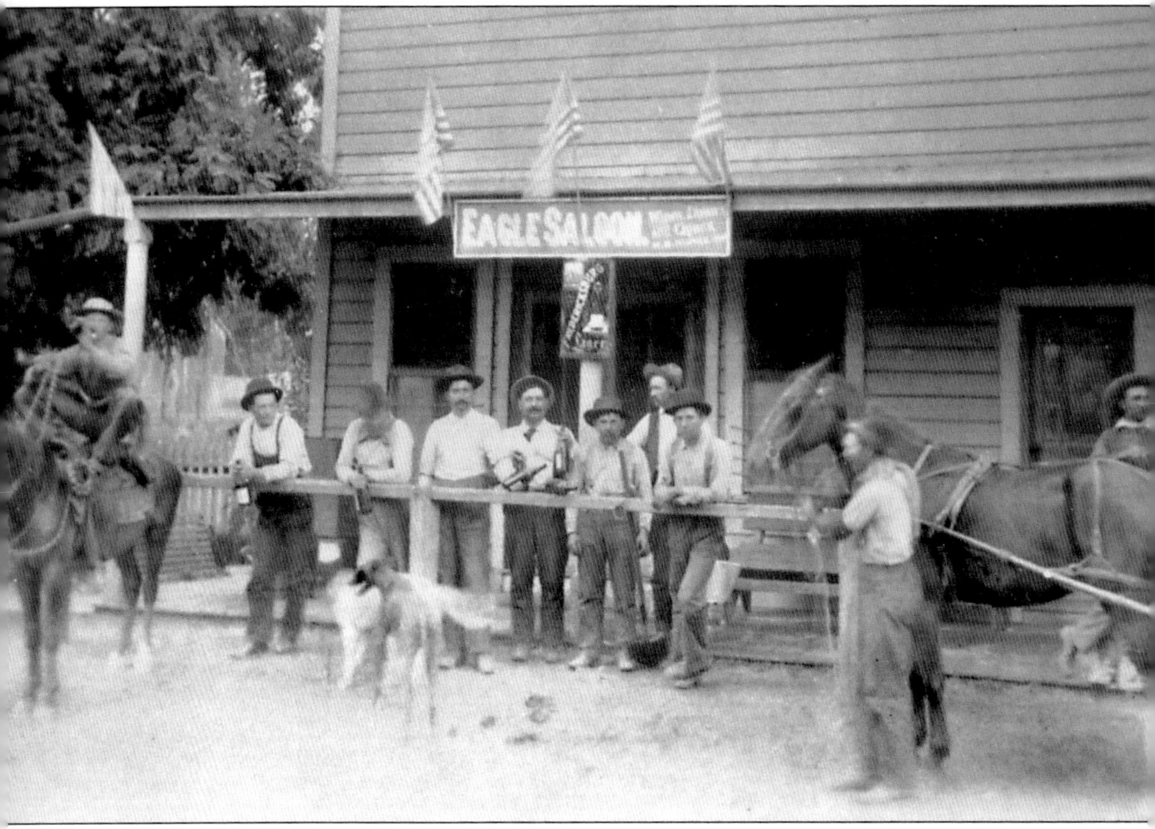

In the early 1900s, the Eagle Saloon on Main Street was owned by Manuel B. Nunez. Pictured here, from left to right, are Wylie McGrew, Matt Schwendel, unidentified, unidentified, "Cap" Mitchell, Otto Schwartz, Doug Mitchell, Billy Wilson, and unidentified. When the Nunez/Bloching home burned in the 1920s, the family took up residence in the saloon while the new house was being built.

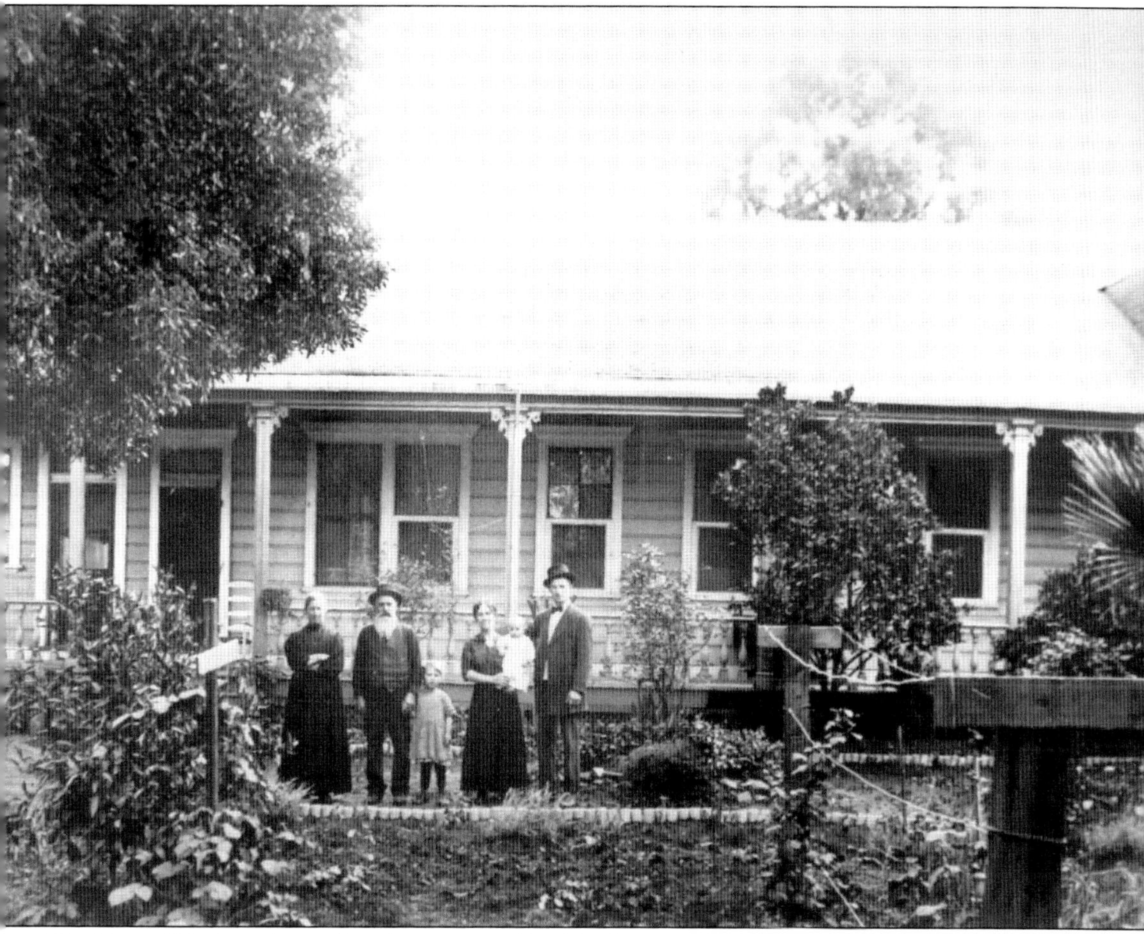

The Nunez/Bloching home faced west toward Diablo Street. It burned in a 1920s fire that most residents suspected was caused by faulty wiring. Pictured in front of the house, from left to right, are Mary Josephine Nunez, Manuel Nunez, Virginia Orlando, Mary Bloching, Fred Bloching, and William R. Bloching. The house was the original residence of Charles Rhine.

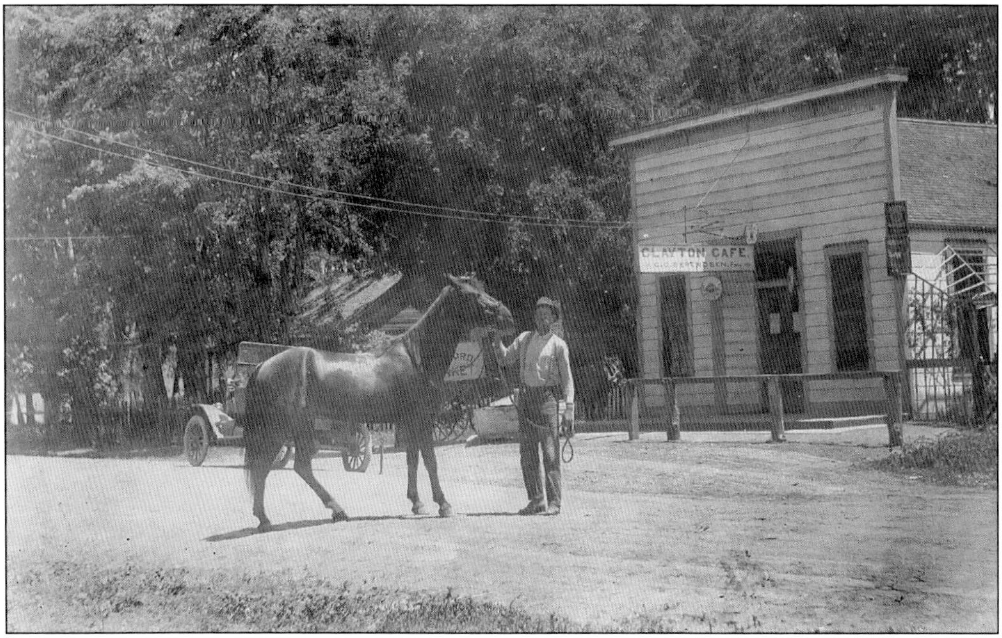

In this c. 1920 photograph, Leslie "Doug" Mitchell parades a fine-looking horse in front of the Clayton Cafe on Main Street at Morris Street.

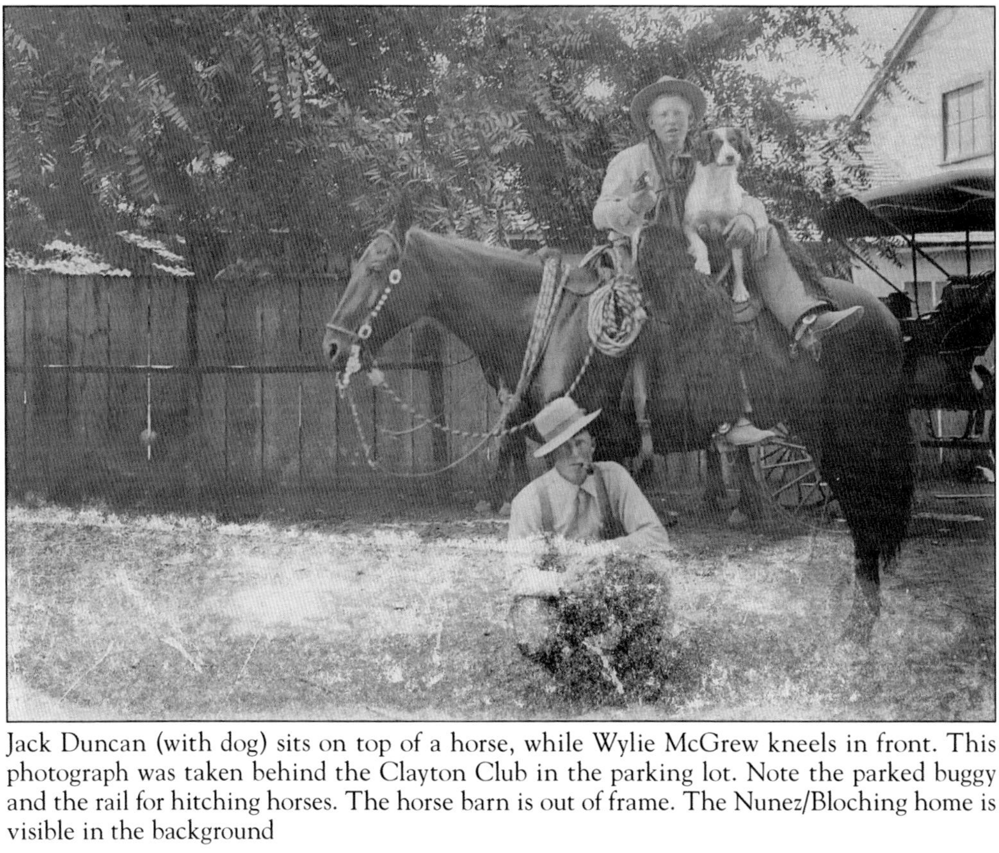

Jack Duncan (with dog) sits on top of a horse, while Wylie McGrew kneels in front. This photograph was taken behind the Clayton Club in the parking lot. Note the parked buggy and the rail for hitching horses. The horse barn is out of frame. The Nunez/Bloching home is visible in the background

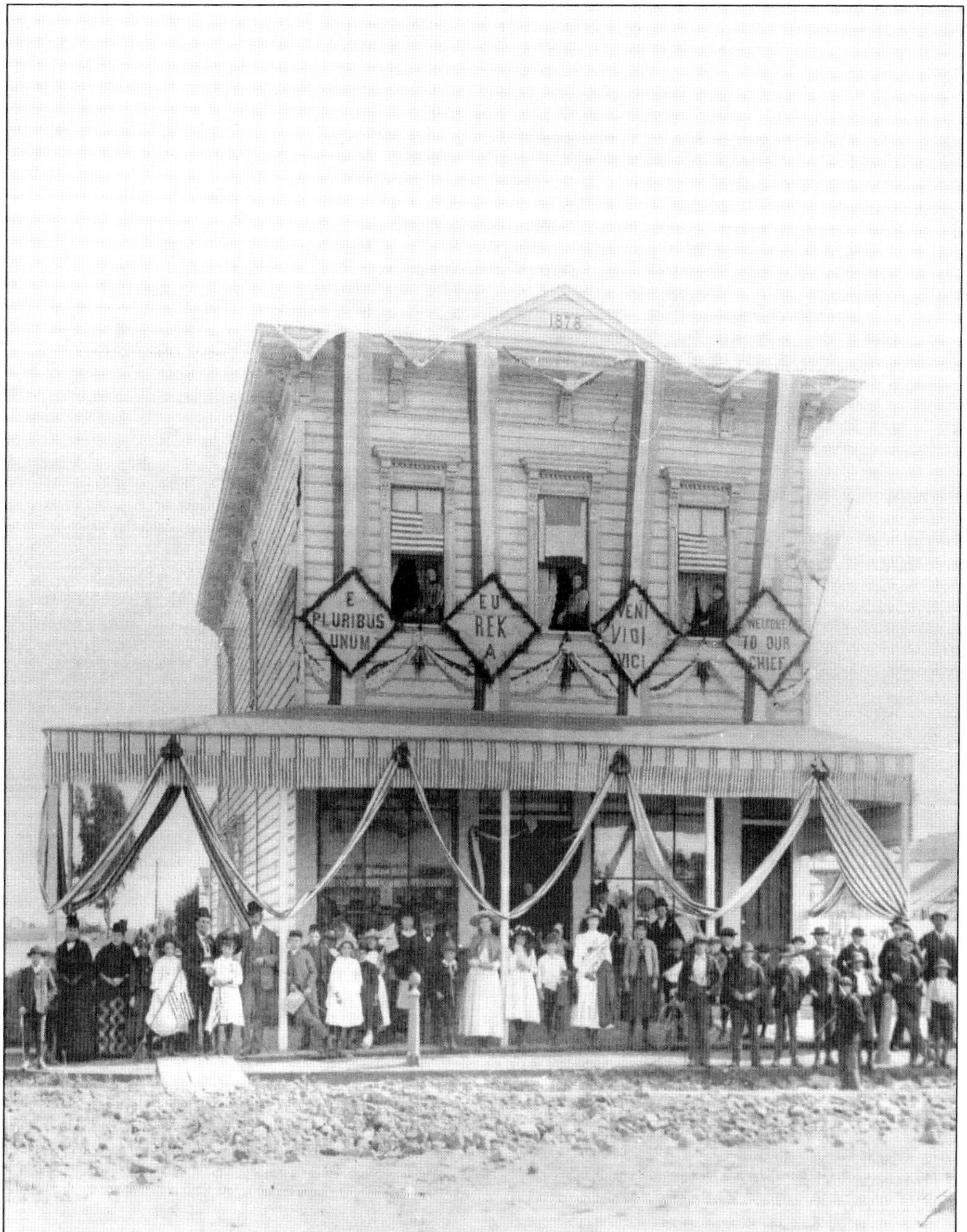

The Rhine Hotel, built by Jacob Rhine in the 1880s, was located on the southwest corner of Main and Morris Streets. After it burned down, the National Saloon replaced it.

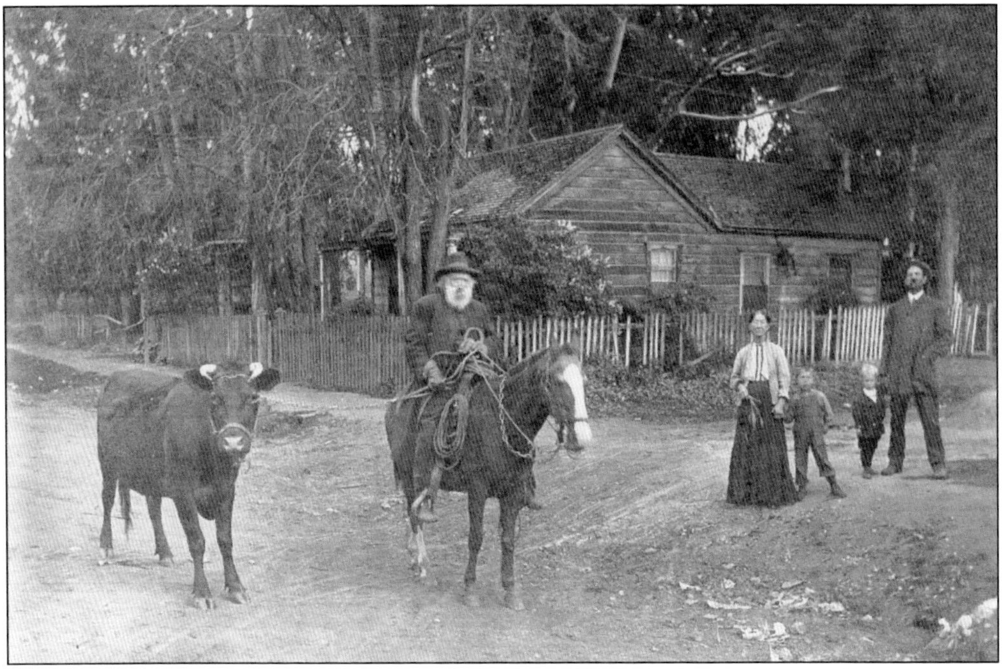

In this *c.* 1895 photograph, the Mitchell family poses at the intersection of Main and Morris Streets. Pictured, from left to right, are Isaac Newton Berry Mitchell; his wife, Louise Nottingham Mitchell; two young boys; and Cary Phelps "Cap" Mitchell.

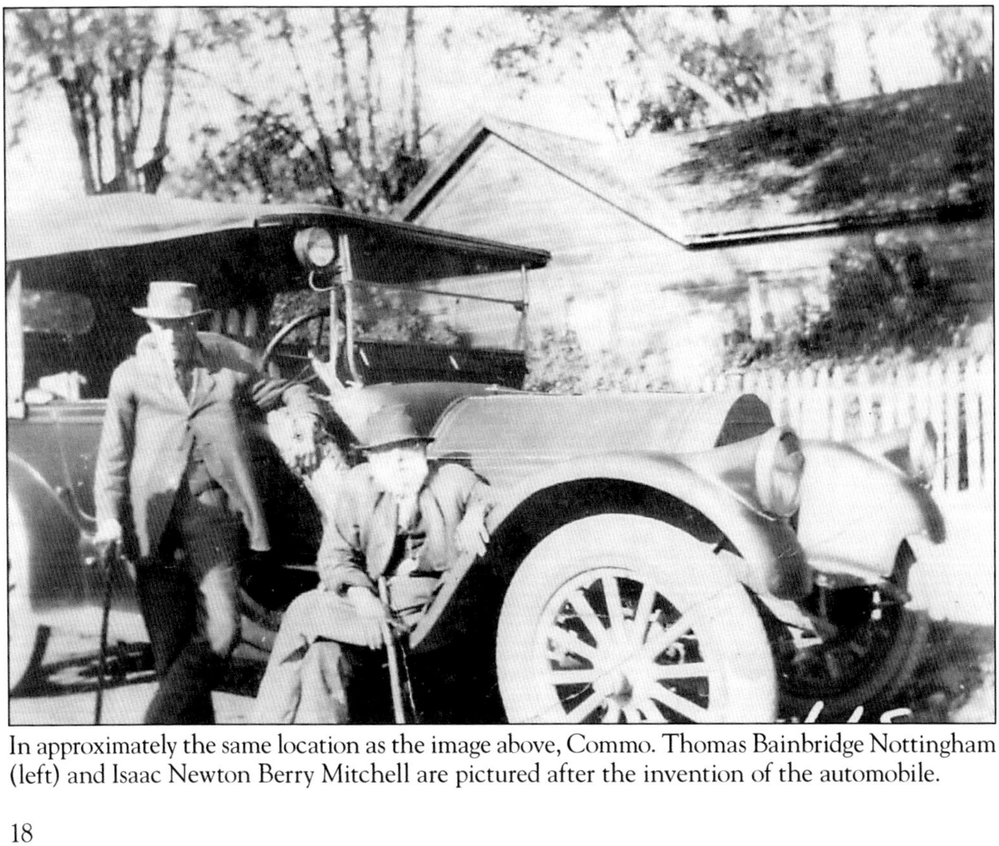

In approximately the same location as the image above, Commo. Thomas Bainbridge Nottingham (left) and Isaac Newton Berry Mitchell are pictured after the invention of the automobile.

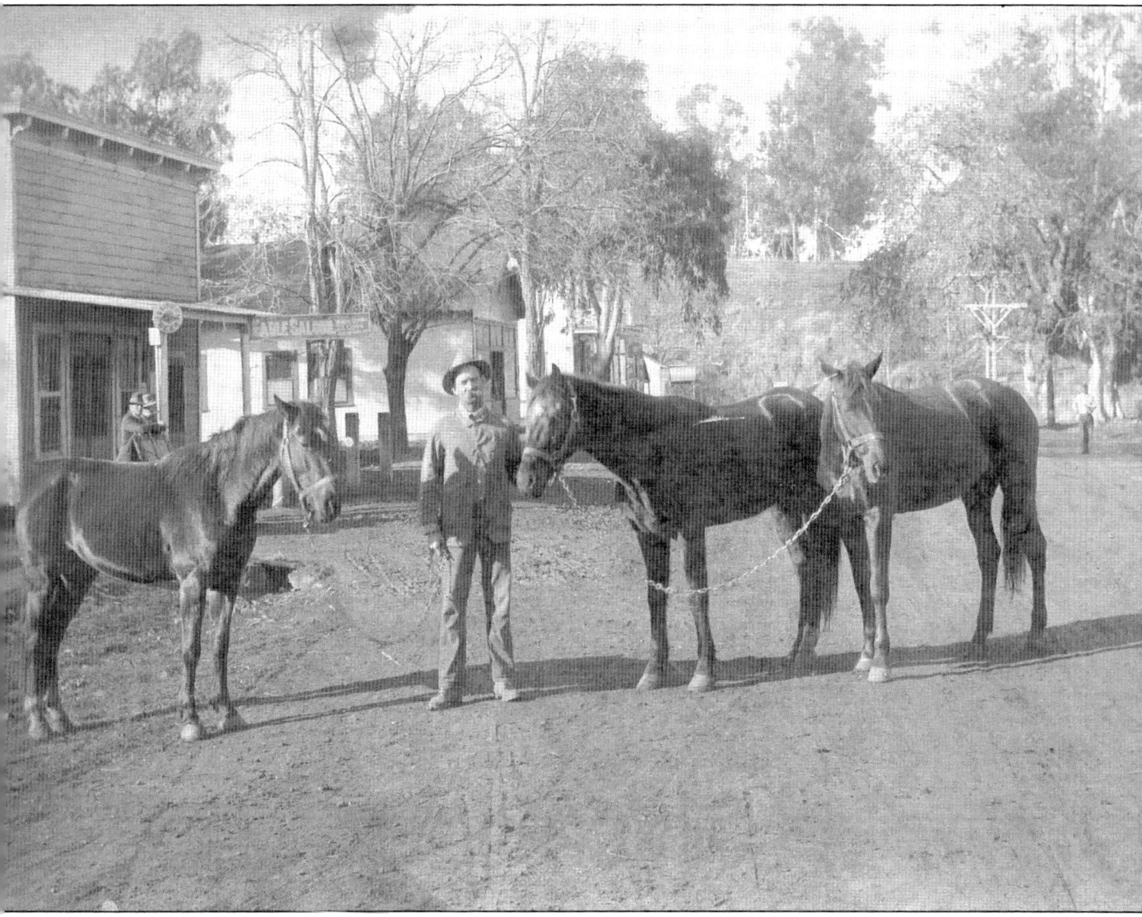

In 1936, Cary Phelps "Cap" Mitchell shows off his horses on Main Street near the Eagle Saloon. It does not appear that Main Street is yet paved.

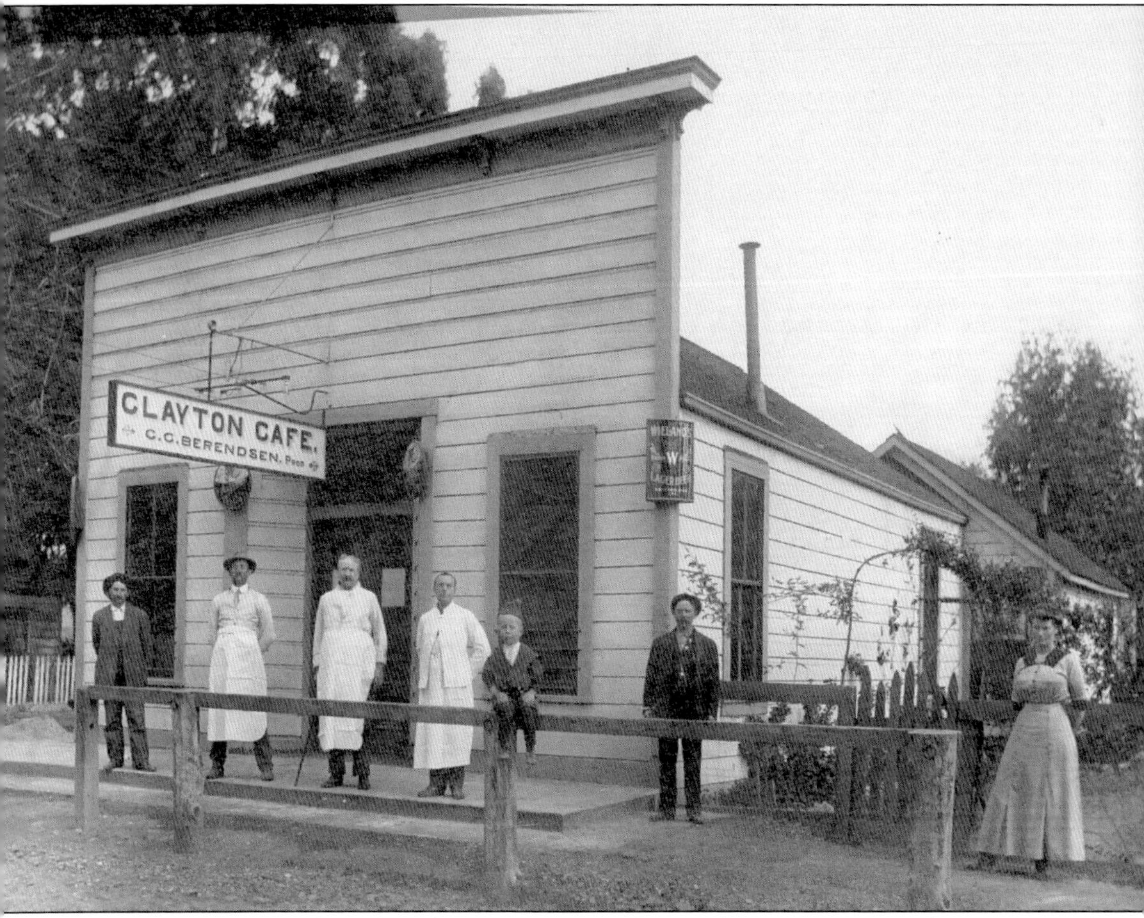

With the passage of the Volstead Act in 1919, the Clayton Club, a Main Street saloon, was forced to undergo a name change to the Clayton Cafe. Carl Berendsen was the proprietor. Pictured, from left to right, are Joe Matz, "Cap" Mitchell, Lou Ivory, Jack Goethals, Mikkel A. Berendsen, Carl Berendsen, and his wife, Mary.

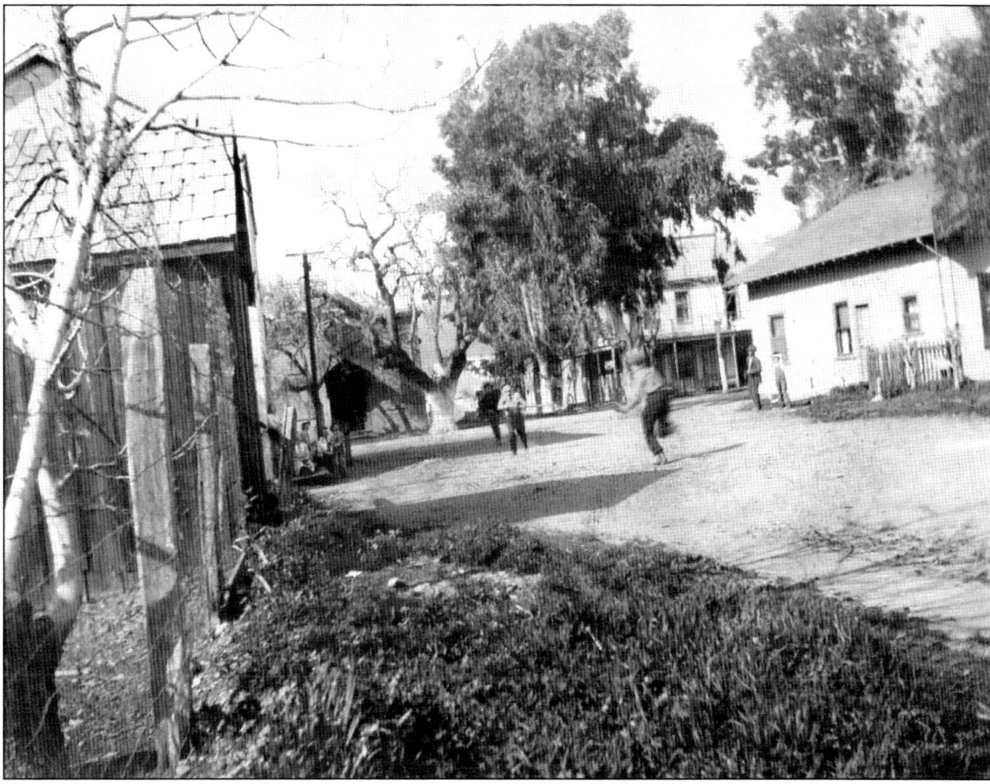

These children were playing baseball on Diablo Street in the 1930s. Hans Rasmussen's Clayton Cash Store can be seen on the right, and the Clayton Hotel and Rhine's Hall are visible on Main Street.

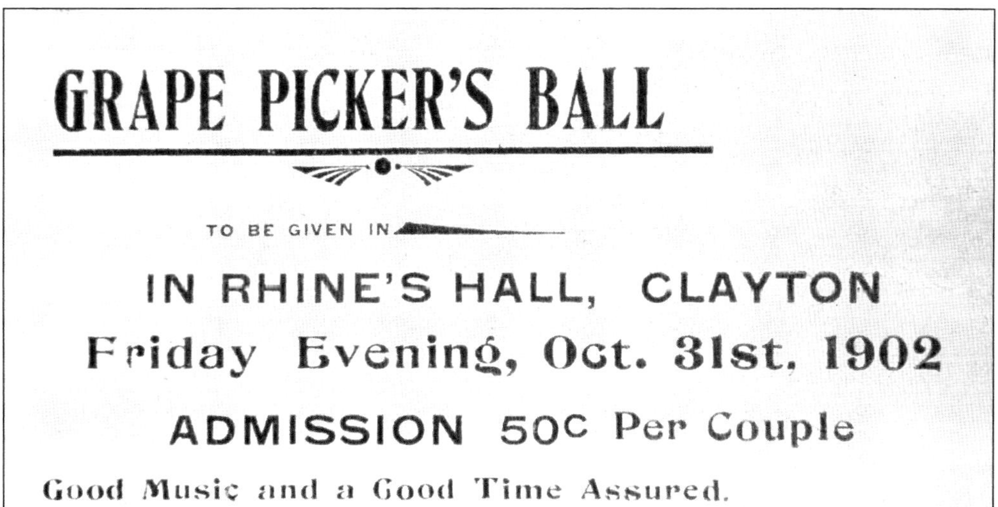

GRAPE PICKER'S BALL

TO BE GIVEN IN

IN RHINE'S HALL, CLAYTON

Friday Evening, Oct. 31st. 1902

ADMISSION 50C Per Couple

Good Music and a Good Time Assured.

Local events such as receptions, flower shows, dances, and the Grape Picker's Ball were held at Rhine's Hall on Main Street

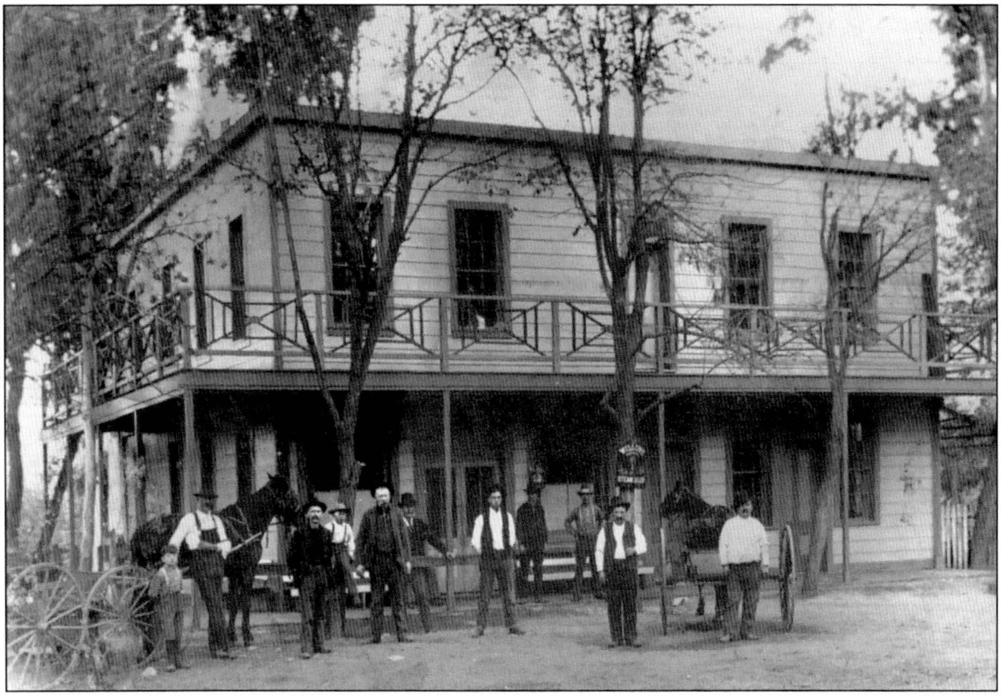

In 1858, Clayton's first hotel and tavern opened and was operated by Romero Mauvais. It burned in a fire in 1864 but was rebuilt. The above photograph shows the Clayton Hotel in 1875, while the one below depicts it in 1938. The post office was also located there.

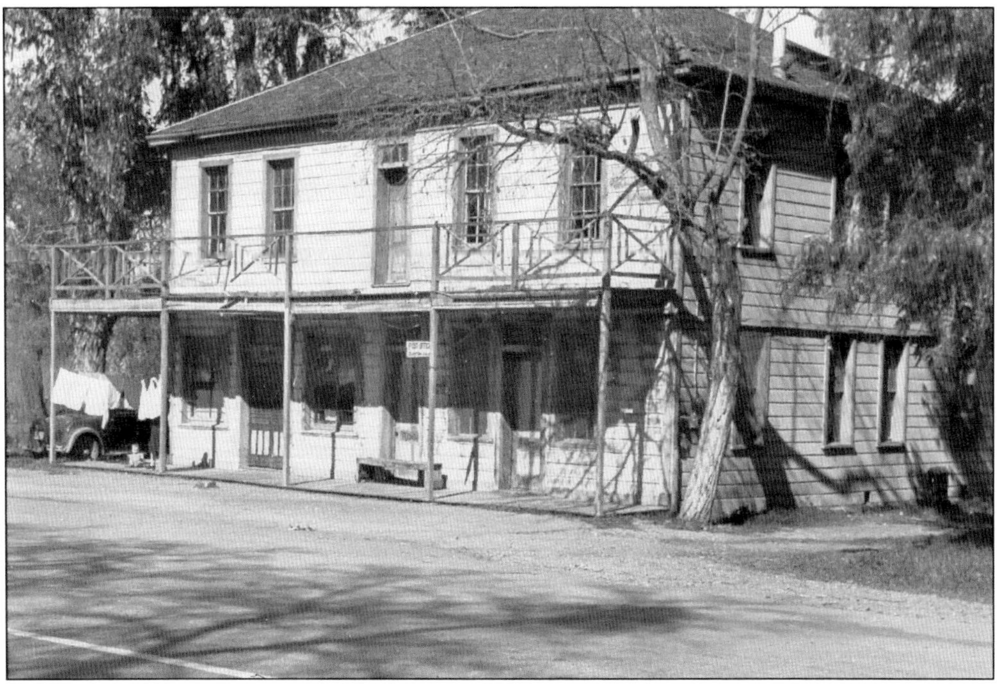

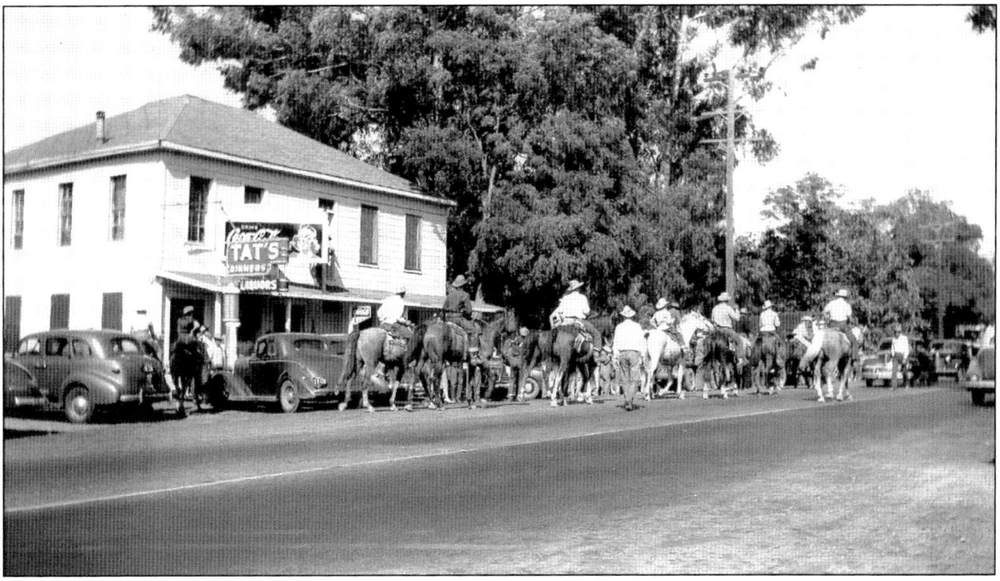

Until about 1947, Francis "Tat" Murchio operated the old Clayton Hotel as Tat's. Below, Randall "Chubby" Humble opened a steakhouse and changed the name to Chubby Humble's Pioneer Inn.

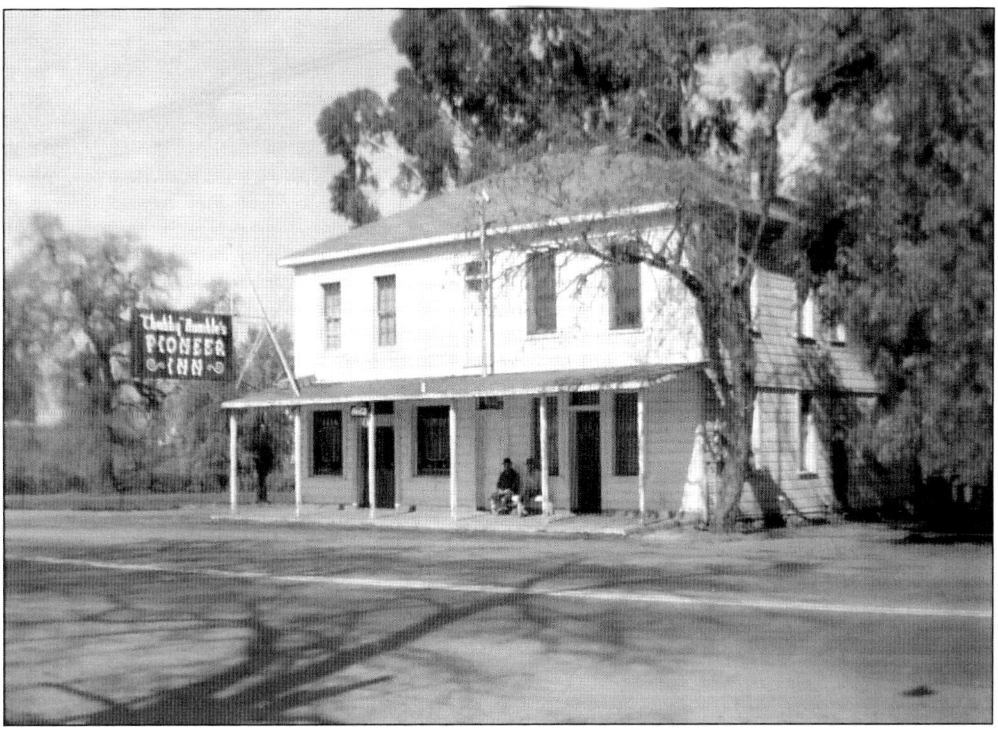

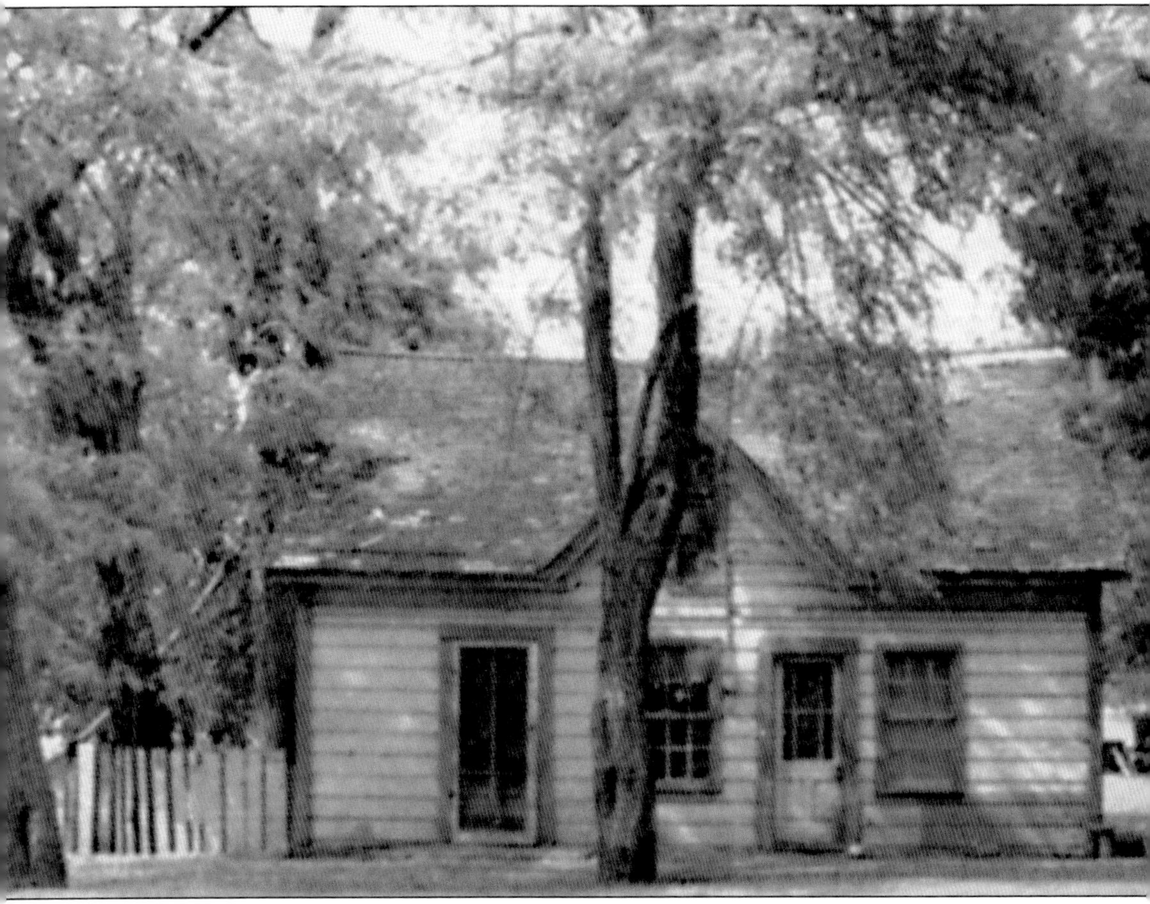

The home of hero Morgan James is pictured here on Main Street. During a cave-in at a Nortonville coal mine, Morgan James climbed through a maze of tunnels, risking his own tiny frame, and led 150 men to safety.

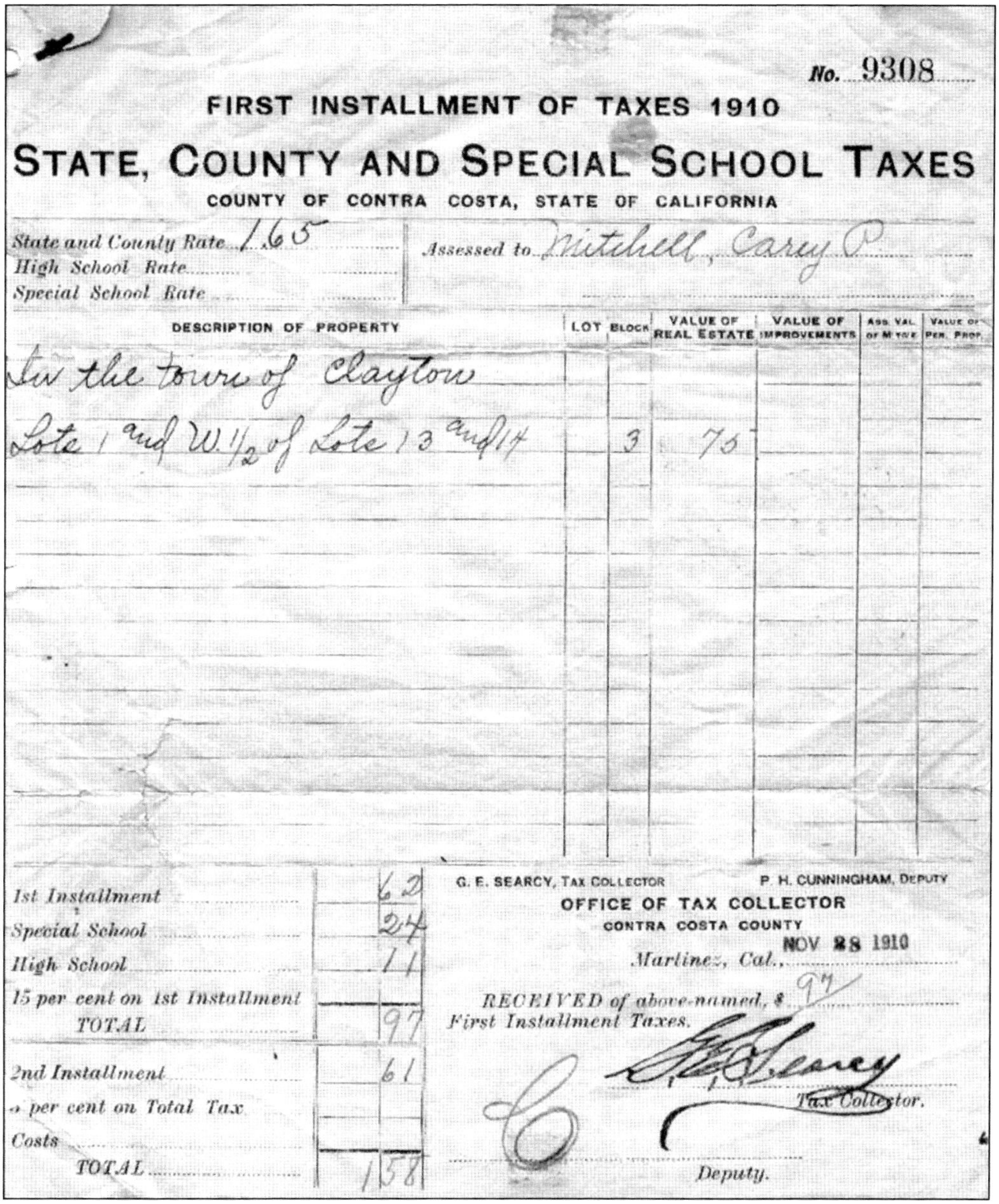

No. 9308

FIRST INSTALLMENT OF TAXES 1910

STATE, COUNTY AND SPECIAL SCHOOL TAXES

COUNTY OF CONTRA COSTA, STATE OF CALIFORNIA

State and County Rate 1.65
High School Rate
Special School Rate

Assessed to Mitchell, Carey P.

DESCRIPTION OF PROPERTY	LOT	BLOCK	VALUE OF REAL ESTATE	VALUE OF IMPROVEMENTS	ASS. VAL. OF M. TG'E	VALUE OF PER. PROP.
In the town of Clayton						
Lots 1 and W. 1/2 of Lots 13 and 14		3	75			

1st Installment	62
Special School	24
High School	11
15 per cent on 1st Installment	
TOTAL	97
2nd Installment	61
5 per cent on Total Tax	
Costs	
TOTAL	158

G. E. SEARCY, TAX COLLECTOR   P. H. CUNNINGHAM, DEPUTY

OFFICE OF TAX COLLECTOR
CONTRA COSTA COUNTY
Martinez, Cal., NOV 28 1910

RECEIVED of above-named, $ 97
First Installment Taxes.

G. E. Searcy
Tax Collector.

Deputy.

Carey [sic] P. Mitchell purchased two lots downtown in 1907 from John Dugan for $10, with payment of delinquent taxes in the amount of $27.28. This 1910 tax bill shows that the total property tax assessed was $1.58.

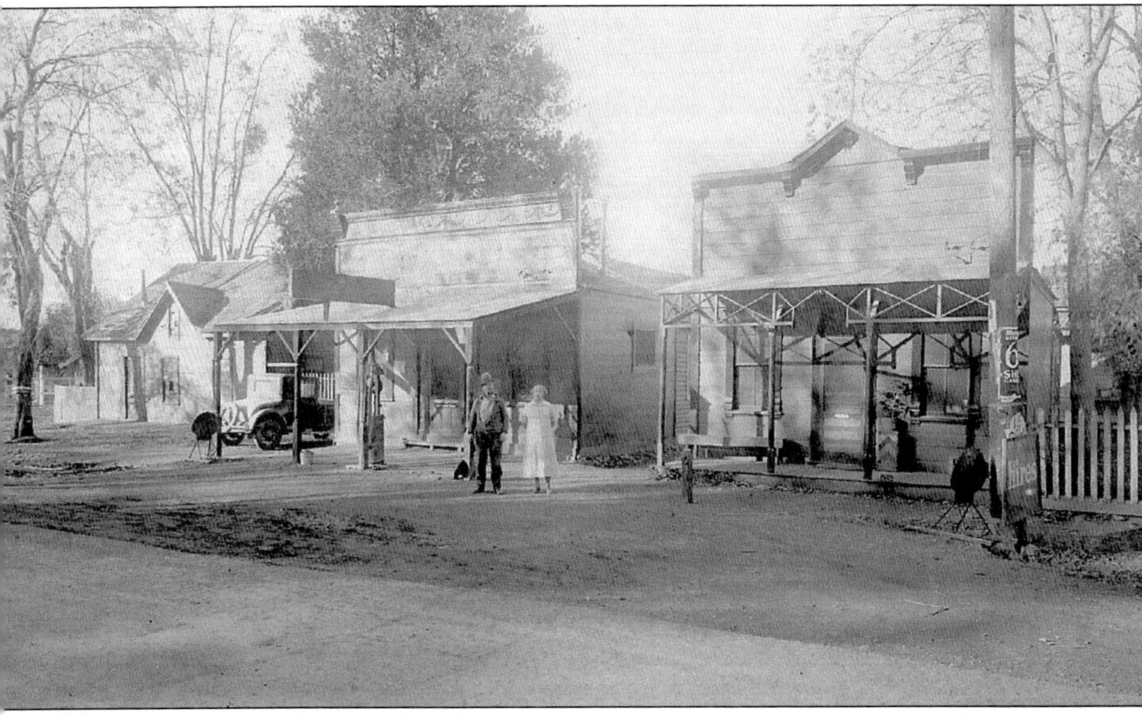

Mr. and Mrs. LeClaire stand in front of the Growler on Main Street in the 1920s. Note the gasoline pump in front. The Morgan James house is on the left and the office of Gus L. Goethals is on the right.

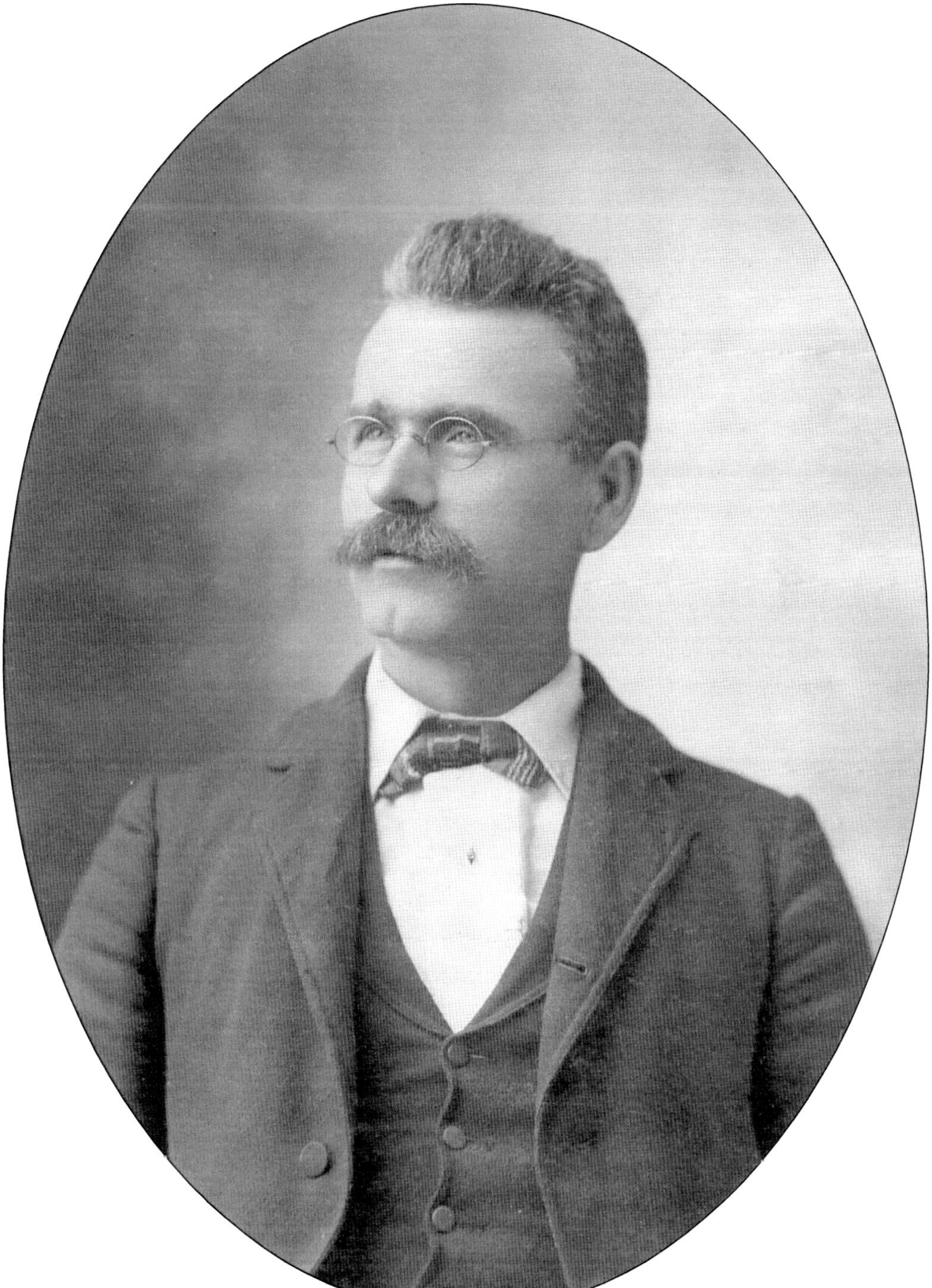

Gustave Louis "Gus" Goethals was born in France and came to Clayton in 1888. He was a skilled carpenter and built his home and office on Main Street. He wrote for several newspapers, served as justice of the peace, and sold real estate and insurance.

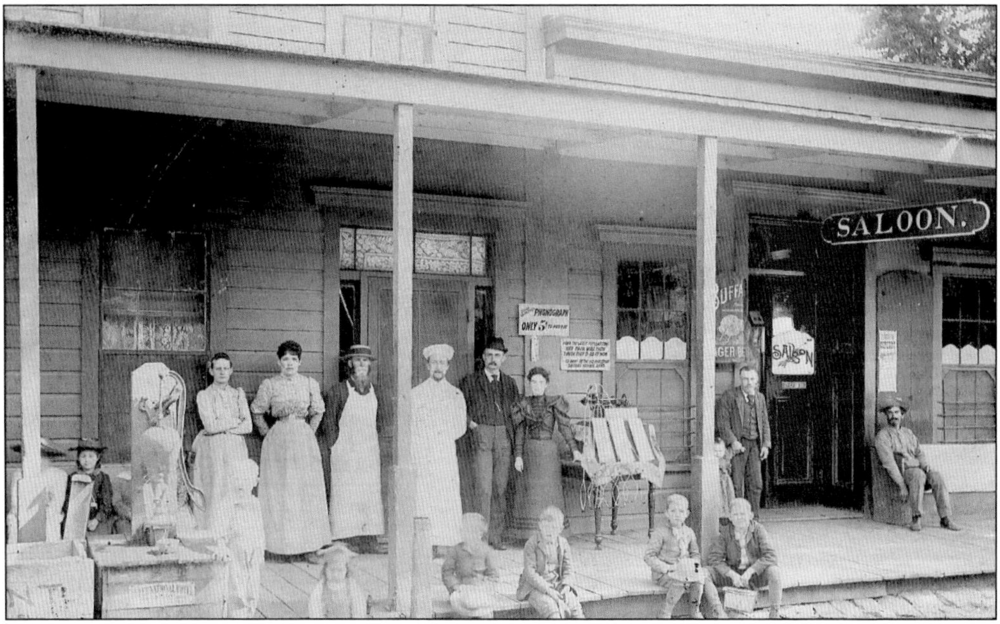

This photograph, taken before 1900, shows the front of Jacob "Jake" Rhine's Hotel and Saloon on Main Street.

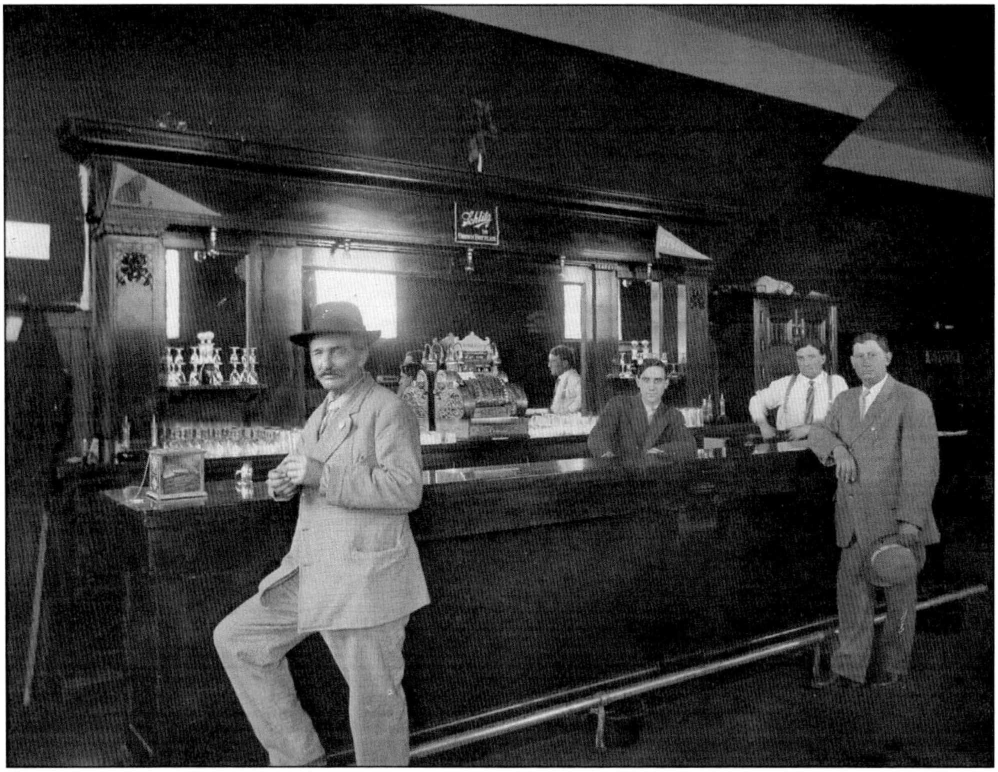
Behind the bar in Jake Rhine's Saloon was a very ornate cash register when this photograph was taken around 1900. The gentleman on the far right is John "Jack" Atchinson, one of Clayton's last stagecoach drivers.

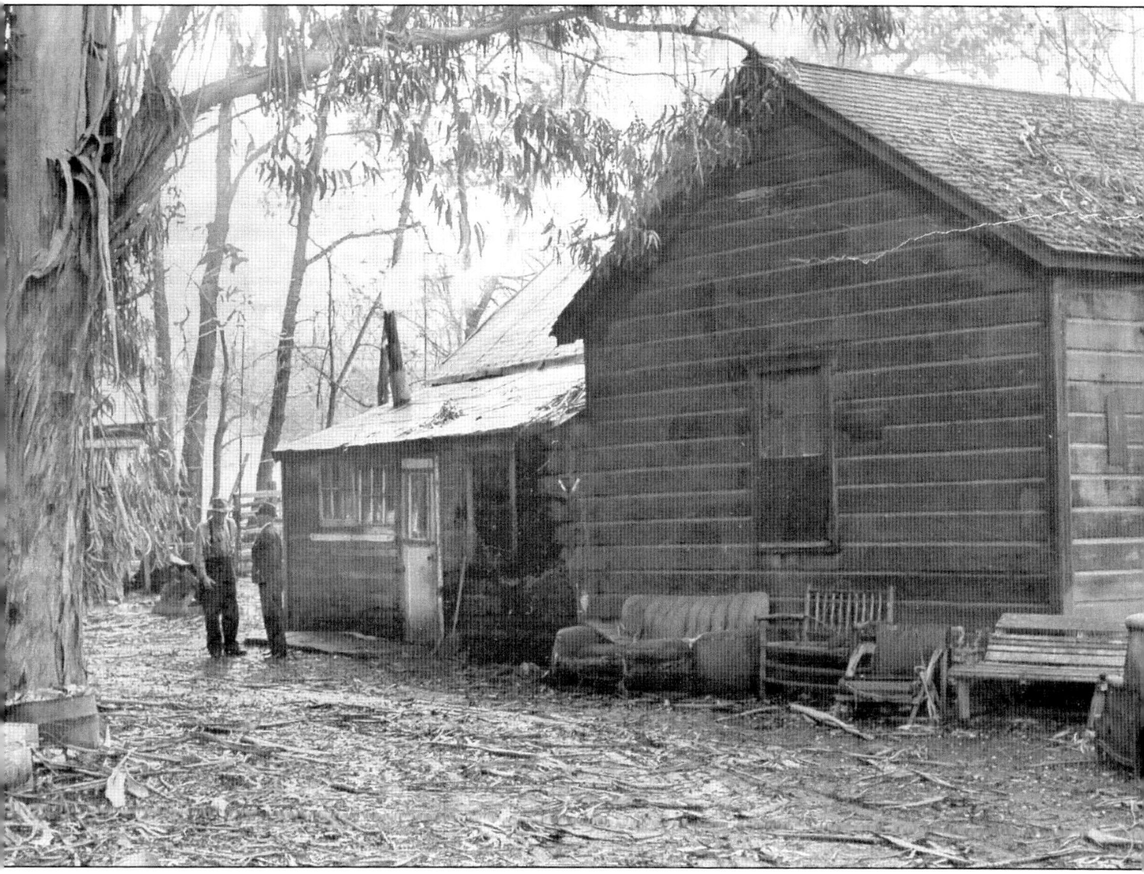

The Mitchell home on the southeast corner of Main and Morris Streets had outdoor furniture for the many people who gathered regularly to pass the time of day. An afternoon horseshoe game was routine behind Mitchell's house and barn.

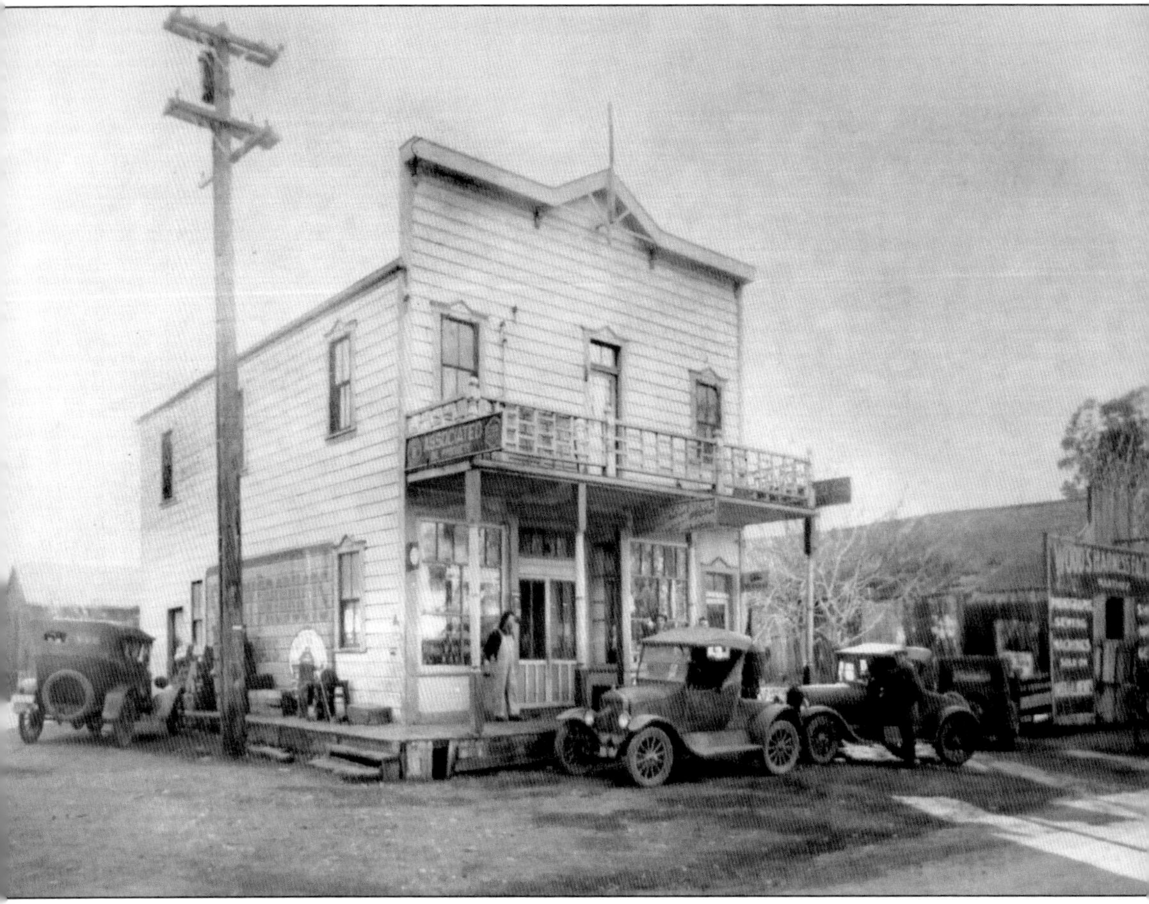

Charles Rhine's store sat on the southwest corner of Main Street and Diablo Street. The sign on the building to the right says Wood's Harness Shop. The advertisement posted on the balcony hawks Associated Oil Products.

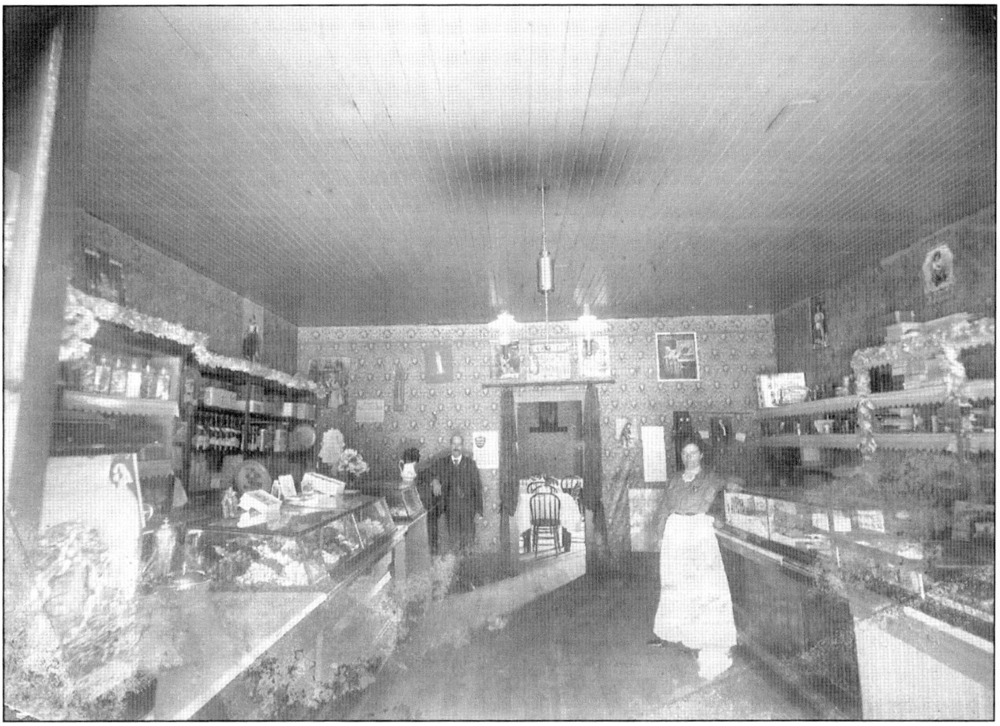

The interior of Rhine's store shows that everything from food to hardware was for sale. Just about anything anyone needed could be purchased at Rhine's store.

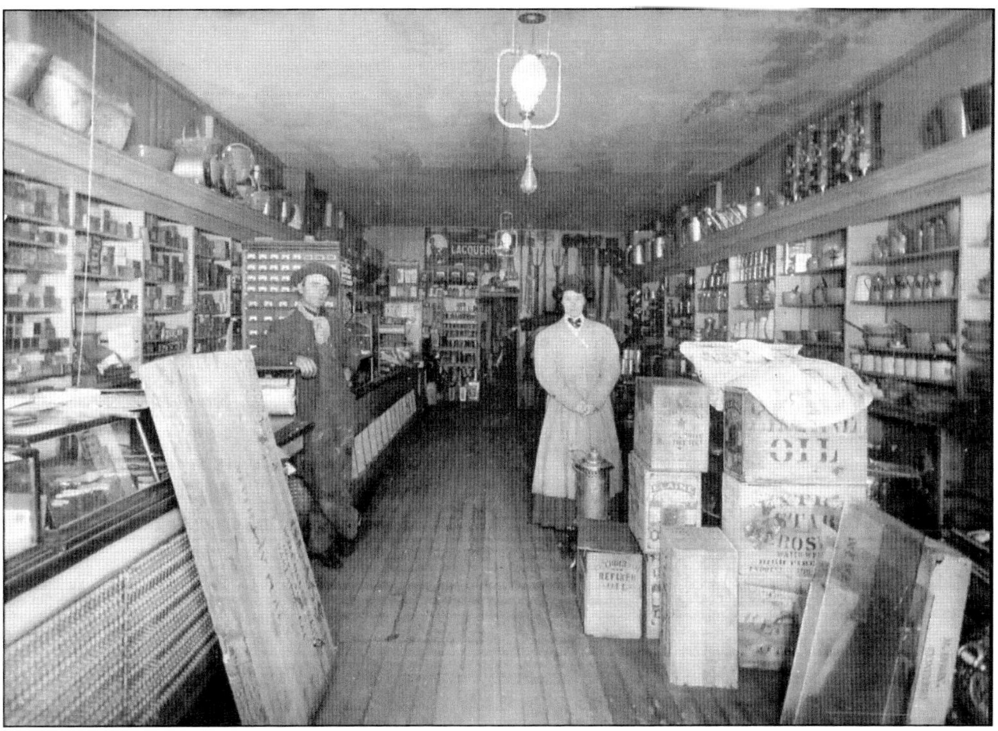

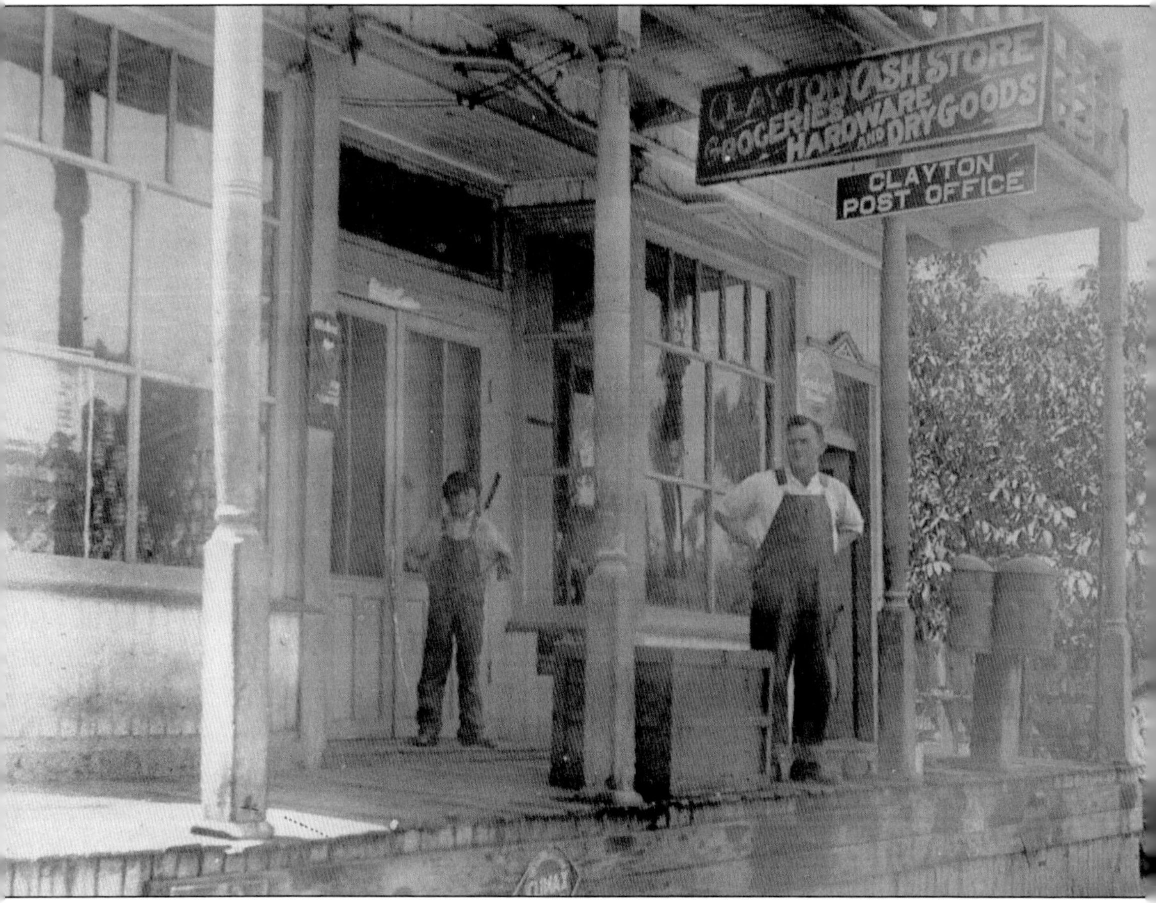

In the early 1910s, Hans Rasmussen purchased the general store from Charles Rhine. Hans is pictured on the front porch around 1925 with Georgie "Tut" Tavarossi. The Clayton Cash Store served as the post office at this time as well as selling Gold Crown gasoline.

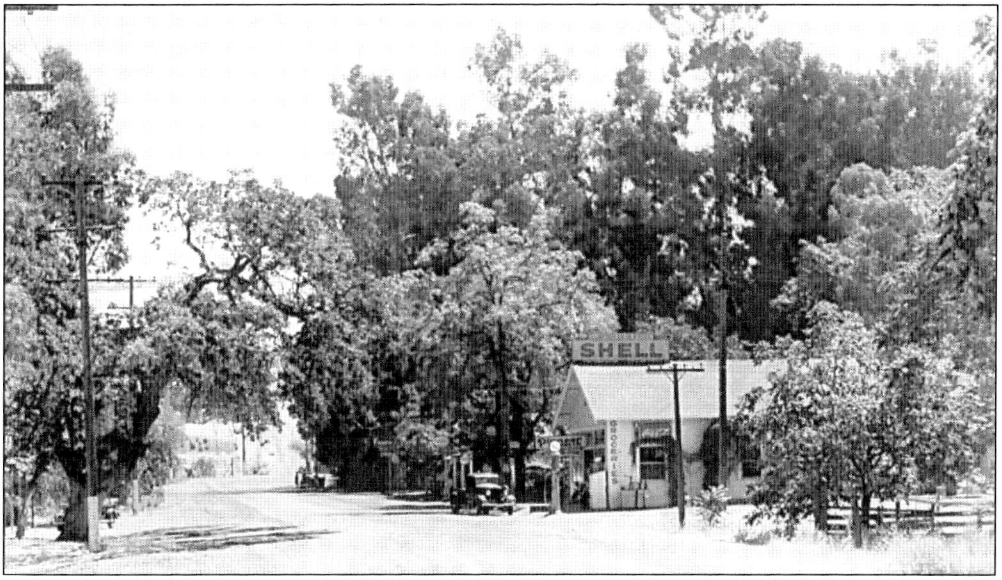

Hans Rasmussen's Clayton Cash Store moved across the street to this one-story building, with living quarters in the rear where he resided with his wife, Bertha Sargent Rasmussen. He prominently featured Shell gasoline; the gas pump is visible in front.

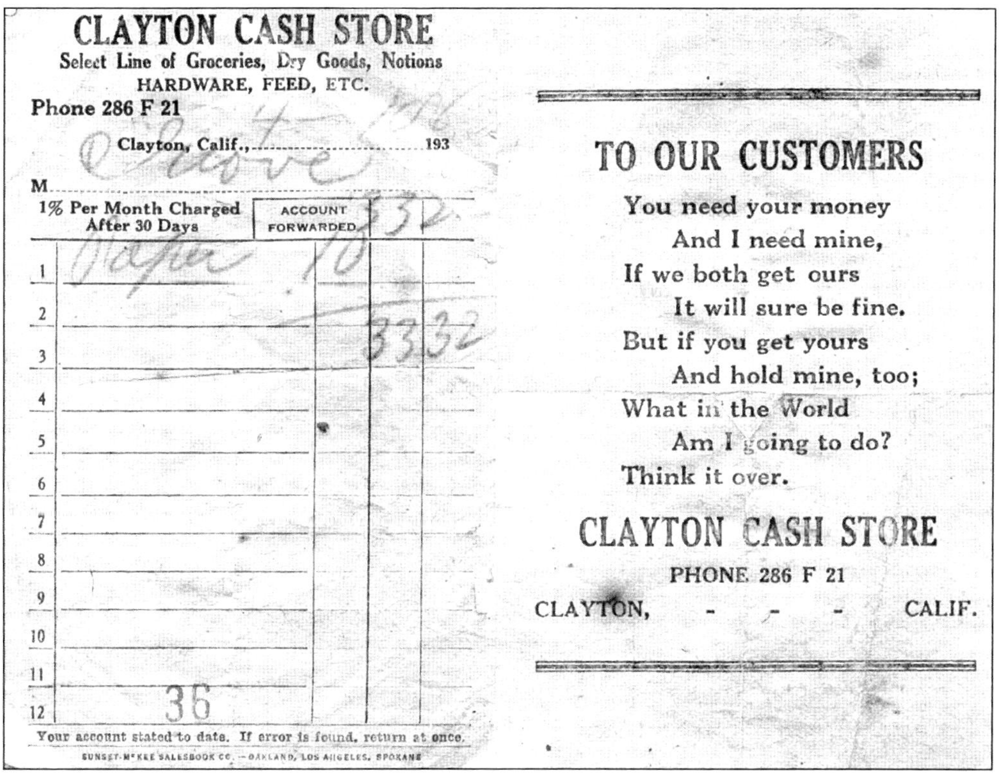

CLAYTON CASH STORE

Select Line of Groceries, Dry Goods, Notions

HARDWARE, FEED, ETC.

Phone 286 F 21

Clayton, Calif., ... 193

M.............................

1% Per Month Charged After 30 Days | ACCOUNT FORWARDED

1
2
3
4
5
6
7
8
9
10
11
12

Your account stated to date. If error is found, return at once.

SUNSET-McKEE SALESBOOK CO. — OAKLAND, LOS ANGELES, SPOKANE

TO OUR CUSTOMERS

You need your money
And I need mine,
If we both get ours
It will sure be fine.
But if you get yours
And hold mine, too;
What in the World
Am I going to do?
Think it over.

CLAYTON CASH STORE

PHONE 286 F 21

CLAYTON, - - - CALIF.

The Clayton Cash Store was really a misnomer. Although this slogan appeared on the reverse side of sales receipts, Hans Rasmussen routinely carried the accounts of his customers.

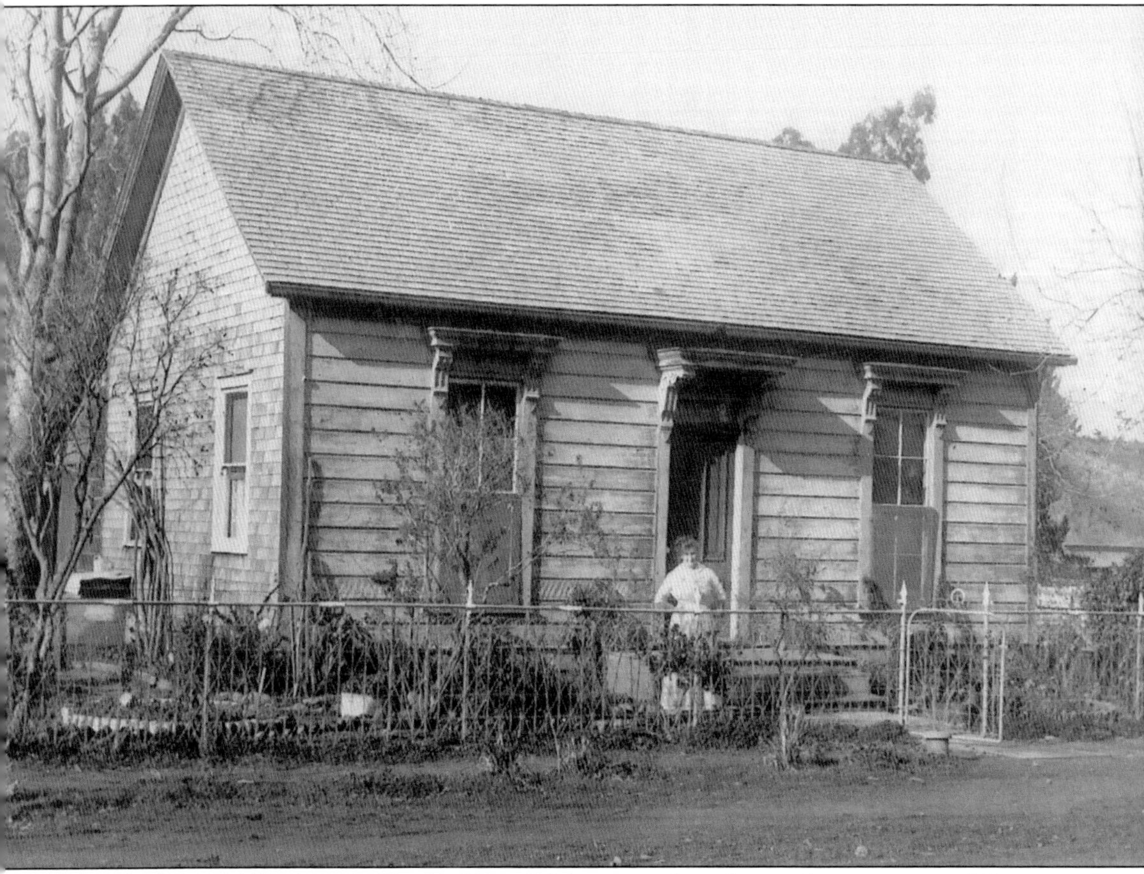

The home of blacksmith Charles "Harry" Trette stood on the southwest corner of Center and Diablo Streets, with the front facing Diablo Street. Pictured is his wife, Emma Jane Robertson Trette, who was born in Nortonville. It is believed the house was originally built in Nortonville and moved to Clayton.

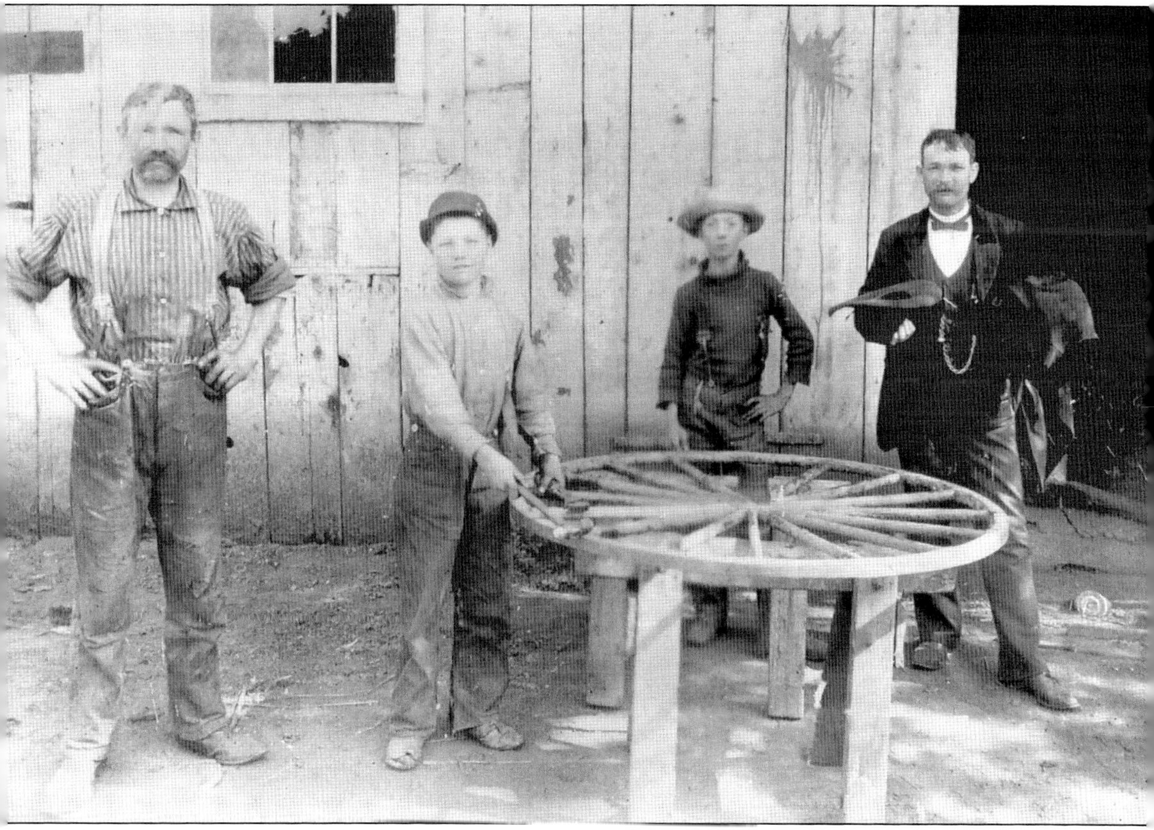

In 1880, the Charles "Harry" Trette family came to Clayton. Trette bought the blacksmith shop on the corner of Main and Oak Streets from Matthew "Doc" Nottingham. Pictured, from left to right, are Harry Trette; his son Rudolph "Dutch" Trette; Bert Curry, son of James Curry (the livery stable owner); and actor and dance teacher John Collins. Harry Trette ran the blacksmith shop for 50 years before turning the operation over to his son Dutch.

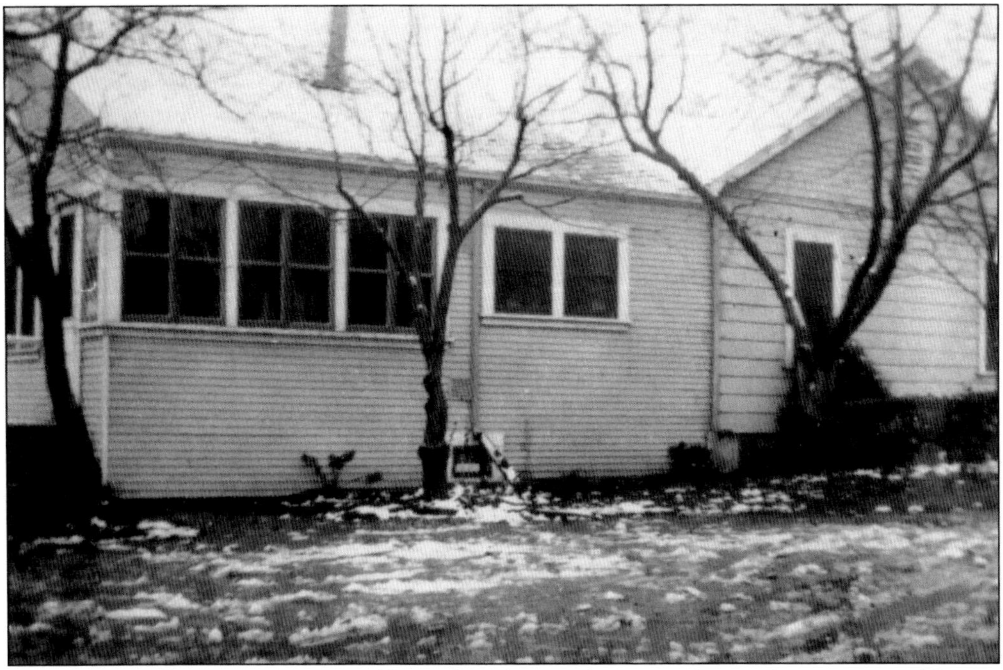

The home of Albert C. Trette Sr. and his wife, Ada Myrick, was on the northwest corner of Center and Diablo Streets. It is pictured here in January 1937, with snow on the ground.

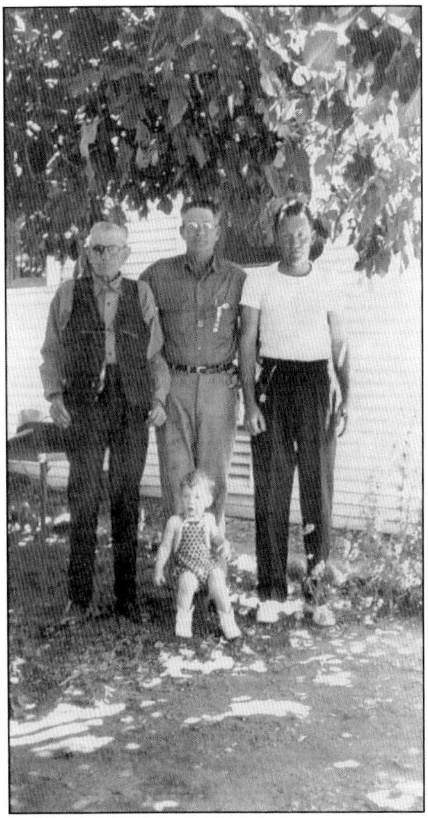

In 1942, four generations of Trette men pose at the home of Albert C. Trette Sr. Standing, from left to right, are Charles "Harry" Trette, Albert Sr. (known as "Tater"), and Albert Jr. (known as "Ike"). The baby is Albert C. "Mickey" Trette.

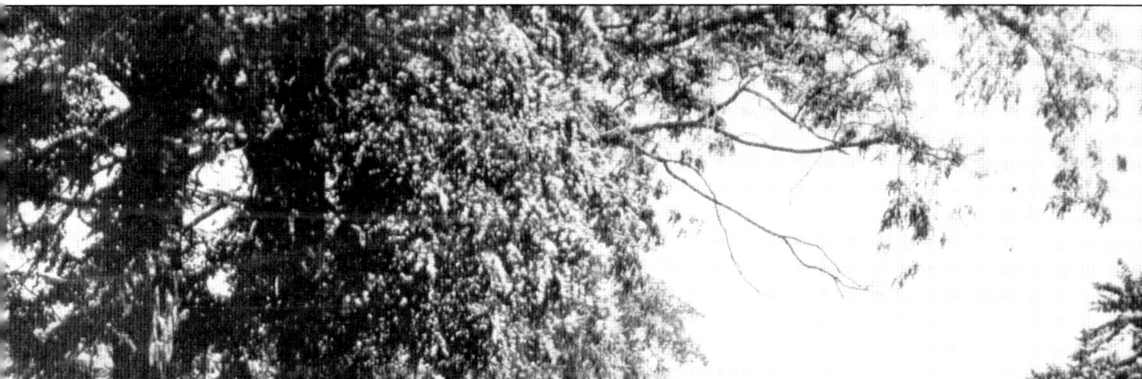

Oak Street, before it was paved, was idyllic. The closest building on the right is Clayton's jail, and the house further up the street is the Gomez/Pape home. An 1884 petition for building the jail said that it was necessary to have one in Clayton for the temporary housing of criminals, as transportation of lawbreakers to Martinez caused inconvenience, extra expense, and delays. A typical case in 1893 charged Charles Johnson of "willfully and maliciously driving his horse at a fast and unusual speed on the public streets of the Town of Clayton." The penalty was a fine of $30 or 30 days imprisonment.

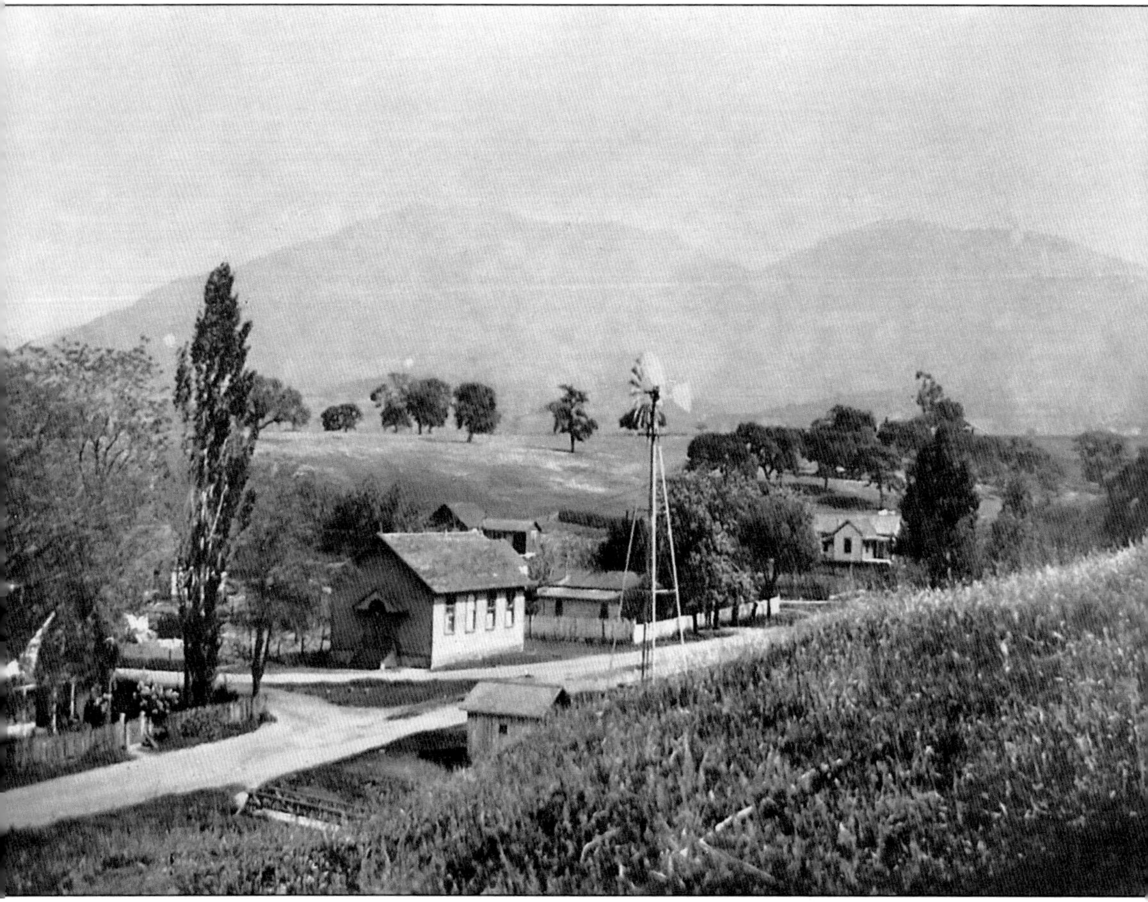

In the 1860s, the Methodists built a stone foundation church on the southeast corner of Oak and Center Streets. Services were provided by circuit-riding preachers from Martinez on their way through Clayton to conduct services in the coal mine area. Clayton was unable to support two churches, so the Congregational Church Christian Endeavor Society acquired the Methodist church in 1896 and thereafter the building was known as Christian Endeavor Hall. The Clayton jail can be seen in this photograph, just to the right of the school bridge.

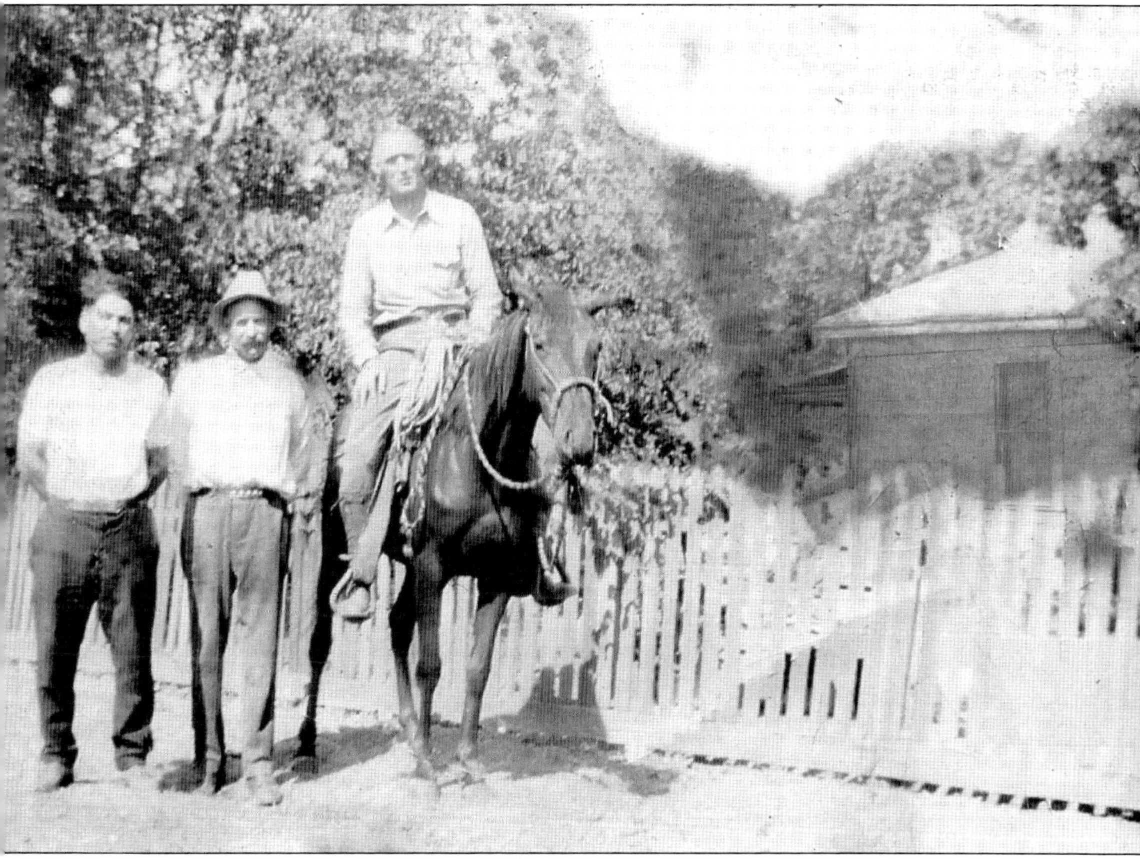

Tony Gomez, Cary P. "Cap" Mitchell, and Bill Biglow (on horse) are pictured at the side of the Gomez house on the northeast corner of Oak and High Streets. This was the second home of the Gomez family (the first was just across the street). Tony Gomez was renowned for his superior skills at tanning leather, then braiding it into reins and other horse-tack items.

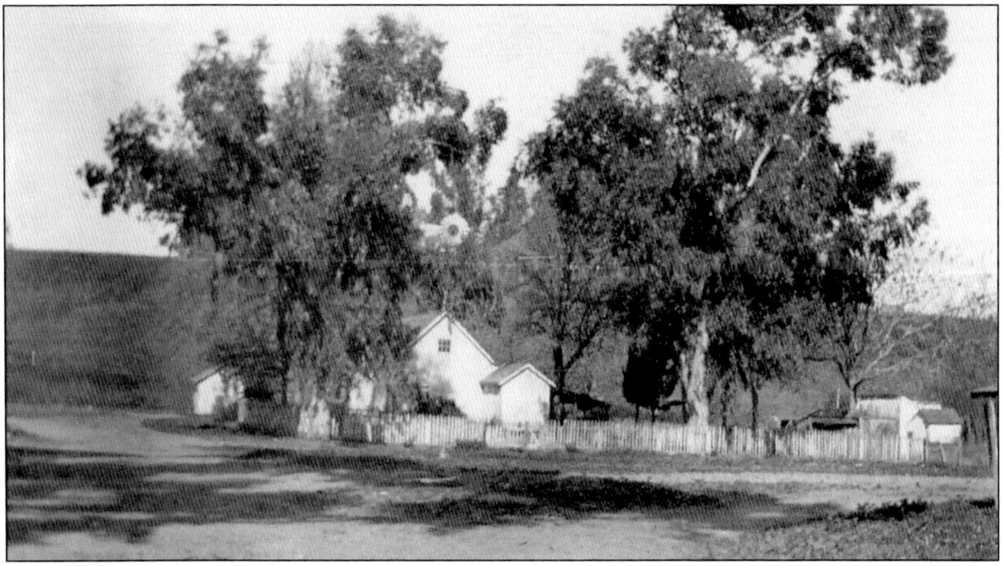

In 1903, the Curry house is pictured on Oak Street. It was later owned by the Kirkwood family.

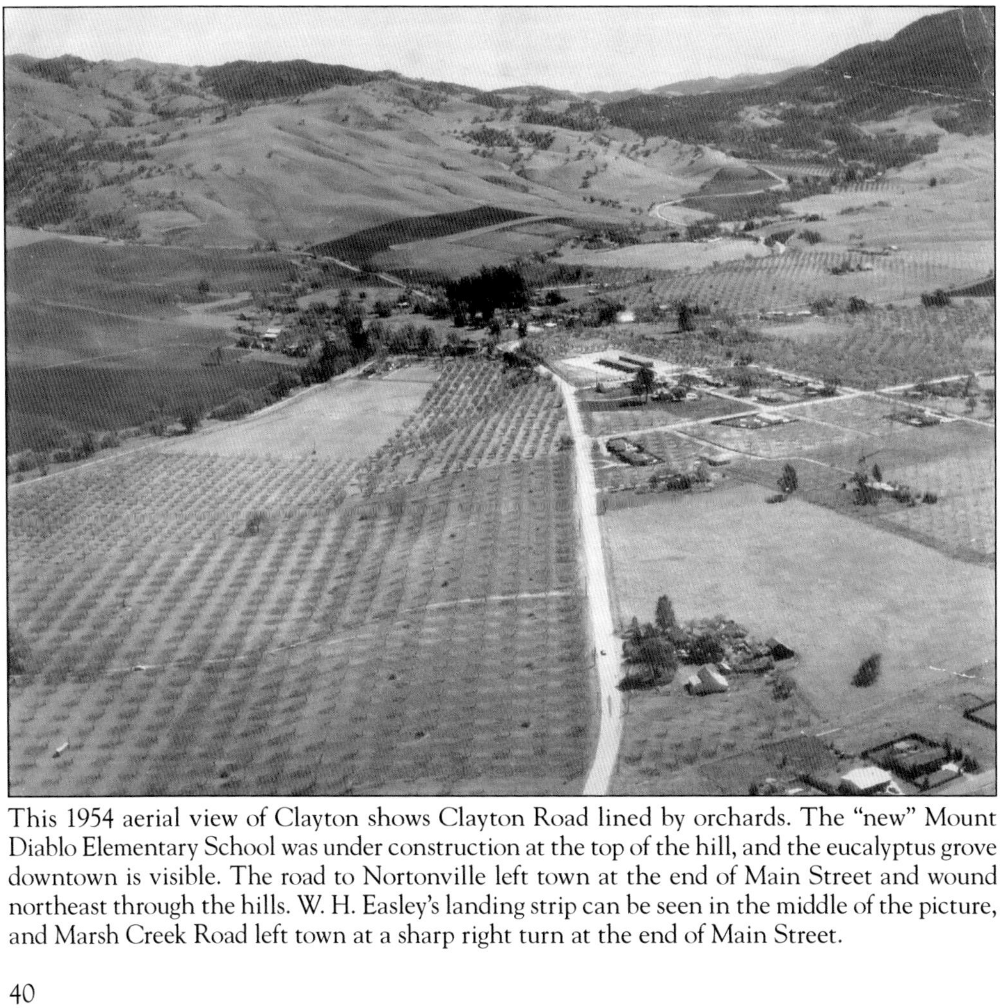

This 1954 aerial view of Clayton shows Clayton Road lined by orchards. The "new" Mount Diablo Elementary School was under construction at the top of the hill, and the eucalyptus grove downtown is visible. The road to Nortonville left town at the end of Main Street and wound northeast through the hills. W. H. Easley's landing strip can be seen in the middle of the picture, and Marsh Creek Road left town at a sharp right turn at the end of Main Street.

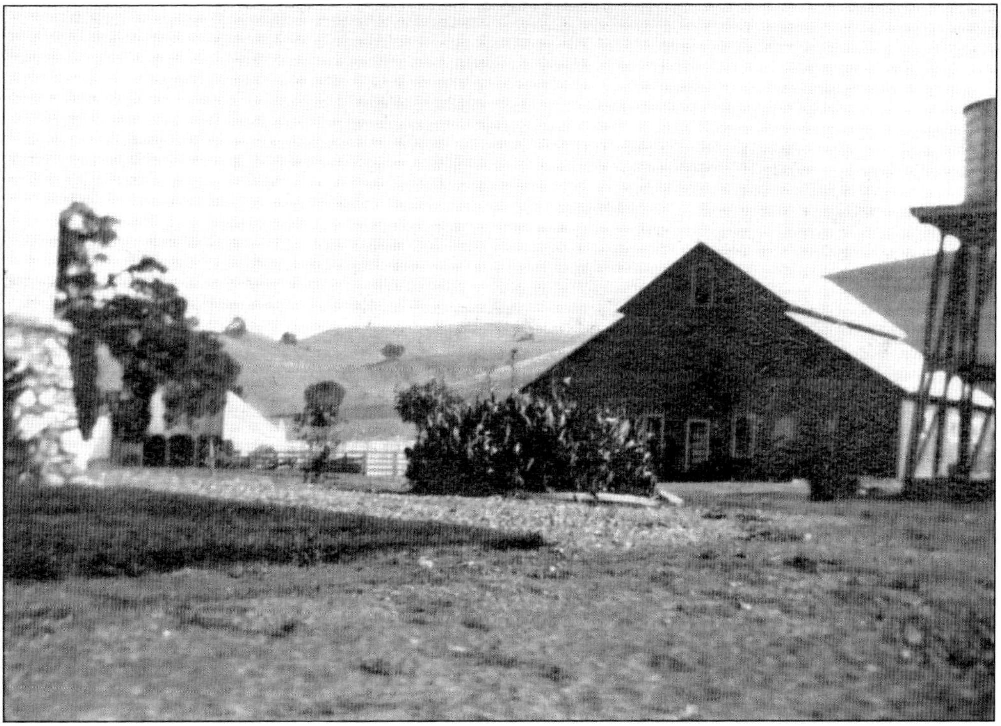

The Keller family barn was visible from Main Street, looking north.

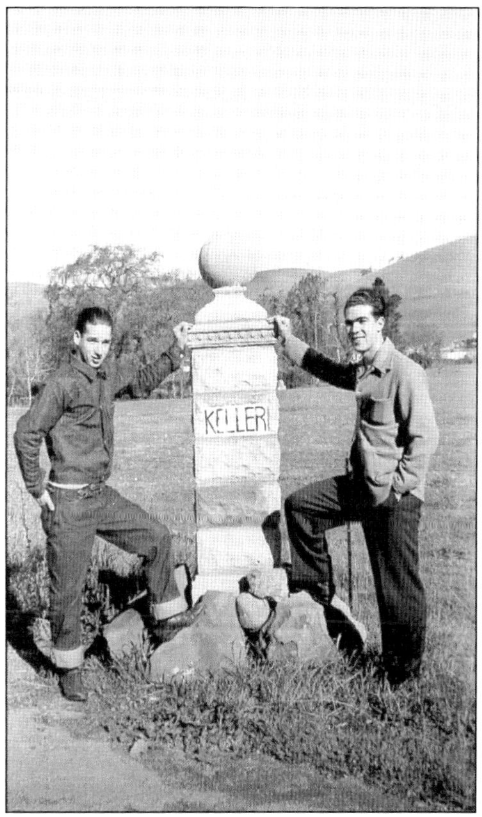

Stuart "Junior" Garrett (left) and Harold Russell pose on Main Street in 1940 near the pillar that stood at the entrance to the Keller ranch. Harold lived on Main Street while growing up.

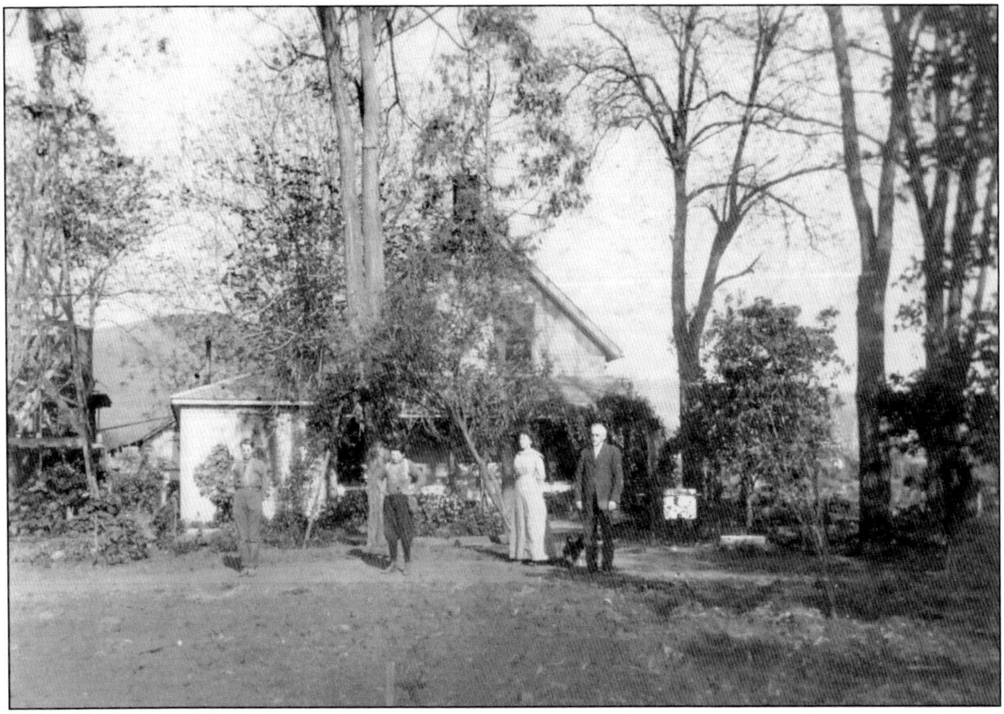

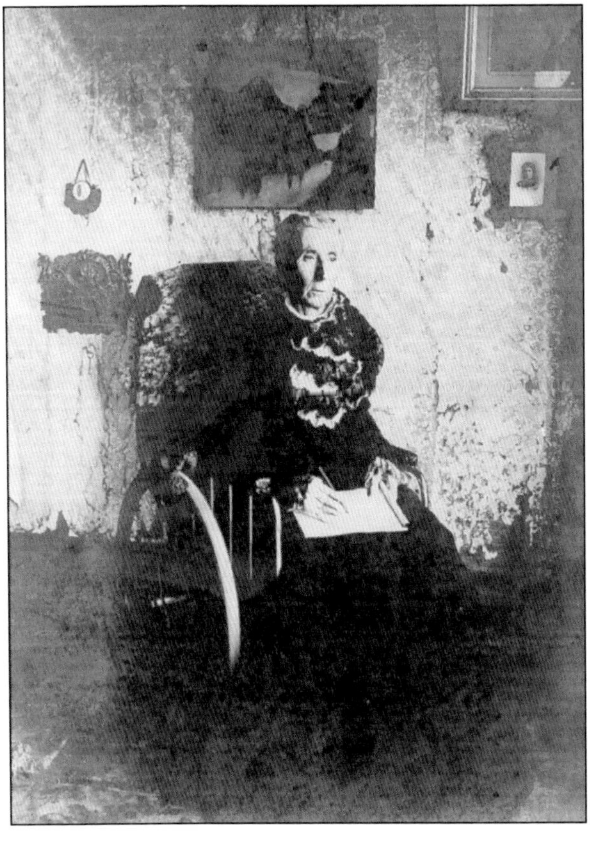

Pictured here in 1913, from left to right, are John Graves, Carl Graves, Pearle Graves, and T. O. Graves in front of the Stranahan house on Swan Street. The Graves family moved in with Sarah Stranahan after the death of her husband. They provided for her and eventually inherited the property from Mrs. Stranahan on the condition that, upon her death, she be buried at the Live Oak Cemetery next to her husband and son.

When her husband, Richard, died in 1900, Sarah Stranahan subsisted by selling off their ranch land in small parcels. In 1907, she had only the house and five acres remaining. To her good fortune, the Graves family moved into her home and helped provide for her.

Two

COMMUNITY ACTIVITIES

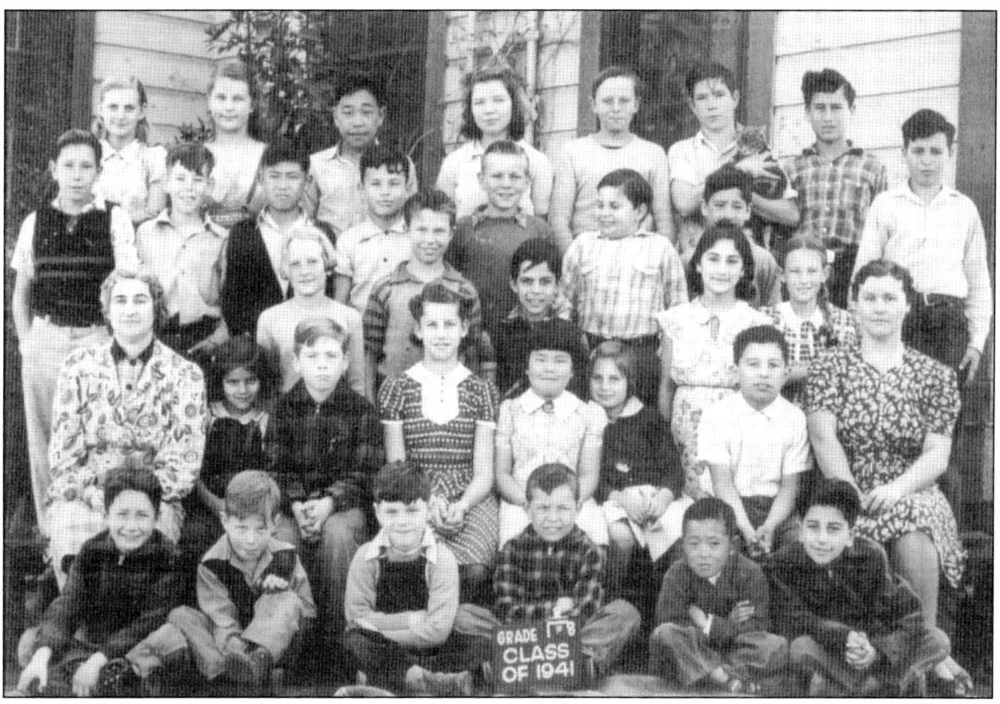

Education of children was important to early residents. Clayton also had its own baseball team, and the 4-H Club flourished.

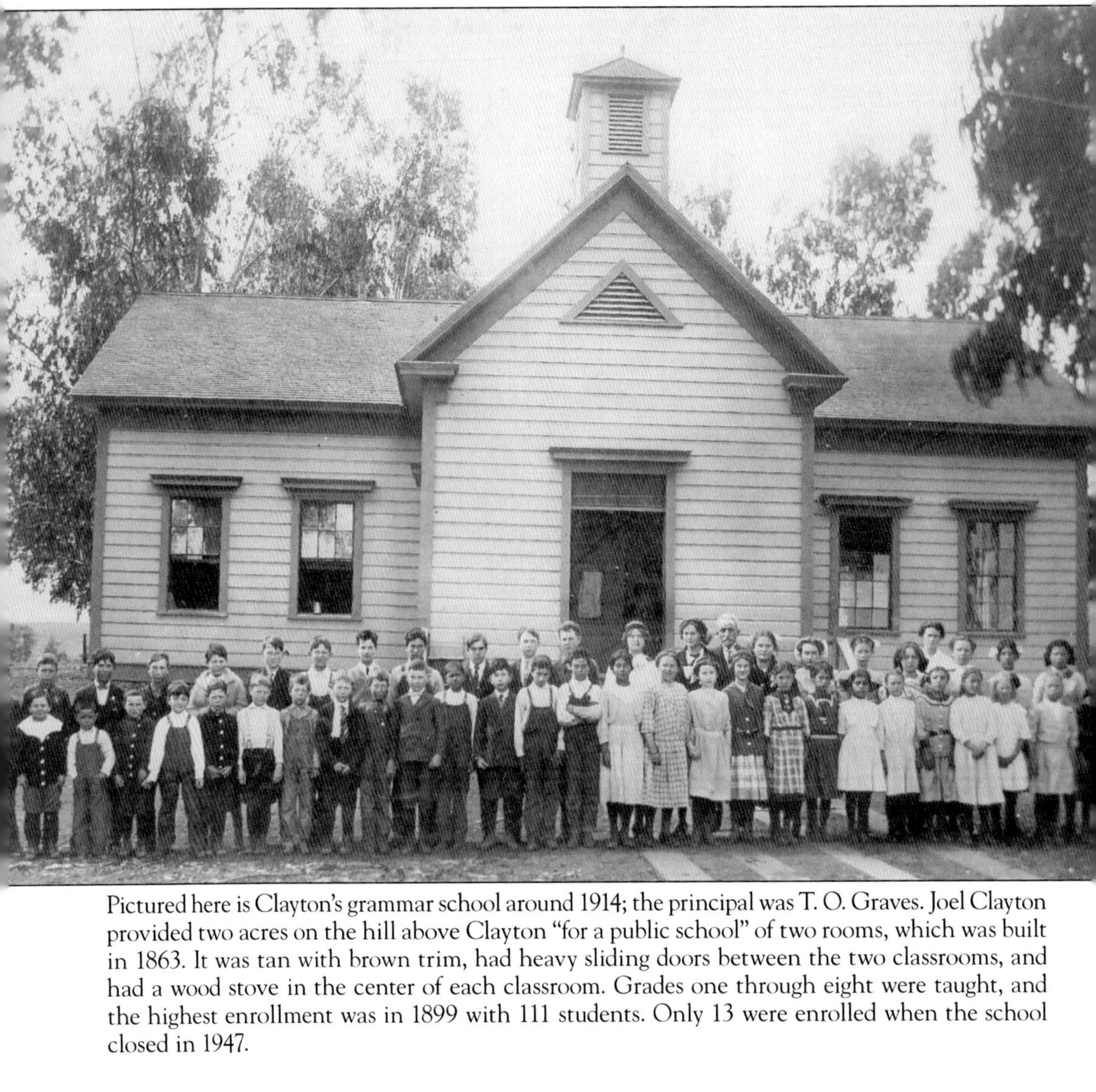

Pictured here is Clayton's grammar school around 1914; the principal was T. O. Graves. Joel Clayton provided two acres on the hill above Clayton "for a public school" of two rooms, which was built in 1863. It was tan with brown trim, had heavy sliding doors between the two classrooms, and had a wood stove in the center of each classroom. Grades one through eight were taught, and the highest enrollment was in 1899 with 111 students. Only 13 were enrolled when the school closed in 1947.

Around 1881, Jessie McGowen was a teacher at the Clayton school.

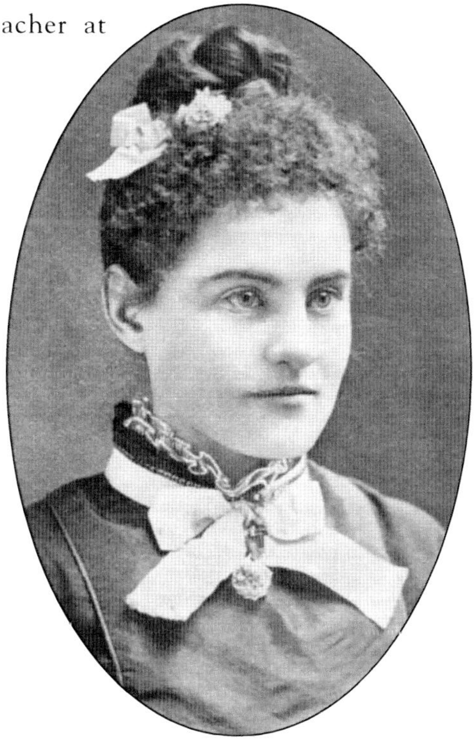

School Rules — 1872

1. Will fill lamps, trim wicks and clean chimneys.
2. Each morning teacher will bring bucket of water and a scuttle of coal for the days session.
3. Make your pens carefully. You may whittle nibs to the individual taste of the pupils.
4. Men teachers may take one evening each week for courting purposes or two evenings a week if they attend church regularly.
5. After 10 hours in school the teachers may spend the remaining time reading the Bible or any other good book.
6. Women teachers who marry or engage in unseemly conduct will be dismissed.
7. Every teacher should lay aside for each pay day a goodly sum of his earnings for his benefit during his declining years so that he will not become a burden on society.
8. Any teacher who smokes, uses liquor in any form, frequents pool or public halls, or gets shaved in a barber shop will give good reason to suspect his worth, intention, integrity and honesty.
9. The teacher who performs his labor faithfully and without fault for five years will be given an increase of $.25 per week in his pay providing the Board of Education approves.

Unmarried teachers typically roomed with a family, who would monitor behavior outside of school.

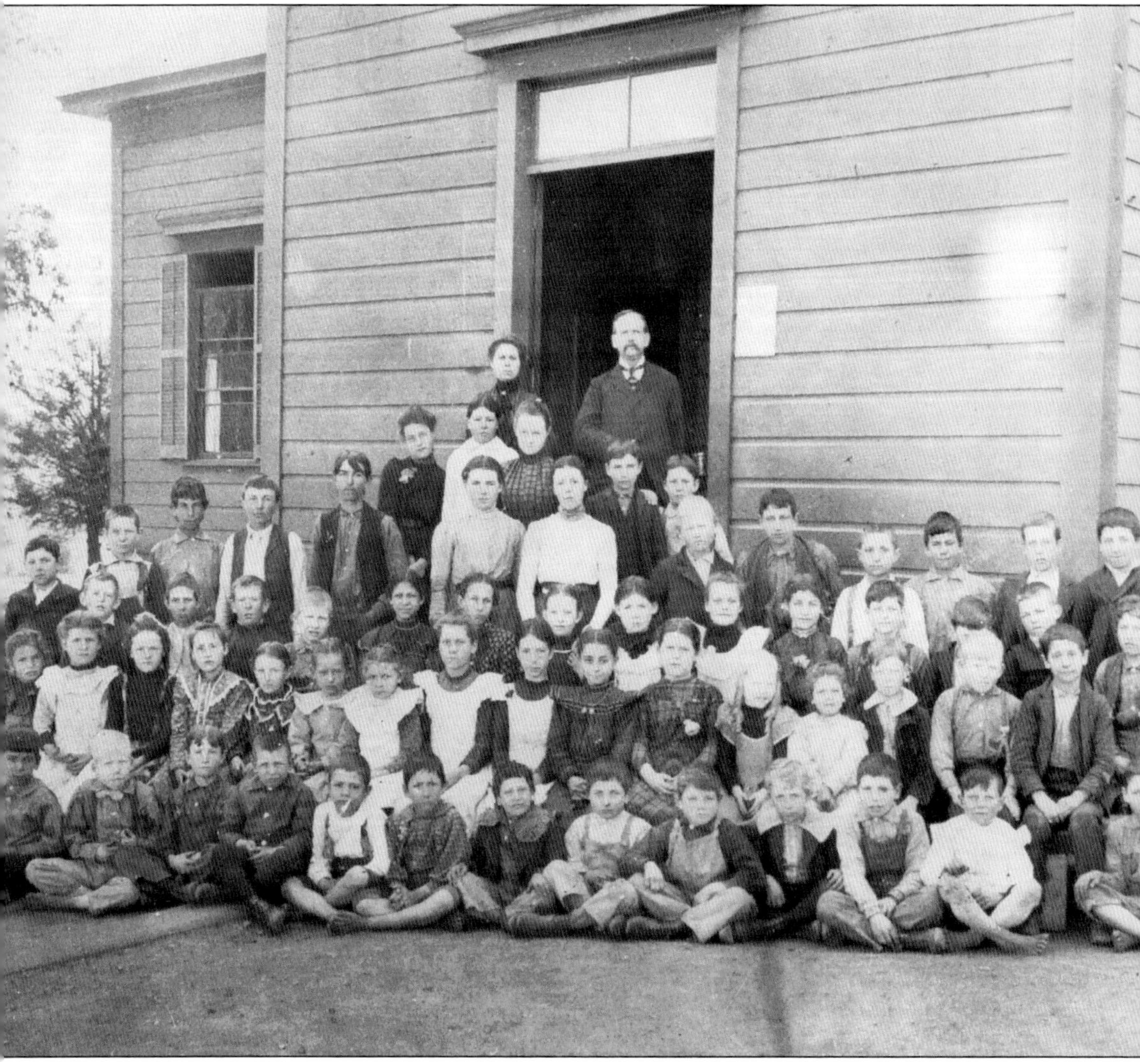

Pictured here is the Clayton grammar school in the late 1890s. The following faculty and students, from left to right, are (first row) Frank Murchio, Henry Duncan, Willie Bloching, Irwin Rhine, Joe Napolitano, Ellie Matheron, Milton Rhine, Mathew Mangini, Orville Trette, Ralph Wetmore, Alec Rhine, Arlo Sperry, and John Napolitano; (second row) Azalia Murchio, Hannah Hurley, Marian Kirkwood, Ada Myrick, Lillie Frank, May Rumgay, Florence Clayton, Lottie Myrick, Wilda Chapman, Mary Mangini, Lois Kirkwood, Gladys Sperry, Ruth Rhine, Bobbie Chapman, Wylie McGrew, and George Napolitano; (third row) Lou Rhine, Willard Ploog, Joe Matheron, Harry Ploog, Willie Duncan, Belle Rhine, Annie Frank, Lillie Chapman, Gertie Hurley, Gladys Sperry, Wilhelmina Trette, Albert Trette, Herbert Chapman, Archie Williams, and Nathan Rhine; (fourth row) Louis Bloching, Dominic Murchio, Leo Frank, Albert Frank, Katie Hurley, Irene Kirkwood, Robert Sweet, Leon Rhine, Tony Napolitano, Louis Murchio, George Stockfleth, and Joe Mangini; (fifth row) May Stockfleth, Mary McGrew, Edna Wetmore, Herman Hebiesn, and Fred Bloching; (sixth row) Miss Lander and W. A. Kirkwood.

Anna Jane O'Connell came to Clayton School to teach around 1908 and boarded with Laura Olofson Condie and Laura's mother on the Atchinson ranch. Miss O'Connell allowed Lucy Correa to attend school even though she was younger than six years old. When Lucy got tired, she would climb up on Miss O'Connell's lap and take a nap.

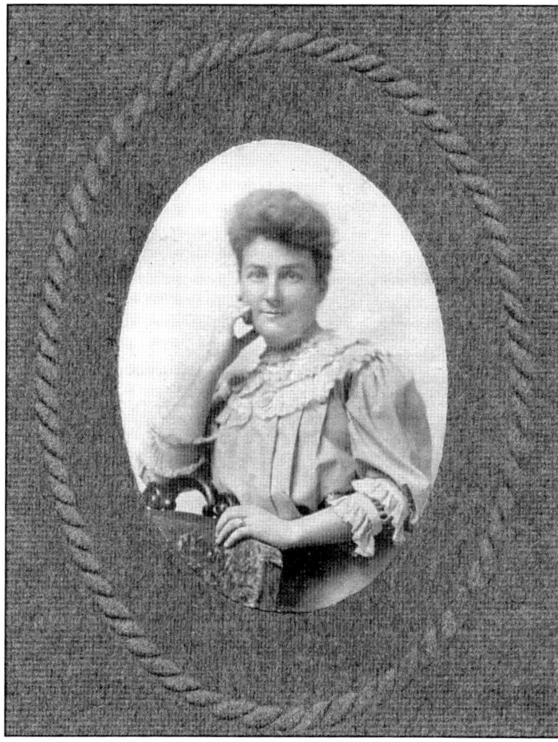

Rules for Teachers — 1915

1. You will not marry during the term of your contract.
2. You are not to keep company with men.
3. You must be home between the hours of 8 PM and 6 AM unless at a school function.
4. You may not loiter downtown in any of the ice cream stores.
5. You may not travel beyond the city limits unless you have permission of the chairman of the chairman of the school board.
6. You may not ride in carriages or automobiles with any man except your father or brother.
7. You may not smoke cigarettes.
8. You may not dress in bright colors.
9. You may under no circumstances dye your hair.
10. You must wear at least 2 petticoats.
11. Your dresses may not be any shorter than 2 inches above the ankles.
12. To keep the classroom neat and clean you must sweep the floor once a day, scrub the floor with hot soapy water once a week, clean the blackboards once a day and start the fire at 7 AM to have the school warm by 8 AM when the scholars arrive.

These rules for women teachers left out an unspoken rule—the teacher was expected to babysit children who were too young to attend school if the children's mothers needed such services.

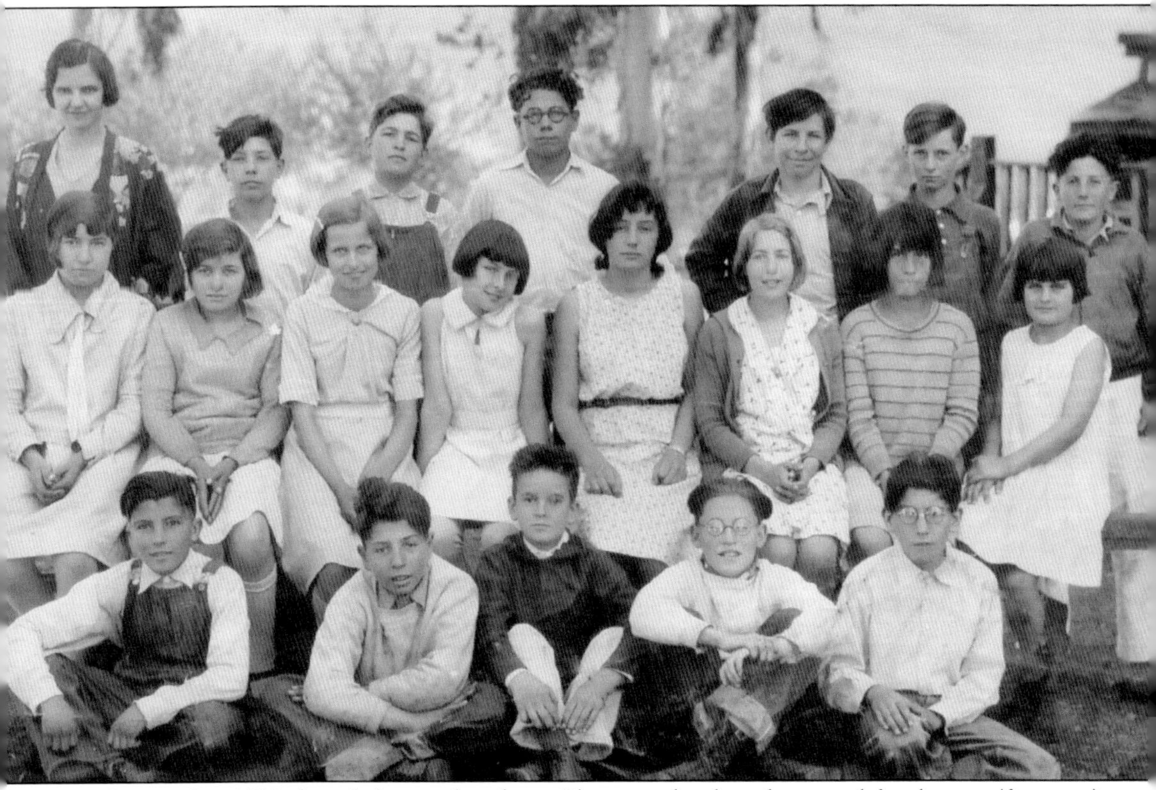

Pictured *c.* 1930, from left to right, these Clayton school students and faculty are (first row) Alvin Joaquin, Edward Gomez, unidentified, Albert Trette, and Eugene Matz; (second row) Olivia Bettencourt, Julia Bettencourt, Camille deWolfe, Gail Dietz, June Maguire, Emma Jane Trette, Lorraine Gomez, and Eleanor deWolfe; (third row) Edna Smith (teacher), Albert Matz, Joe Bettencourt, Alfred Schwartz, unidentified, unidentified, and ? Maggiora.

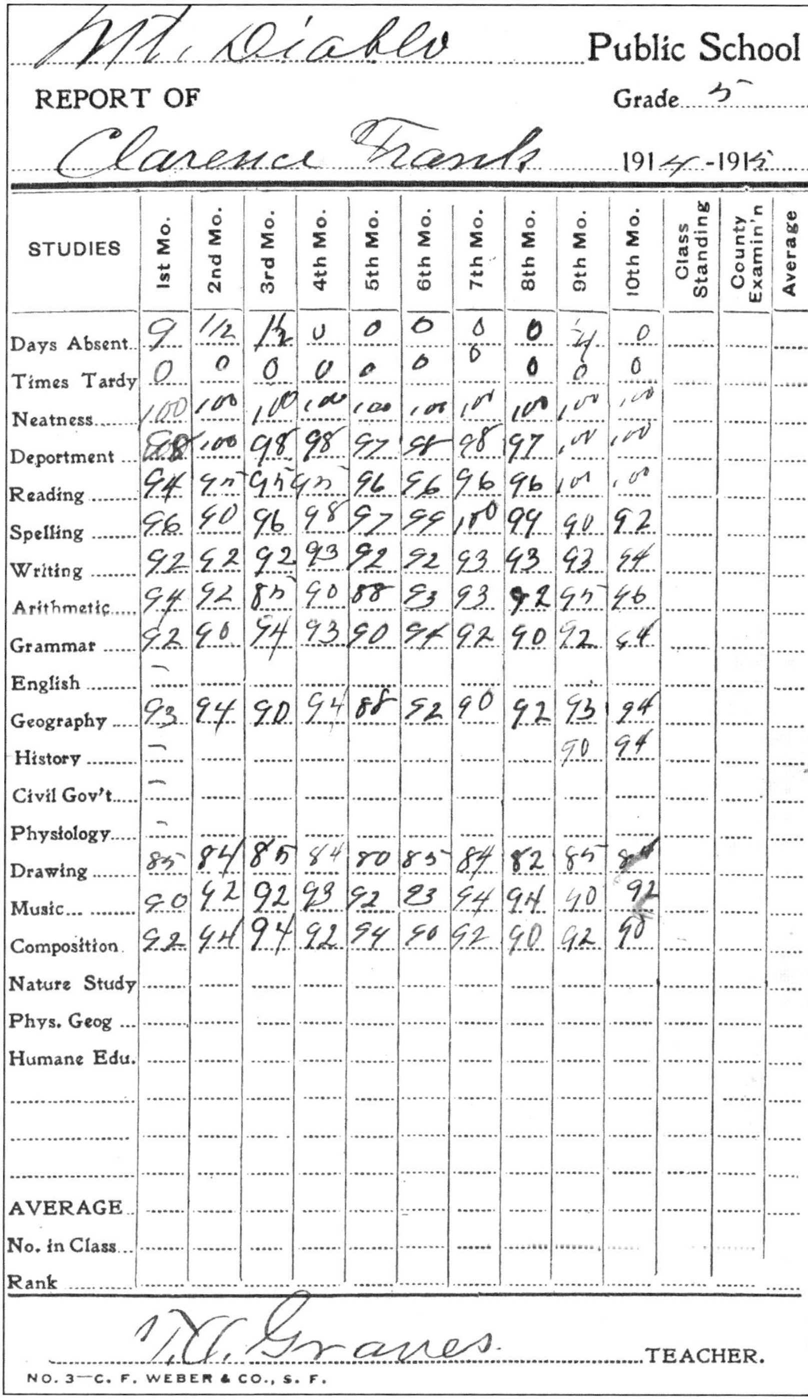

Mt. Diablo Public School

REPORT OF Clarence Franks Grade 5 1914-1915

STUDIES	1st Mo.	2nd Mo.	3rd Mo.	4th Mo.	5th Mo.	6th Mo.	7th Mo.	8th Mo.	9th Mo.	10th Mo.	Class Standing	County Examin'n	Average
Days Absent	9	1/2	1½	0	0	0	0	0	½	0			
Times Tardy	0	0	0	0	0	0	0	0	0	0			
Neatness	100	100	100	100	100	100	100	100	100	100			
Deportment	98	100	98	98	97	98	98	97	100	100			
Reading	94	95	95	95	96	96	96	96	100	100			
Spelling	96	90	96	98	97	99	100	99	90	92			
Writing	92	92	92	93	92	92	93	93	93	94			
Arithmetic	94	92	85	90	88	93	93	92	95	96			
Grammar	92	90	94	93	90	94	92	90	92	94			
English	–												
Geography	93	94	90	94	88	92	90	92	93	94			
History	–								90	94			
Civil Gov't	–												
Physiology	–												
Drawing	85	84	85	84	80	85	84	82	85	80			
Music	90	92	92	93	92	93	94	94	90	92			
Composition	92	94	94	92	94	90	92	90	92	90			
Nature Study													
Phys. Geog													
Humane Edu.													
AVERAGE													
No. in Class													
Rank													

T. A. Graves TEACHER.

NO. 3—C. F. WEBER & CO., S. F.

Although it was commonly called Clayton Grammar School, this report card from 1914–1915 indicates an official name of "Mt. Diablo." Students who graduated from the eighth grade in Clayton went on to Mount Diablo High School in Concord after its construction in 1904. Before 1904, the closest high schools were in Oakland and Berkeley, so few Clayton students had a high-school education before Mount Diablo High was built.

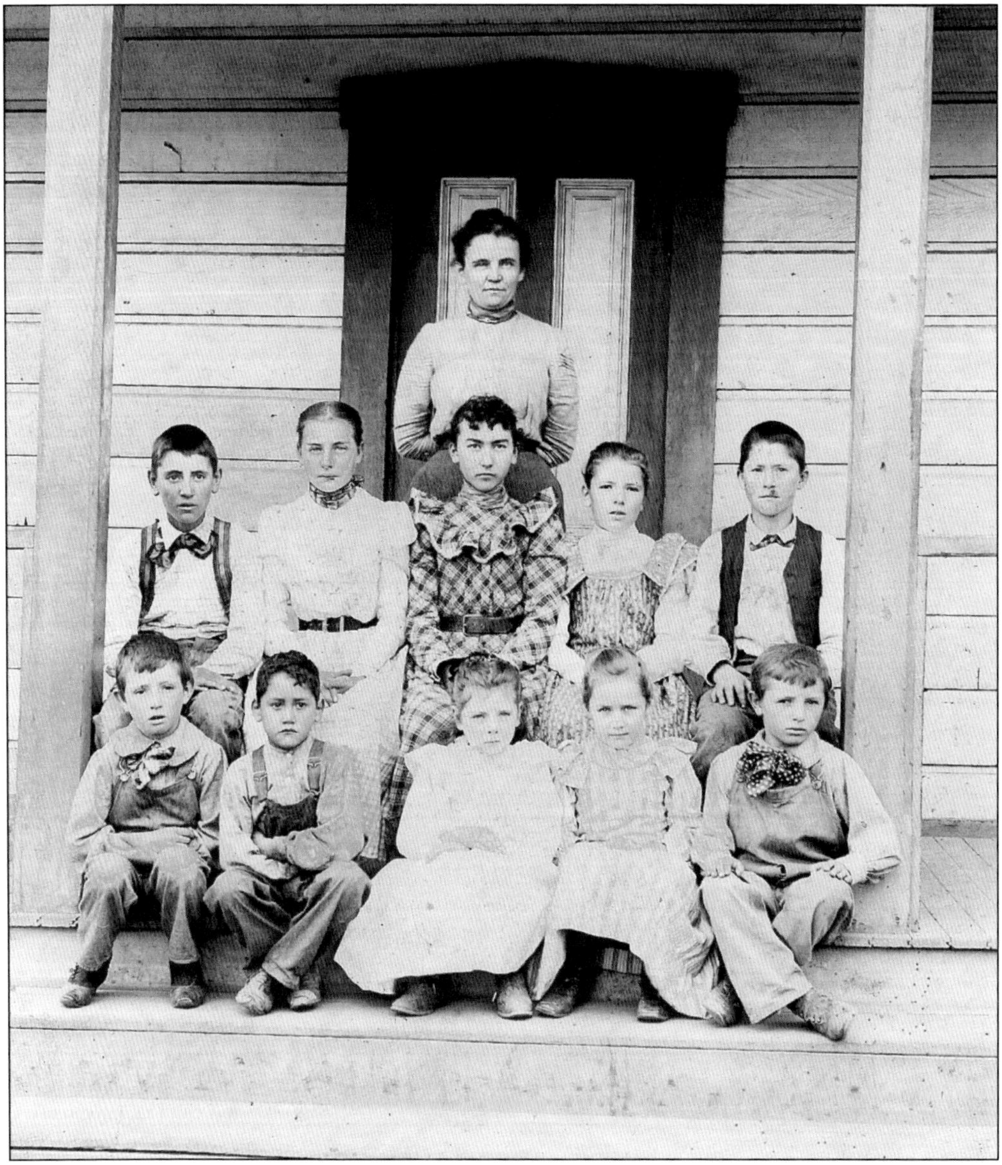

In 1858, the Morgan Territory School opened. Although Jeremiah Morgan could neither read nor write, educating his offspring to do so was important. It was always a one-room school and never employed more than one teacher. Its greatest enrollment was in 1870, when 32 students attended. Pictured here around 1899, from left to right, are (front row) Albert Morgan, unidentified, Lissy Morgan, Edith Olofson, and Jerry Morgan; (second row) Bob Morgan, Sally Morgan, unidentified, Alice Morgan, and Charlie Neary; (third row) Ellen Riley, the teacher.

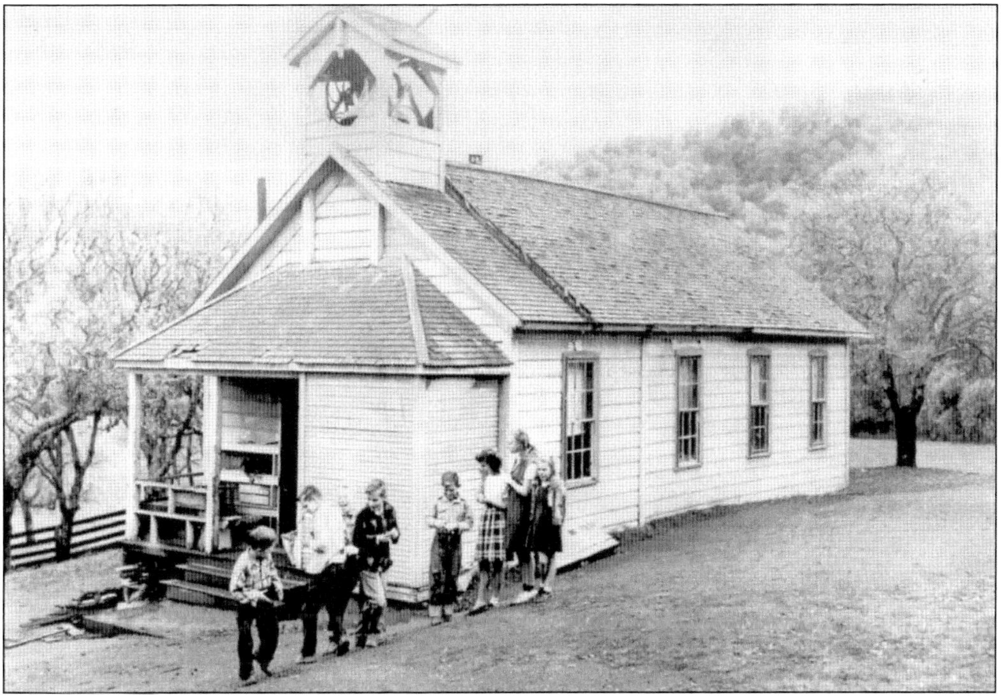

Morgan Territory School closed in 1947, with an enrollment of 15 students. It was difficult finding a teacher willing to live so far out in the country, and to make matters worse, there were no rooms available to board a teacher. After 1947, the students of Morgan Territory were forced to ride a bus to school in Concord. The school building and land were given to the community for use as a hall but shortly thereafter it was consumed by fire.

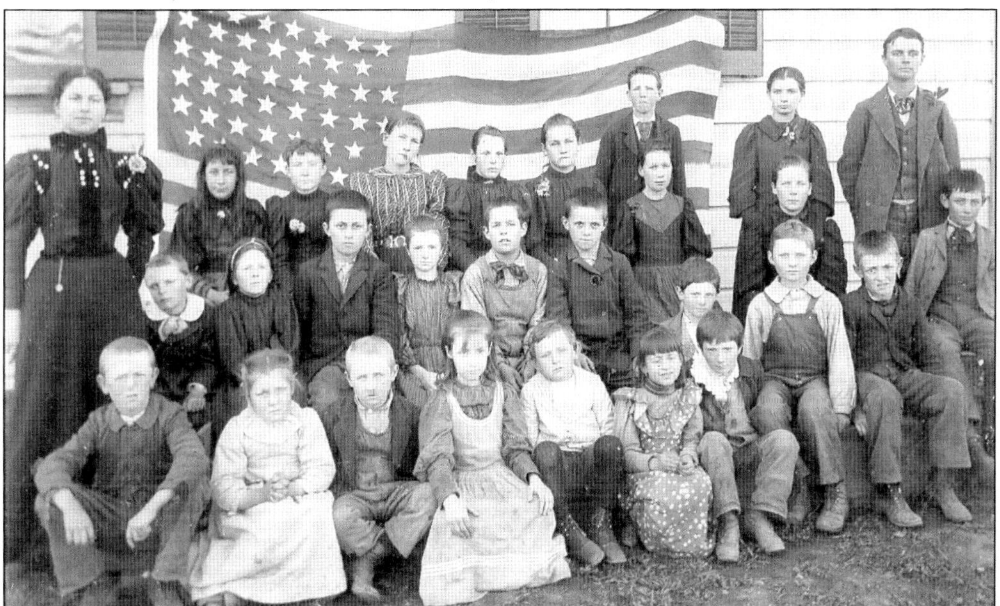

Lime Quarry School, which served Clayton Valley, stood on Clayton Road near Treat. The teacher, standing to the far left, is Esther Rhine. This photograph was taken around 1890.

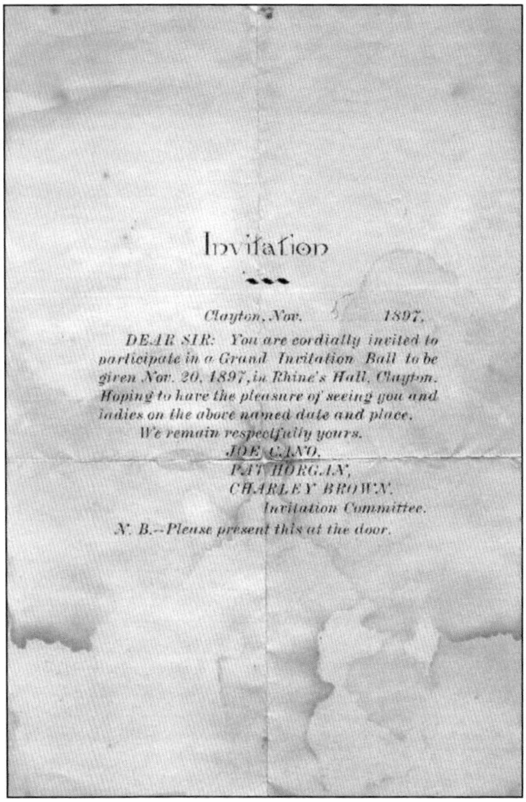

Invitation

Clayton, Nov. 5 1897.

DEAR SIR: You are cordially invited to participate in a Grand Invitation Ball to be given Nov. 20, 1897, in Rhine's Hall, Clayton. Hoping to have the pleasure of seeing you and ladies on the above named date and place.

We remain respectfully yours.

JOE CANO,
PAT HORGAN,
CHARLEY BROWN,
Invitation Committee.

N. B.—Please present this at the door.

On November 5, 1897, a grand invitation ball was held in Rhine's Hall on Main Street. The notation at the end of the invitation, N. B., is Latin for *nota bene* ("take notice").

Looking east on Main Street, Rhine's Hall is visible on the left. Many town events were held in Rhine's Hall including dinners, dances, plays, parties, and flower shows.

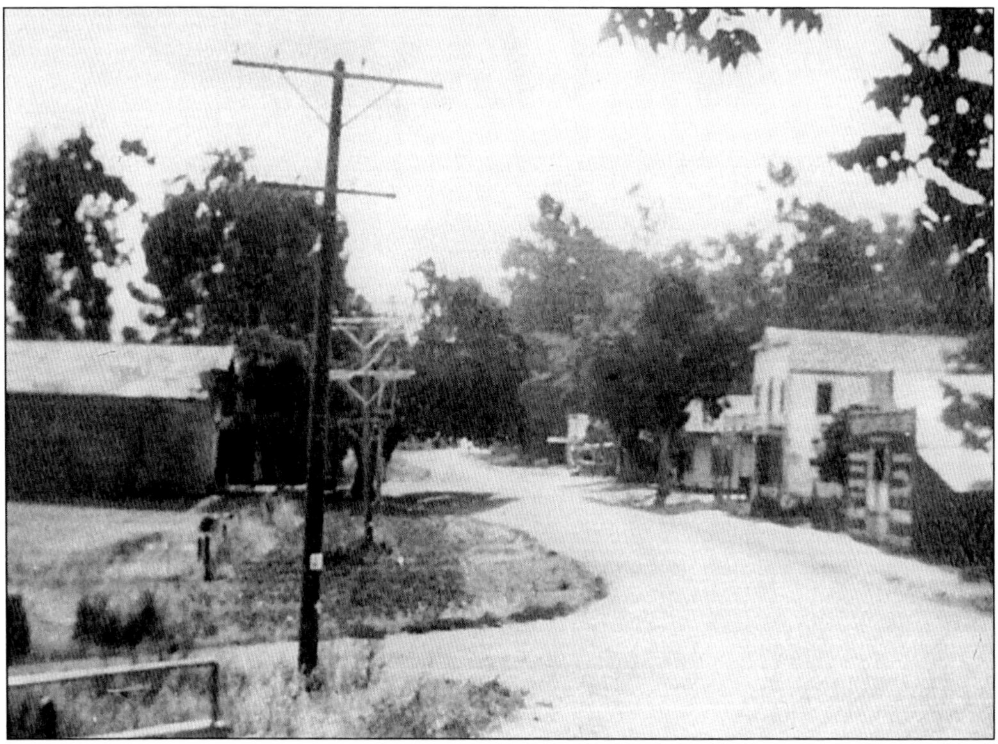

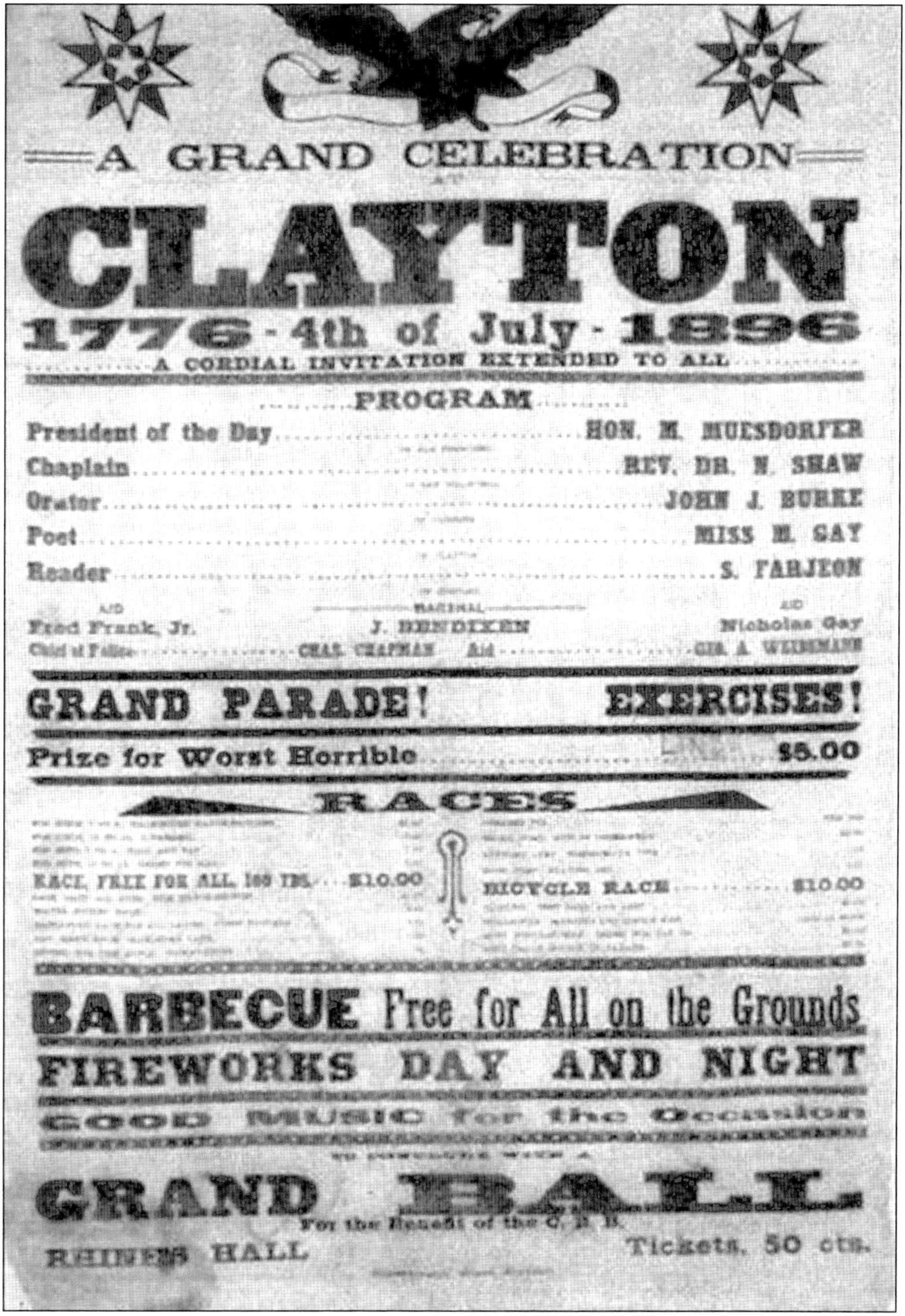

This fabric banner announced the 1896 Fourth of July celebration. It is printed in red, white, and blue on a muslin-type cloth and measures two feet, four inches by three feet, four inches. The dollar amounts of the prizes were handsome sums in 1896.

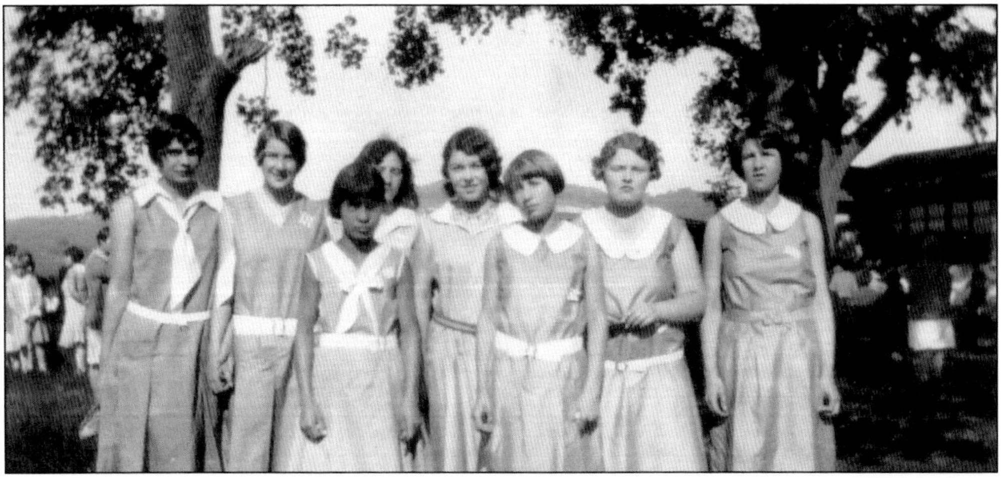

Members of Clayton's 4-H Club posed for this 1930 photograph. Pictured, from left to right, are Doris Kennerley, Willmetta Frank, Lorraine Gomez, June McGuire, Merle McGuire, Emma Jane Trette, Laura May Stockfleth, and Charlotte Trette.

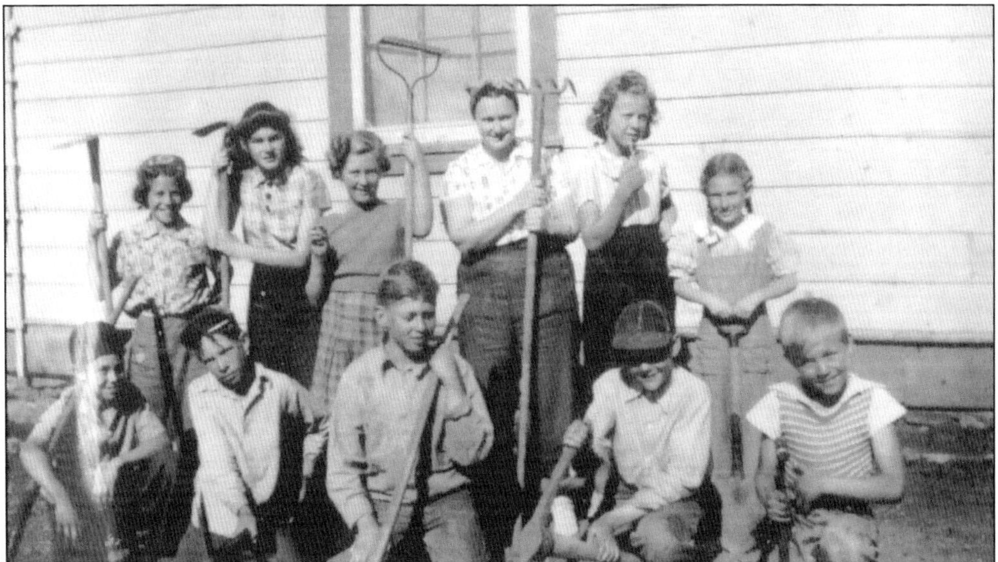

This 1938 photograph shows the Clayton 4-H Club children scouring the area around Clayton School. Pictured, from left to right, are (front row) Andy Bloching, David ?, Earl Duncan, Ronald Duncan, and Roy Chisholm (?); (second row) Phyllis Frank, Betty Arnold, Barbara Duncan, 4-H leader Carmen Frank, Yvonne Chisholm (?), and Lois Duncan.

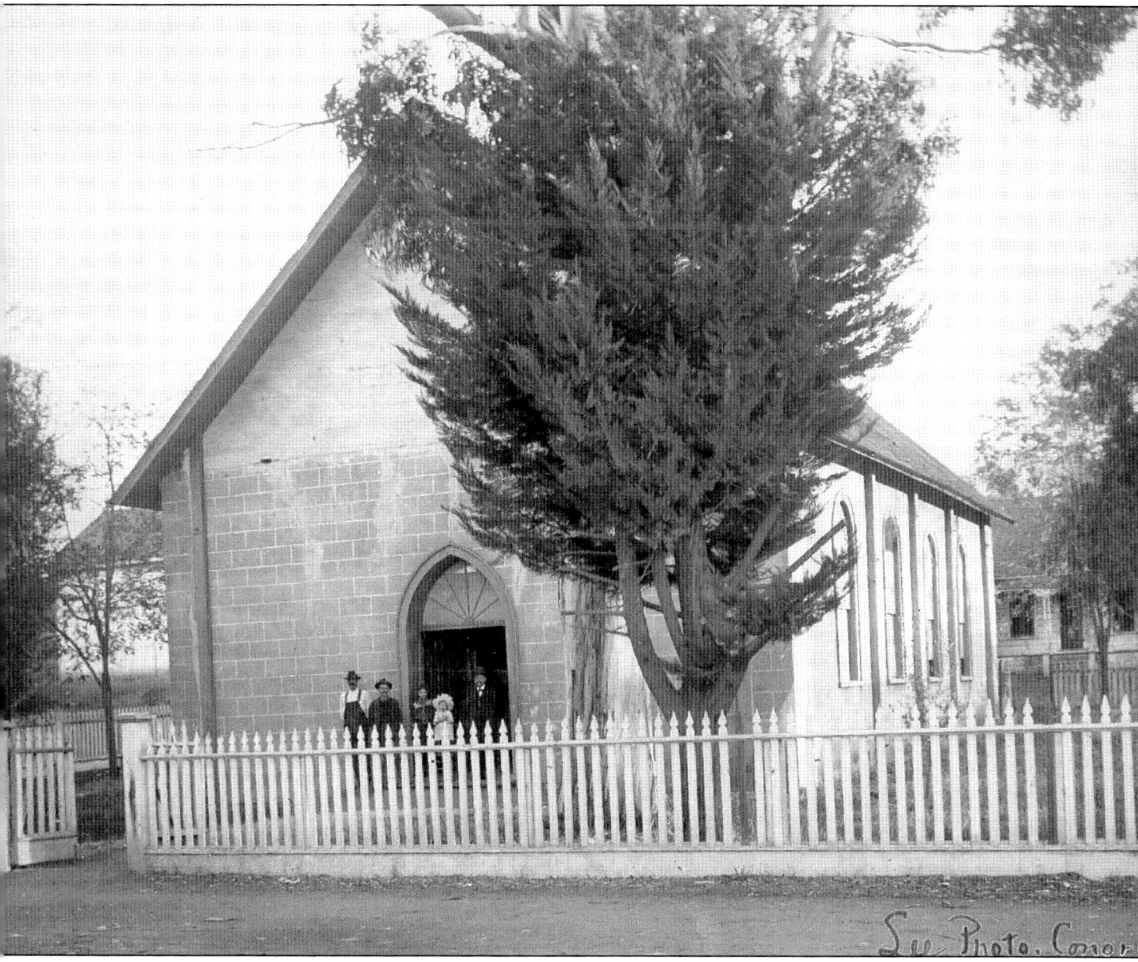

The Congregational church was built in the summer of 1866 of rammed earth. It stood on the southeast corner of Center and Diablo Streets. After the closure of the Methodist church in 1896, because it was the only church in Clayton, most area residents of a church-going nature became members of the Congregational church. This picture, taken around 1900, shows members of the Trette family and others in front of the church. The parsonage is visible behind. The property also had a barn, visible on the left.

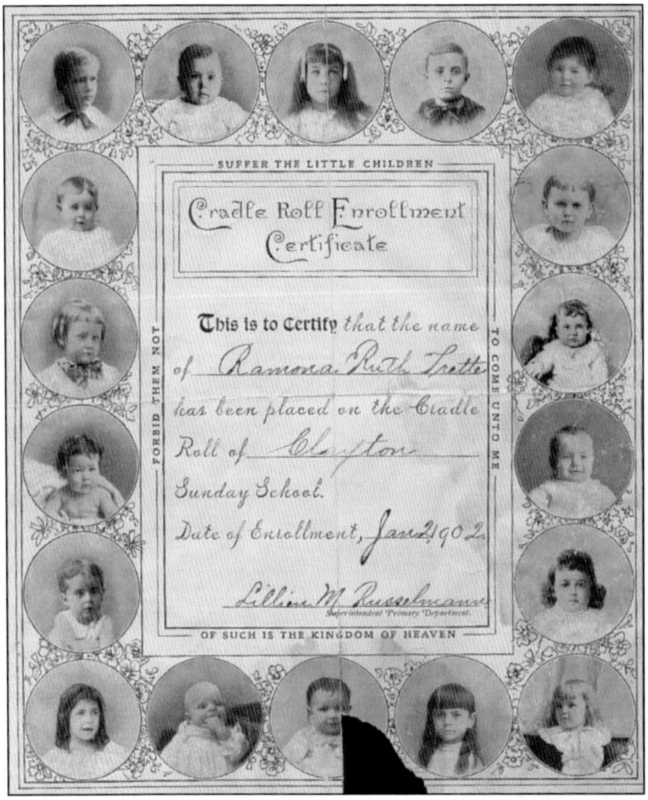

SUFFER THE LITTLE CHILDREN

Cradle Roll Enrollment Certificate

This is to Certify that the name of Ramona Ruth Trette has been placed on the Cradle Roll of Clayton Sunday School.

Date of Enrollment, Jan 2 1902.

Lillien M. Russelmann
Superintendent Primary Department.

FORBID THEM NOT TO COME UNTO ME

OF SUCH IS THE KINGDOM OF HEAVEN

In 1902, Ramona Trette attends Sunday school. The officials of the Congregational church in 1902 were deacons Mary E. Bigelow, William Kirkwood, and C. P. Bigelow; H. C. Wetmore, treasurer and assistant Sunday school superintendent; Glennie Busey, clerk; Sunday school superintendent Lillien Russelmann; and organist Mrs. C. H. Stevens.

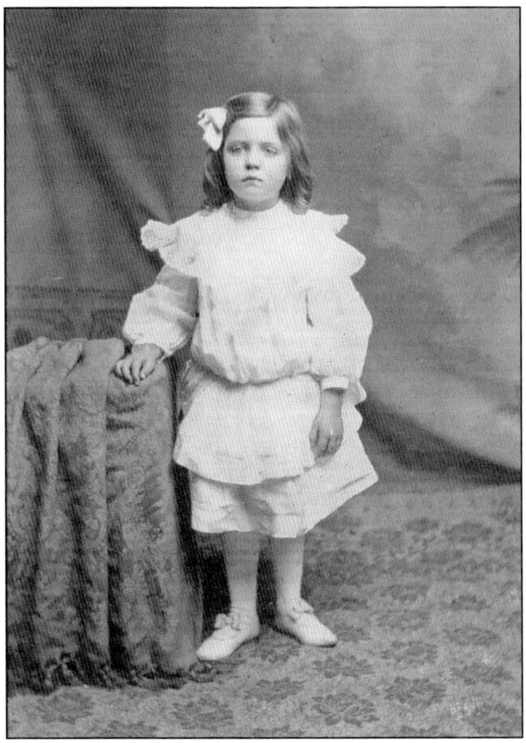

Around 1902, Ramona Trette poses for a portrait.

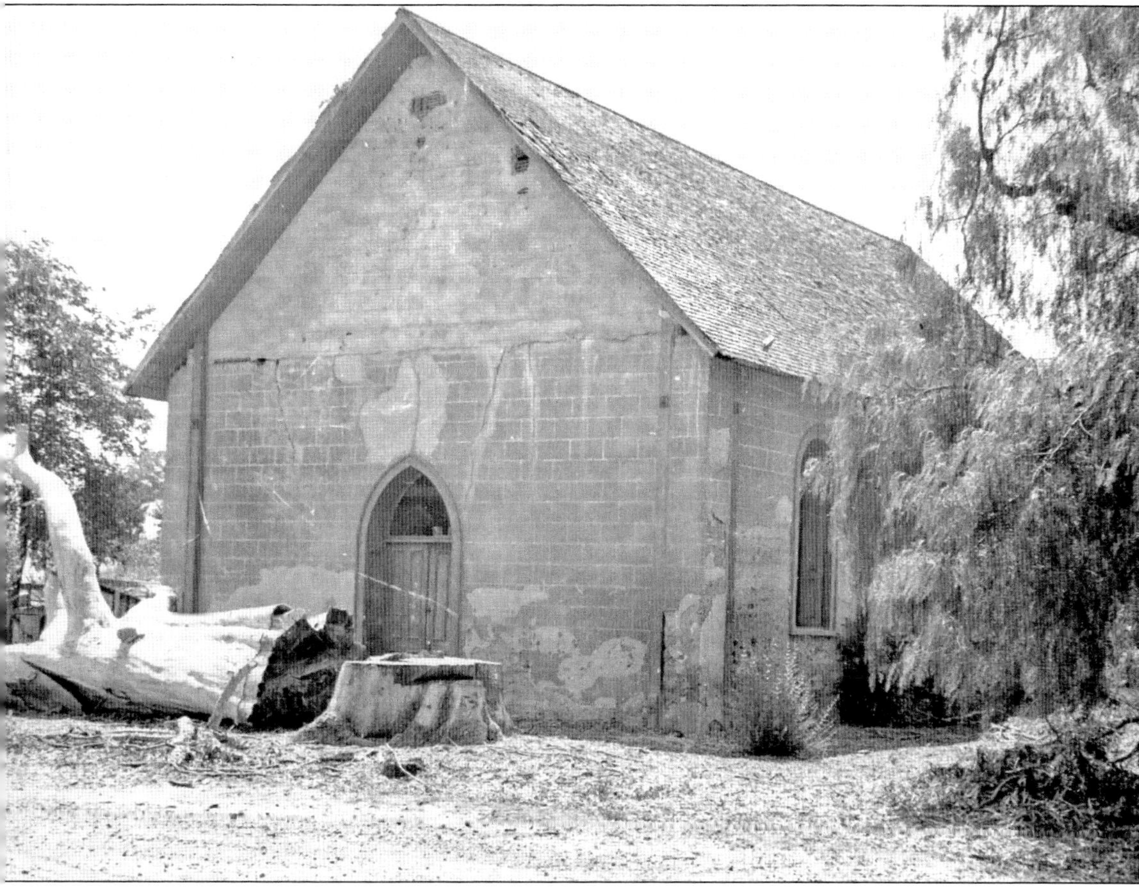

Throughout its existence, the Congregational church was in constant need of repair. Services ceased being held there in 1924 and were held instead in the Christian Endeavor Hall. The church, parsonage, barn, and lots were sold in 1927 to Joe Matz for $1,550. This photograph was taken about 1940.

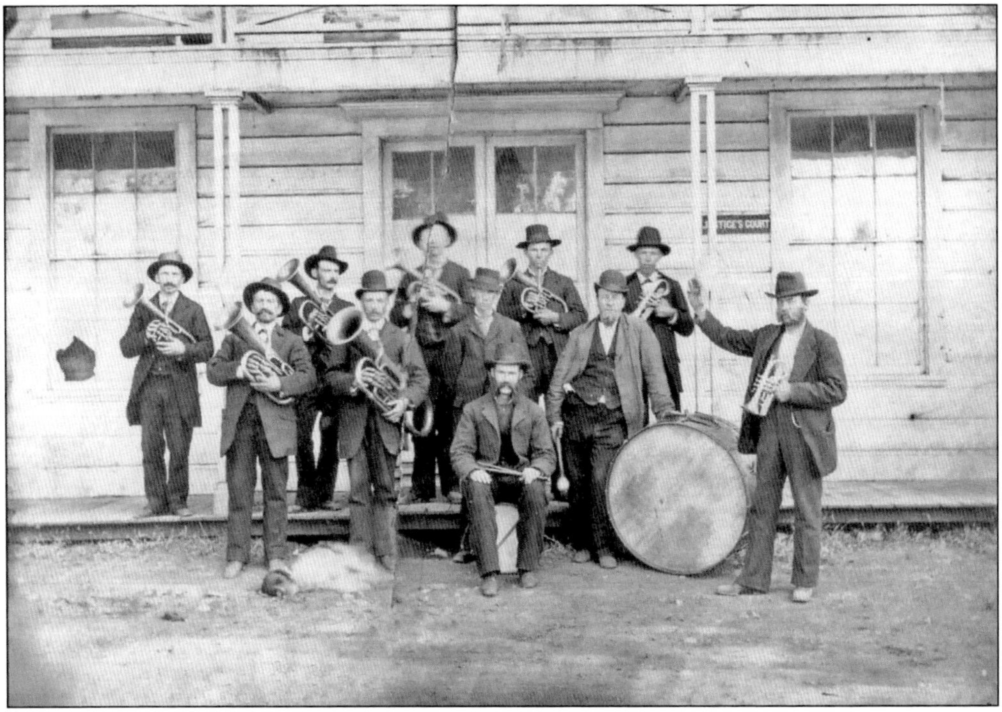

Otto Schwartz was the director of Clayton's Silver Cornet Band. The drummer was Doc Nottingham. Many of the Clayton area musicians who played in the silver cornet band were taught by Josef Schwendel, who was trained in classical music in his native Austria.

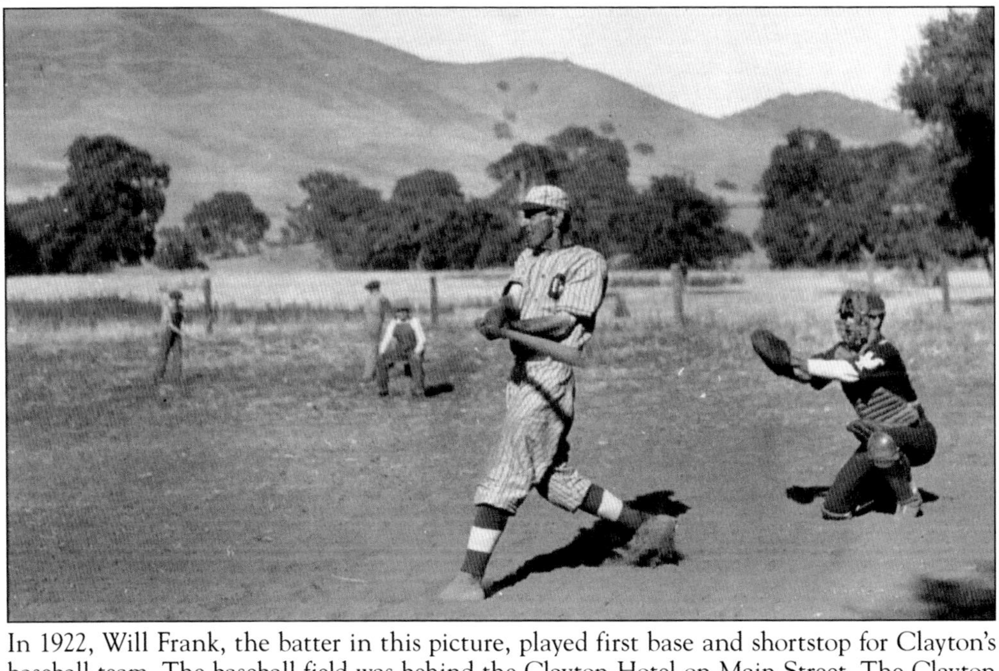

In 1922, Will Frank, the batter in this picture, played first base and shortstop for Clayton's baseball team. The baseball field was behind the Clayton Hotel on Main Street. The Clayton team uniforms were gray with dark red pinstripes and had a red "C" on the chest. Clayton played teams from Black Diamond, Concord, and Martinez.

Three

AGRICULTURE AND THE COUNTRYSIDE

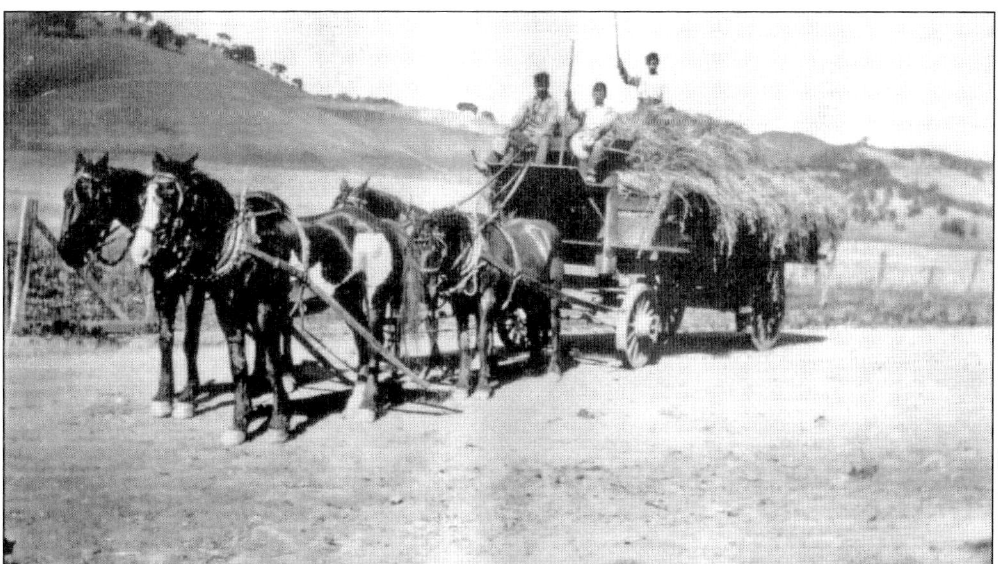

Hay was grown, vineyards thrived, and livestock was produced in the outlying areas of Clayton. The quicksilver mine bore mercury.

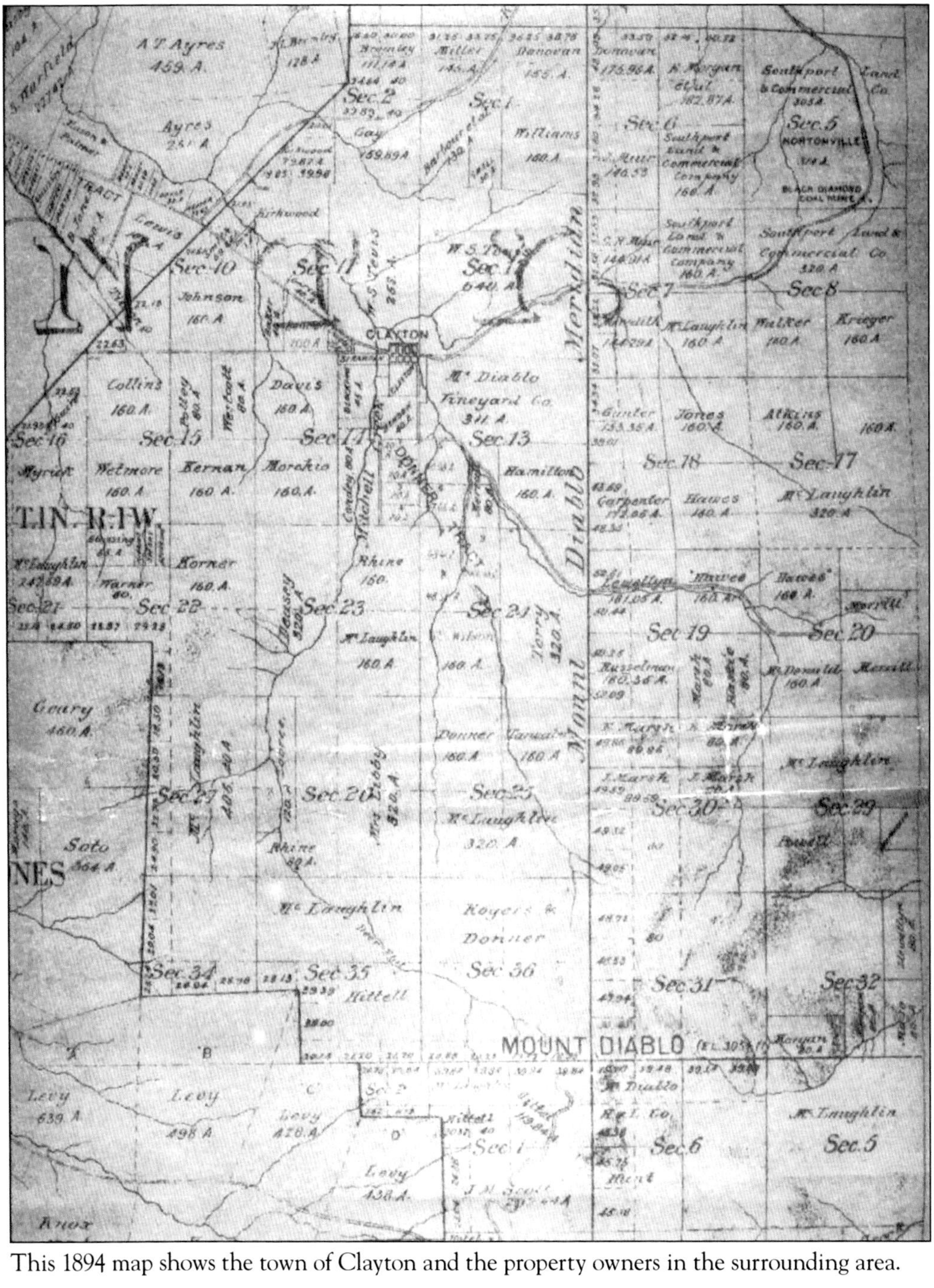

This 1894 map shows the town of Clayton and the property owners in the surrounding area.

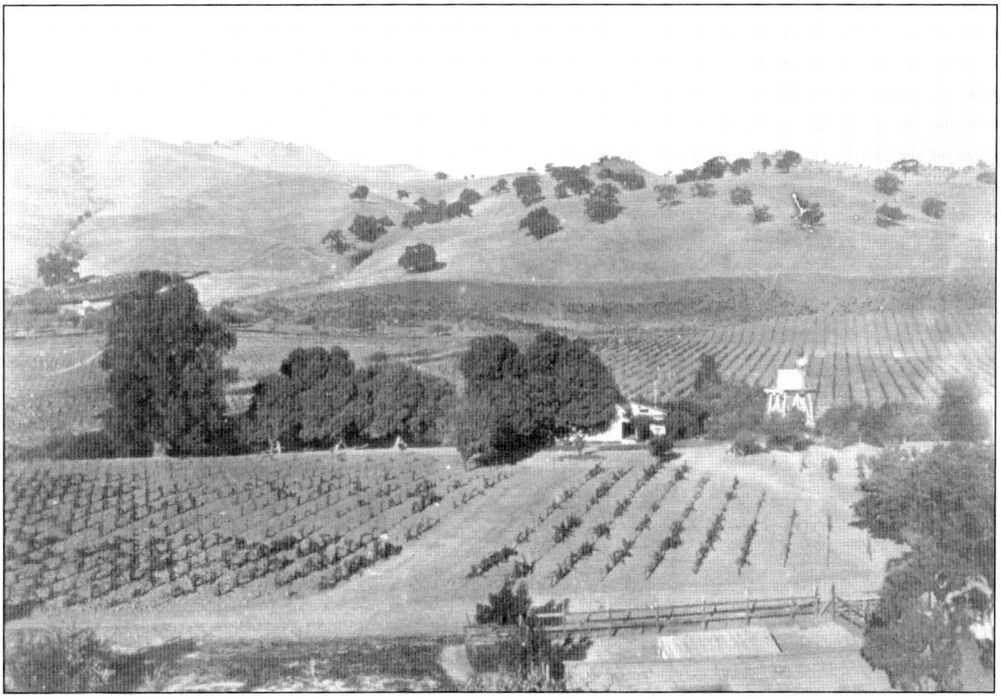

These two photographs of the Mount Diablo Winery were taken in 1911 and show views from both the north and the south angles.

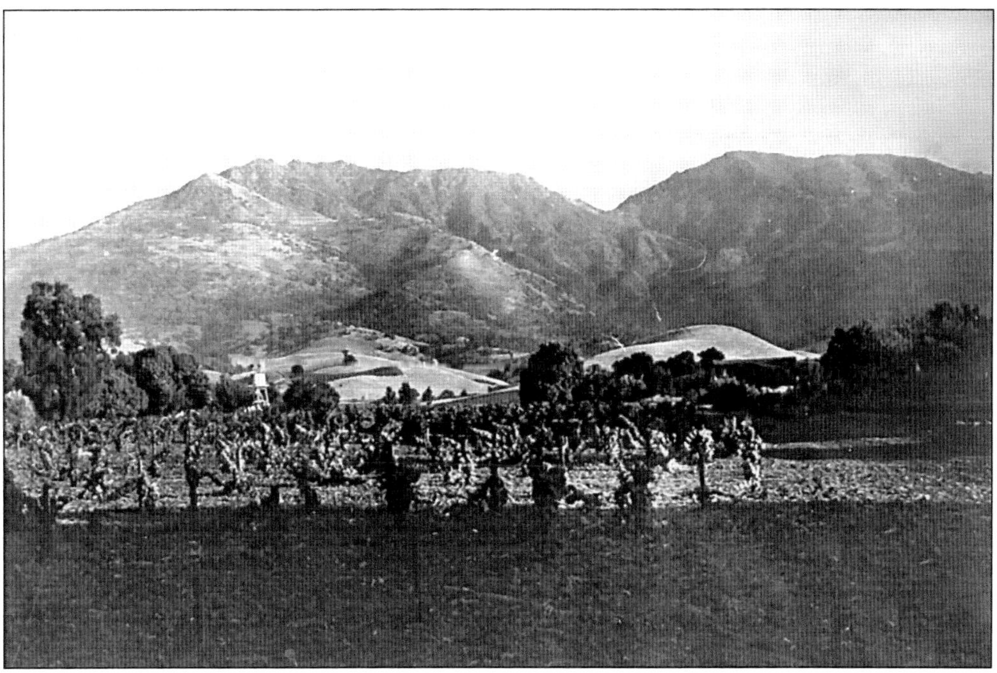

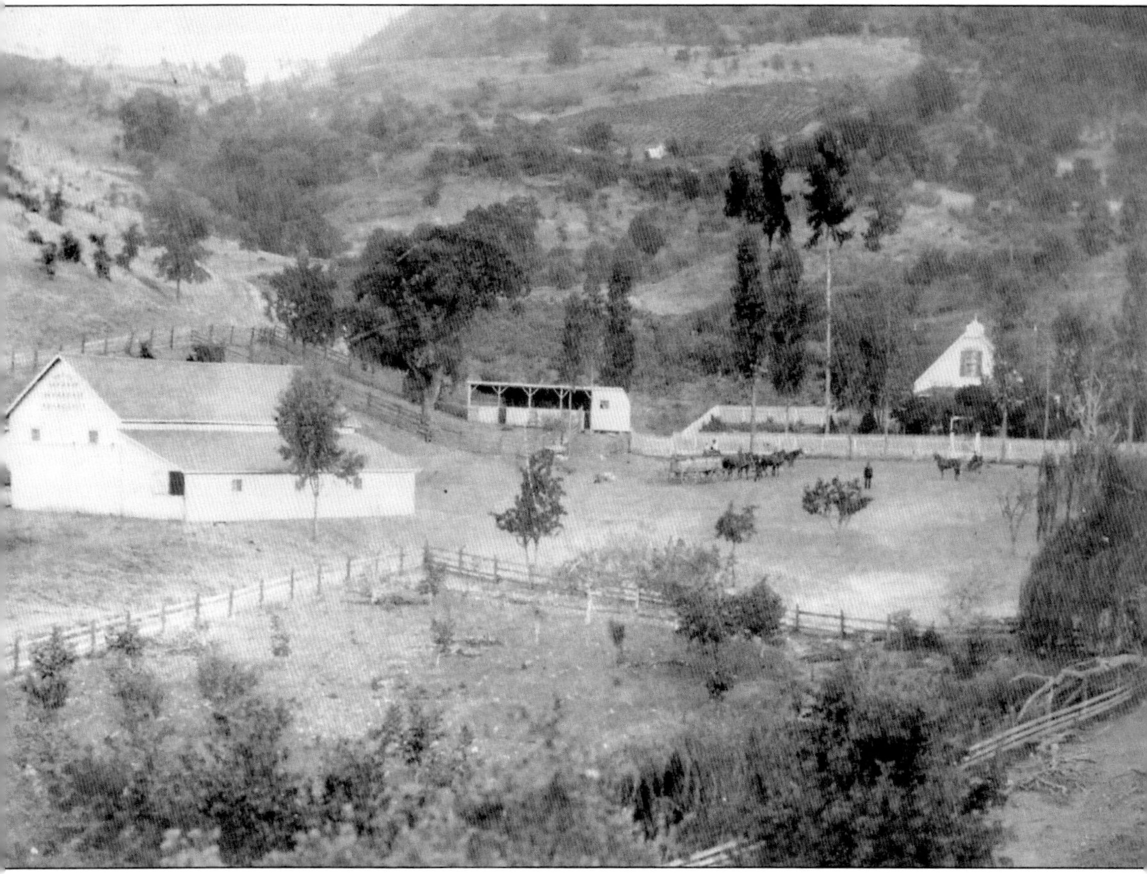

In the 1870s, sea captain Hinrich Friedrich "Fred" Russelmann, a native of Germany, built his ranch house on the slopes of Mount Diablo, about two miles east of Clayton. This photograph was taken in 1880.

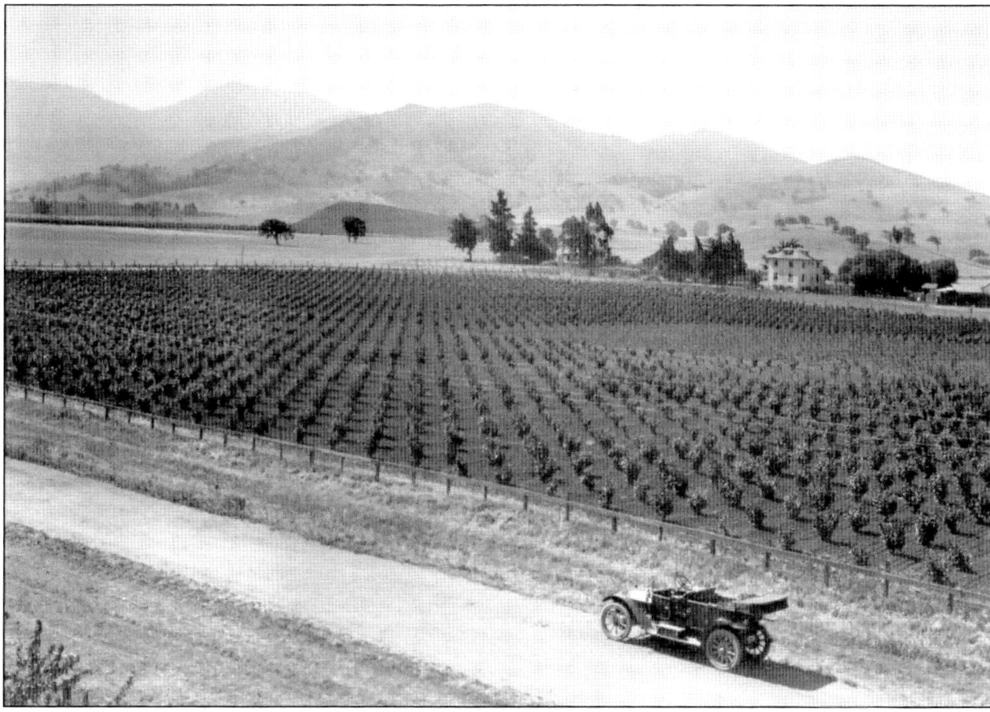

The automobile parked on Clayton Road in this 1915 photograph shows a vineyard and the home of Dr. A. W. Gamble. The property was later owned by the Garaventa family.

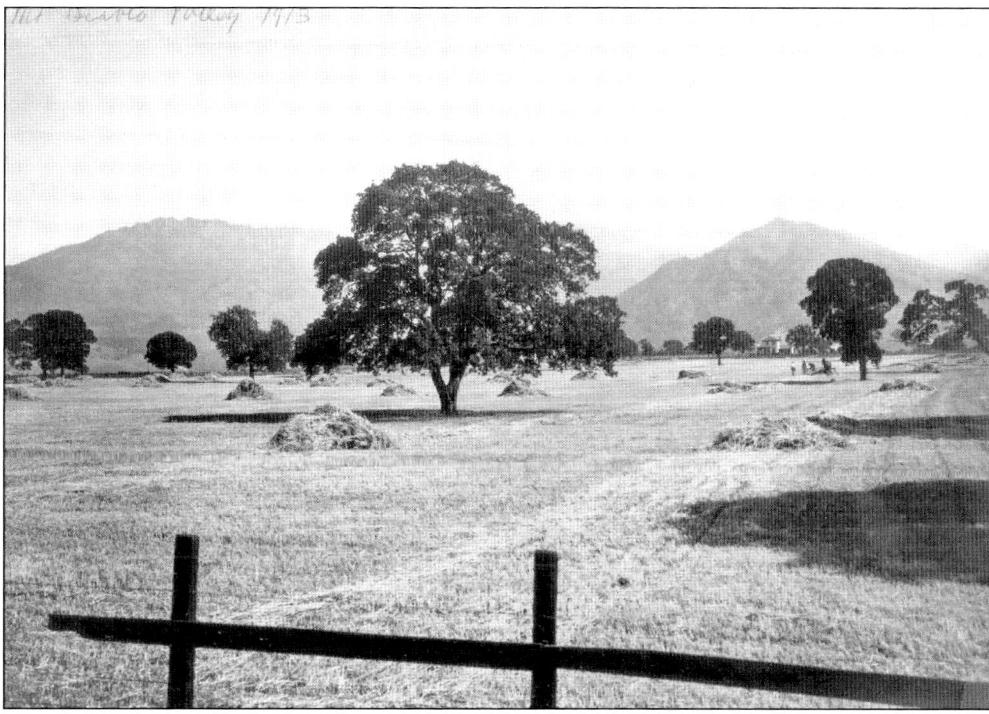

This 1913 photograph, with the Gamble home in the background, shows hay being harvested on the opposite side of Clayton Road.

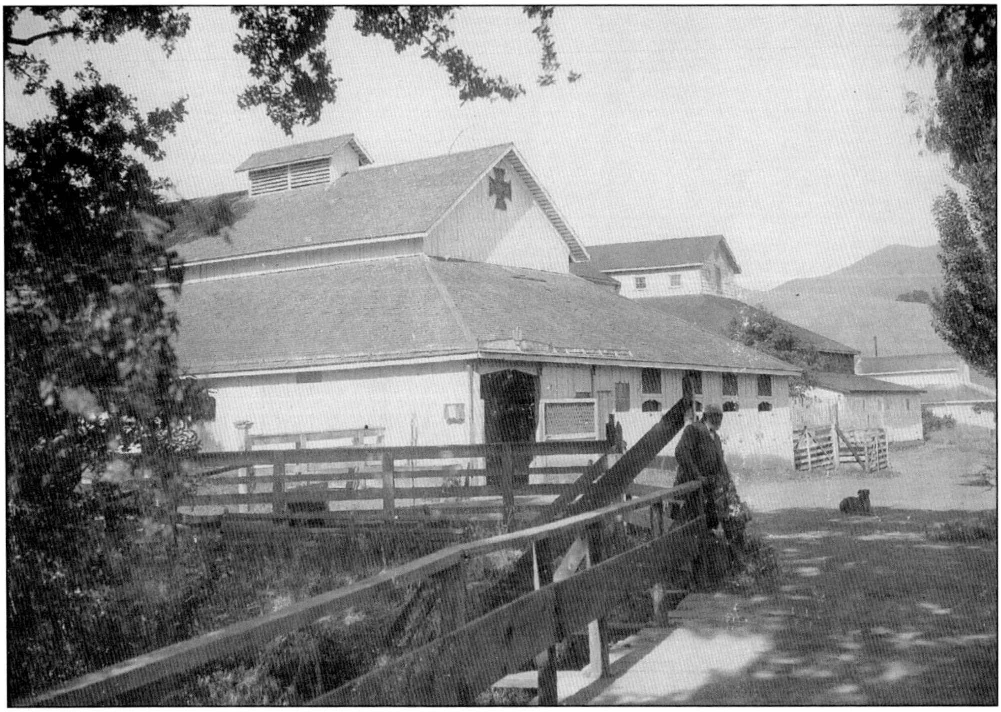

The Glen Terry Winery was located about one mile east of Clayton, off Marsh Creek Road. In the late 1800s, Mr. Terry poses for a picture at this bridge.

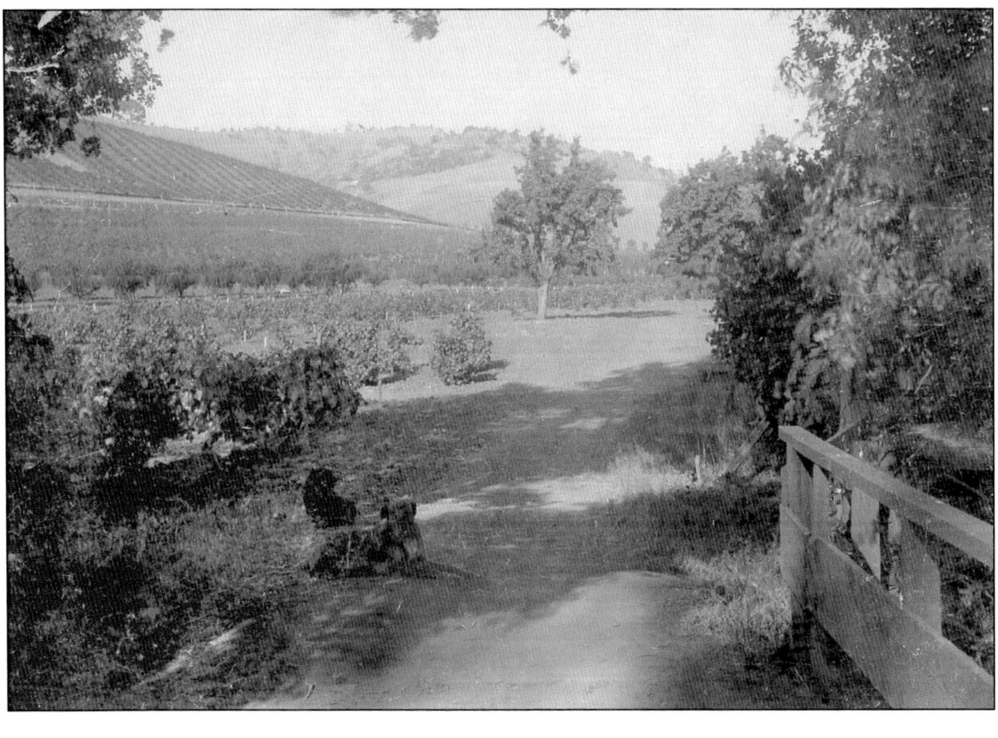

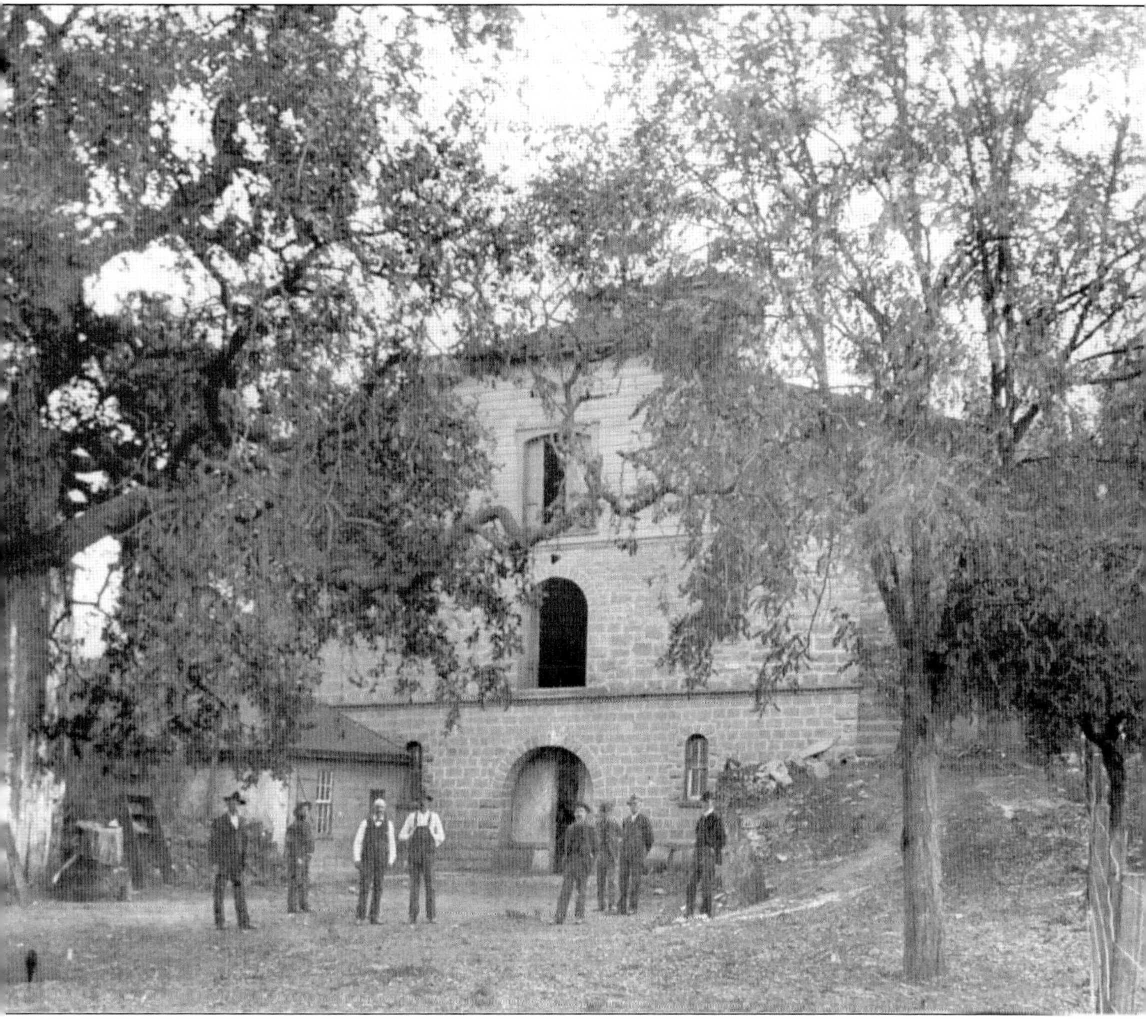

In 1885, Paul DeMartini built Clayton Vineyards Winery. Austrian stone masons used rock quarried on Mount Diablo that was hauled to Clayton by wagon teams. DeMartini port, sherry, white claret, and zinfandel won state, national, and international recognition. DeMartini sherries and ports won first prizes at the 1904 St. Louis Exposition. In 1919, wine production ended when the Congress passed the Volstead Act.

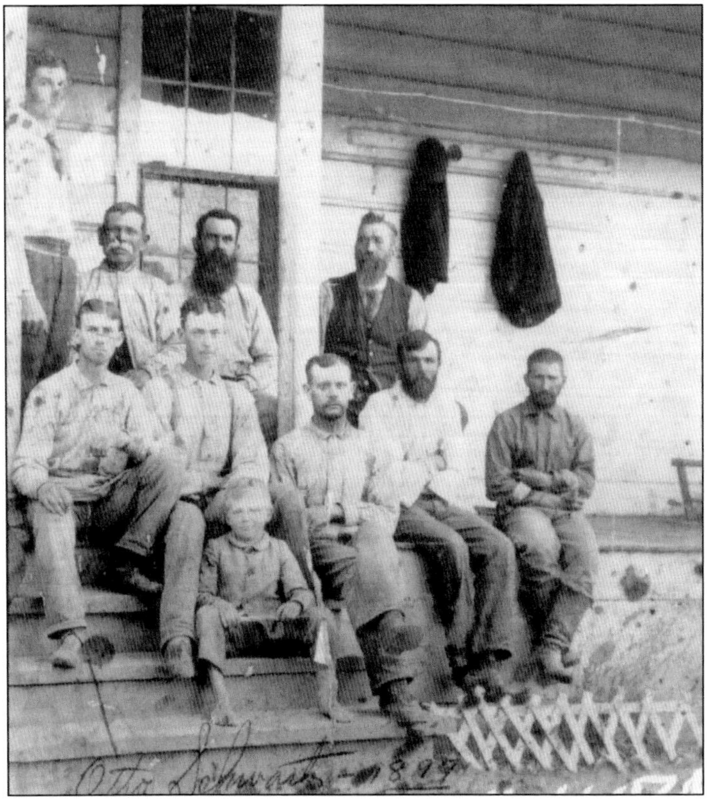

In 1899, the Mount Diablo Winery workers pose on the bunkhouse porch. Otto Schwartz is seated in the lower left.

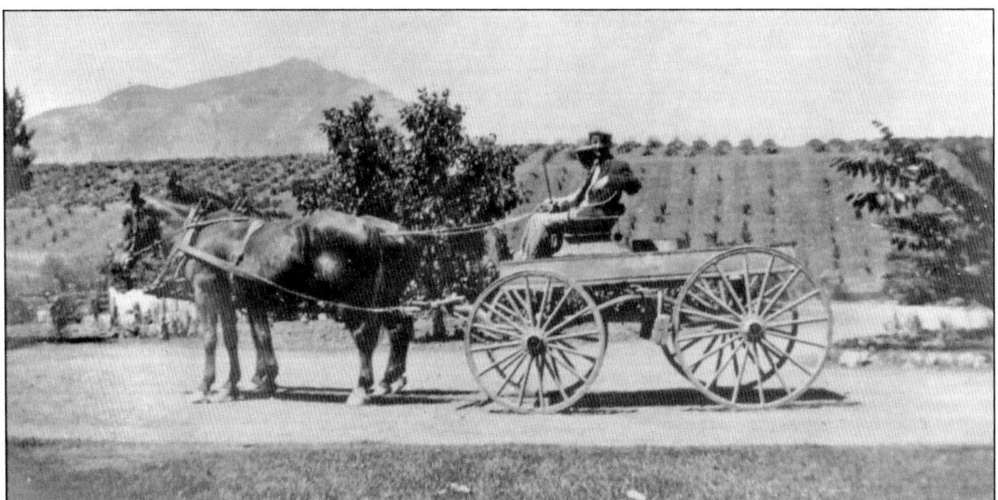

Mr. Salazar, shown here with a wagon and team of horses in 1911, was the manager of the Mount Diablo Winery.

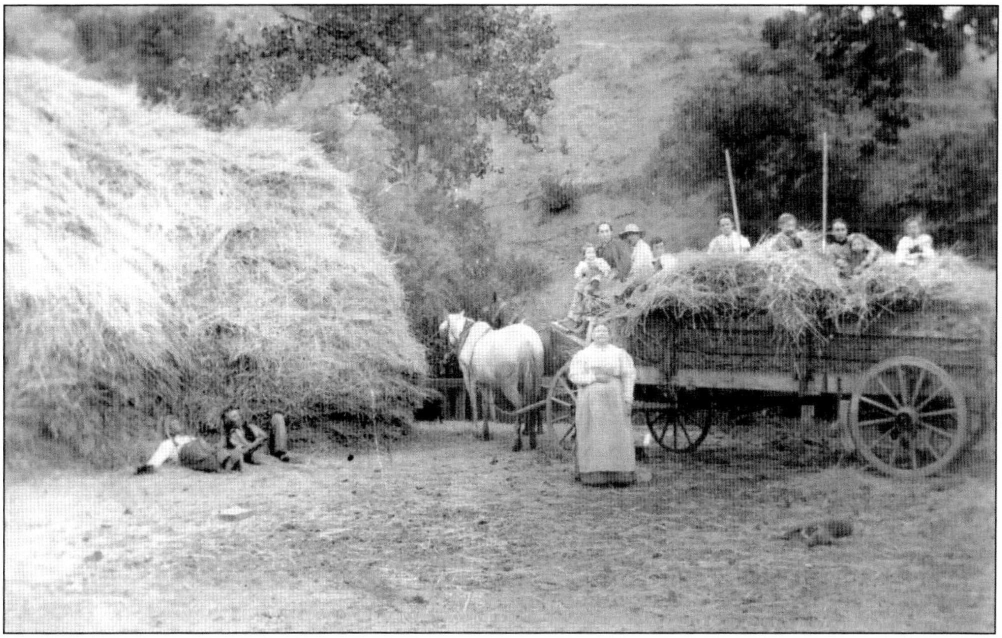

Hay was harvested on the Olofson ranch in Curry Canyon in Morgan Territory.

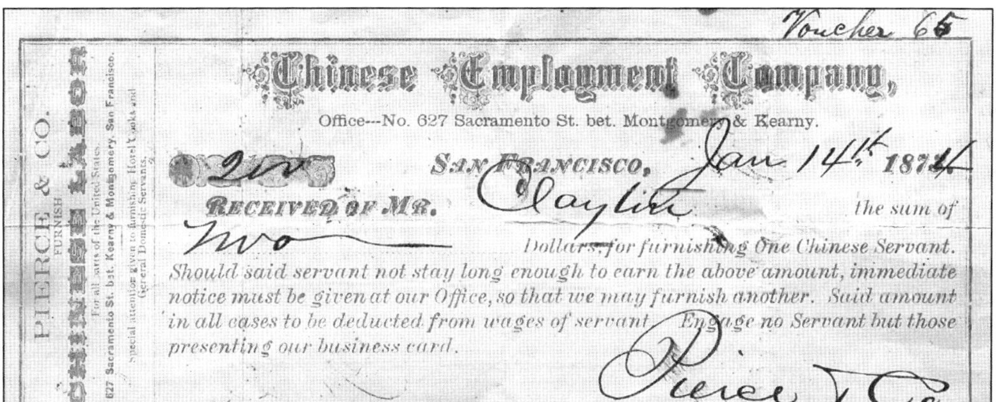

Voucher 65

PIERCE & CO.
FURNISH
CHINESE LABOR
For all parts of the United States.
627 Sacramento St. bet. Kearny & Montgomery, San Francisco.
Special attention given to furnishing Hotel Cooks and General Domestic Servants.

Chinese Employment Company,

Office---No. 627 Sacramento St. bet. Montgomery & Kearny.

$2 San Francisco, Jan 14th 187[illegible]

Received of Mr. Clayton the sum of Two Dollars, for furnishing One Chinese Servant. *Should said servant not stay long enough to earn the above amount, immediate notice must be given at our Office, so that we may furnish another. Said amount in all cases to be deducted from wages of servant. Engage no Servant but those presenting our business card.*

Pierce & Co

DEAKIN'S PRINT, 638 SAC. ST.

In the 1870s, the Clayton family hired Chinese laborers. Chinese labor was readily available after the completion of the transcontinental railroad in 1869.

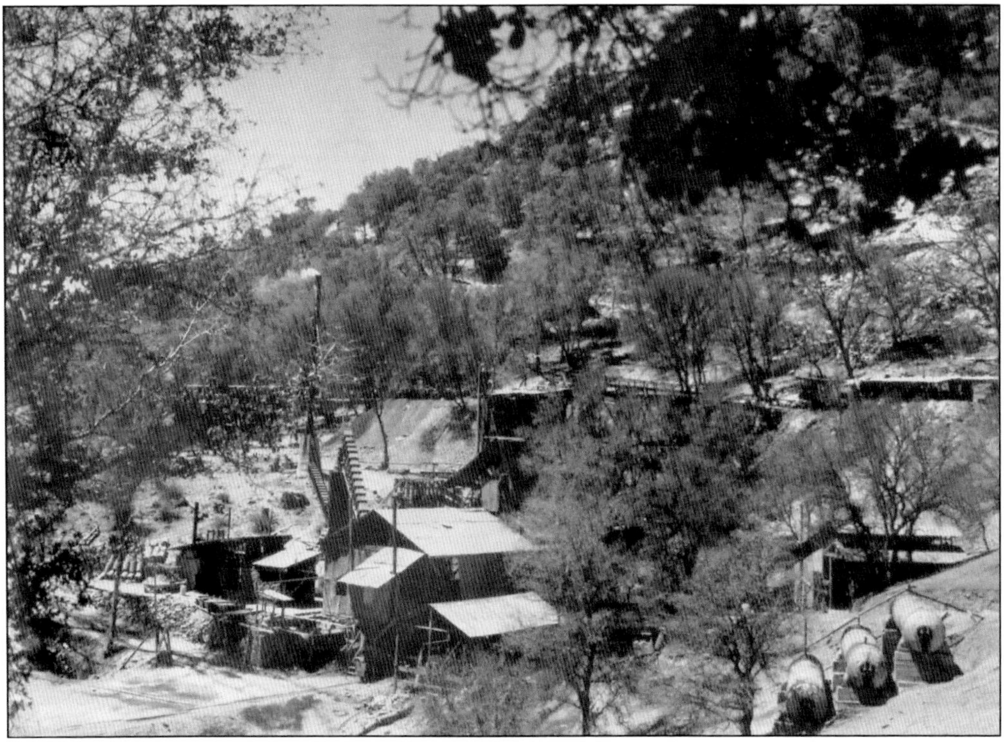

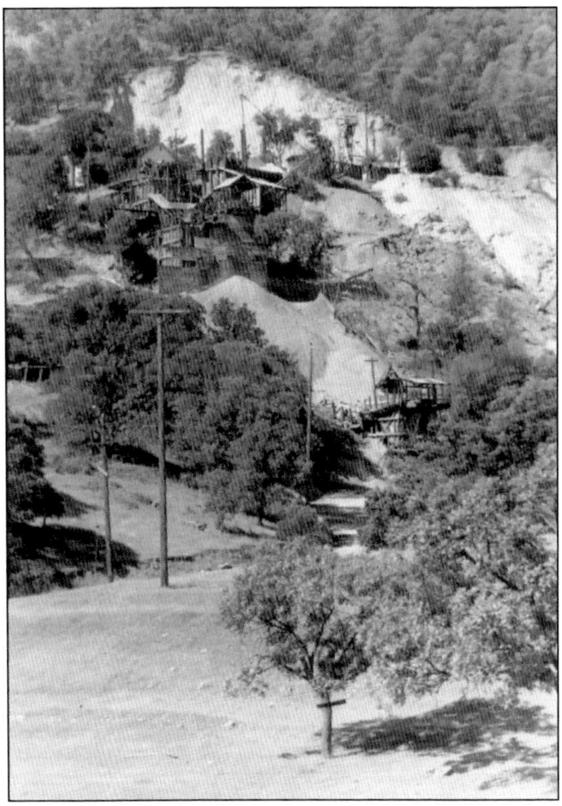

The Bradley Mining Company operated a quicksilver mine near the intersection of Marsh Creek Road and Morgan Territory Road. The mining operation is shown here in 1936.

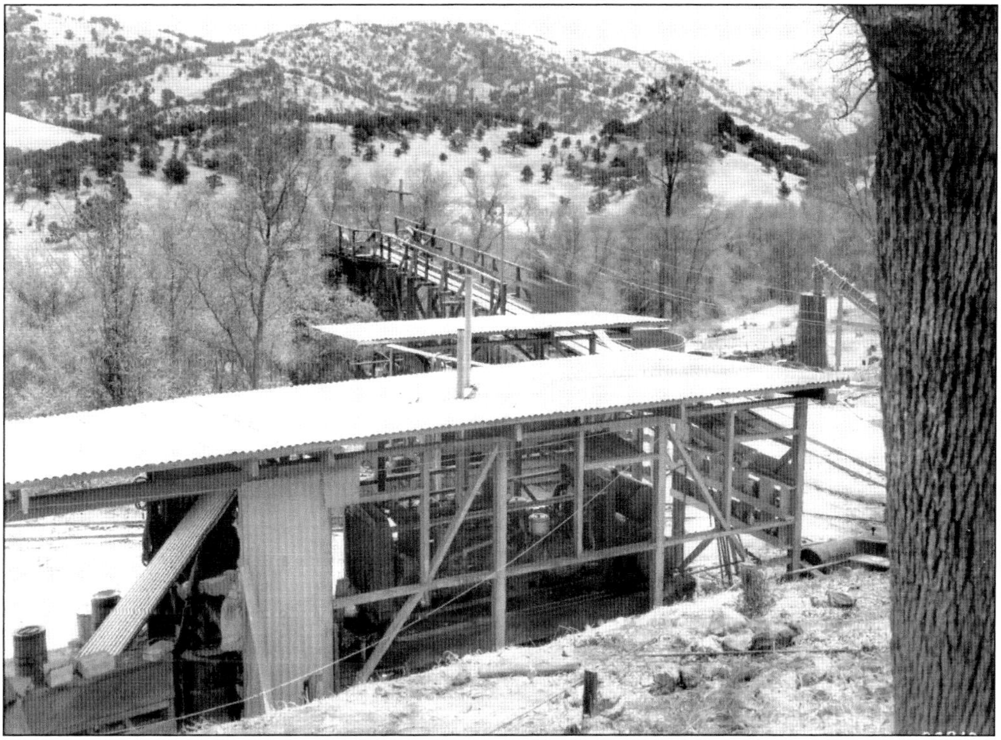

In 1938, the quicksilver mine operated a D7700 210 cubic-foot compressor 20 hours a day. It used two and a half gallons of fuel per hour at 6¢ per gallon.

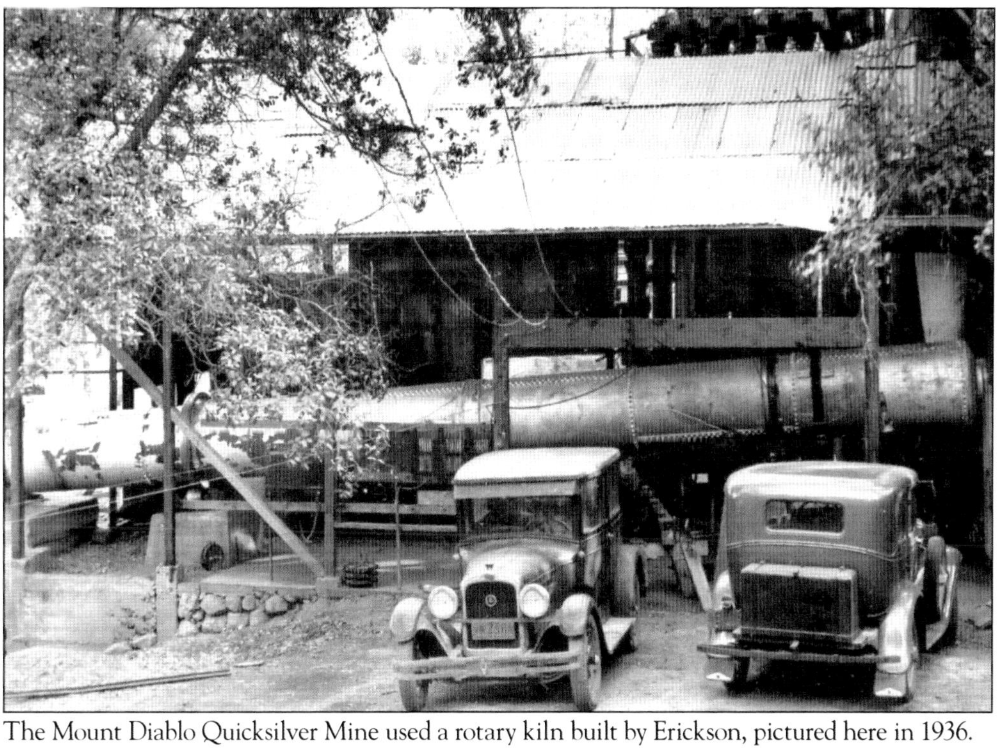

The Mount Diablo Quicksilver Mine used a rotary kiln built by Erickson, pictured here in 1936.

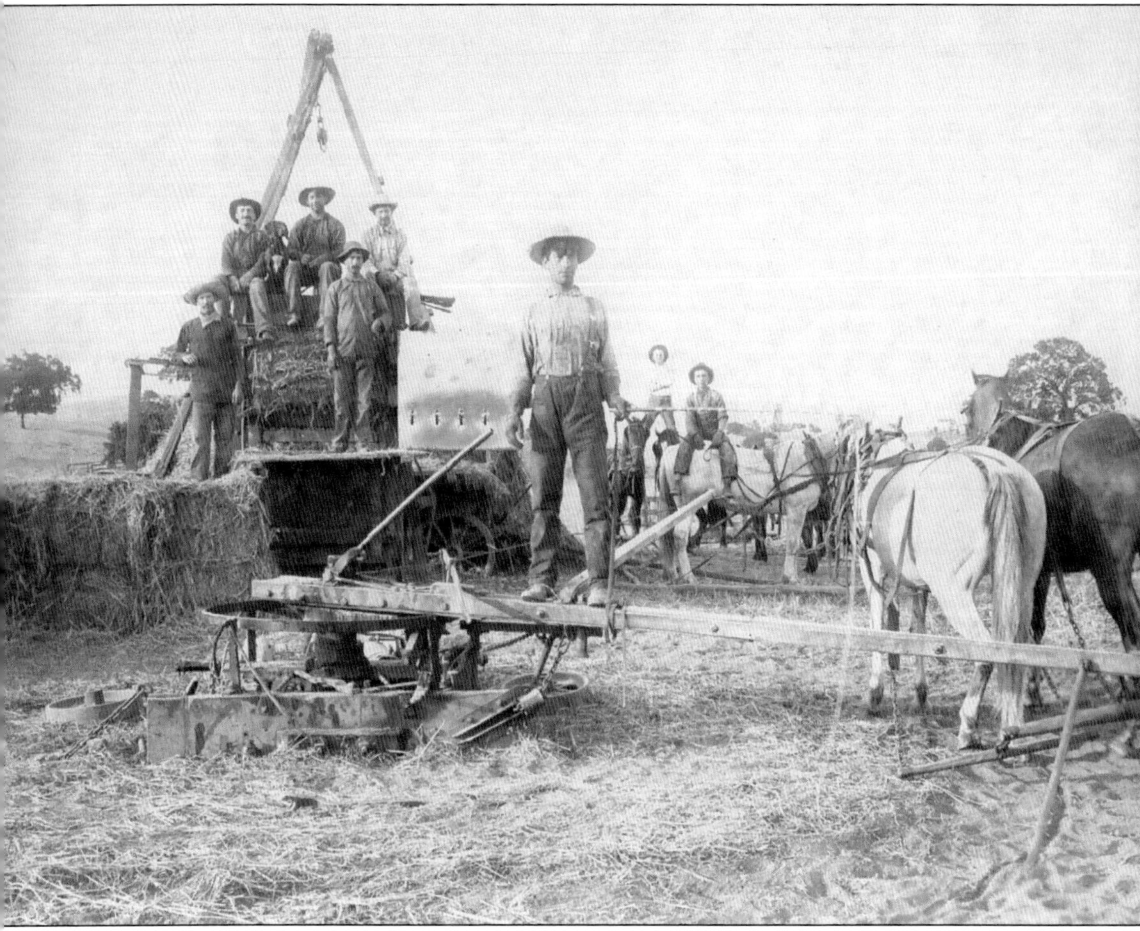

Around 1900, "Boy" Murchio is seen standing prominently in the center of this photograph. The Murchio children were not typically called by their given names as Albert was "Jumbo," Peter was "Jack," Joseph was "Dick," Helen was "Lena," Amelia Dolores was "Dolly," Dominic was "Boy," Francis was "Tat," Louis was "Nig," George was "Lickey," and Emilio was "Dewey." Strangely enough Azalia was called Azalia.

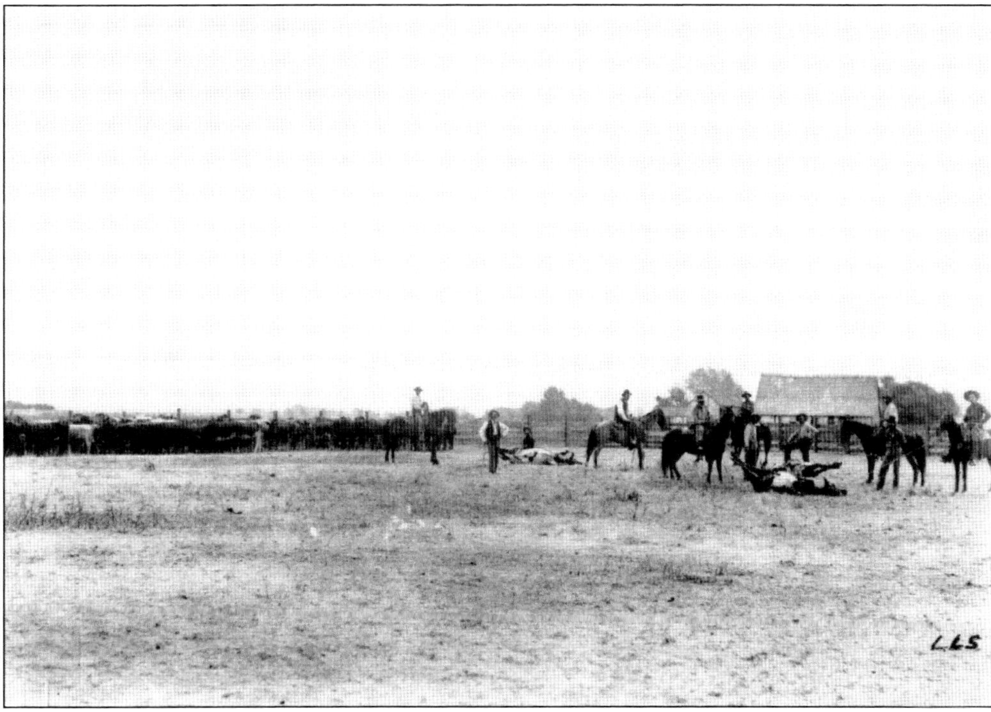

The Foskett and Elworthy crew are seen here roping steers in 1895. Included in the picture are Buck Mitchell, Bert Elworthy, Edd Randall, Jacinto Soto, Peter Pacheco, ? Mesa, Telano Soto, and ? Peralta.

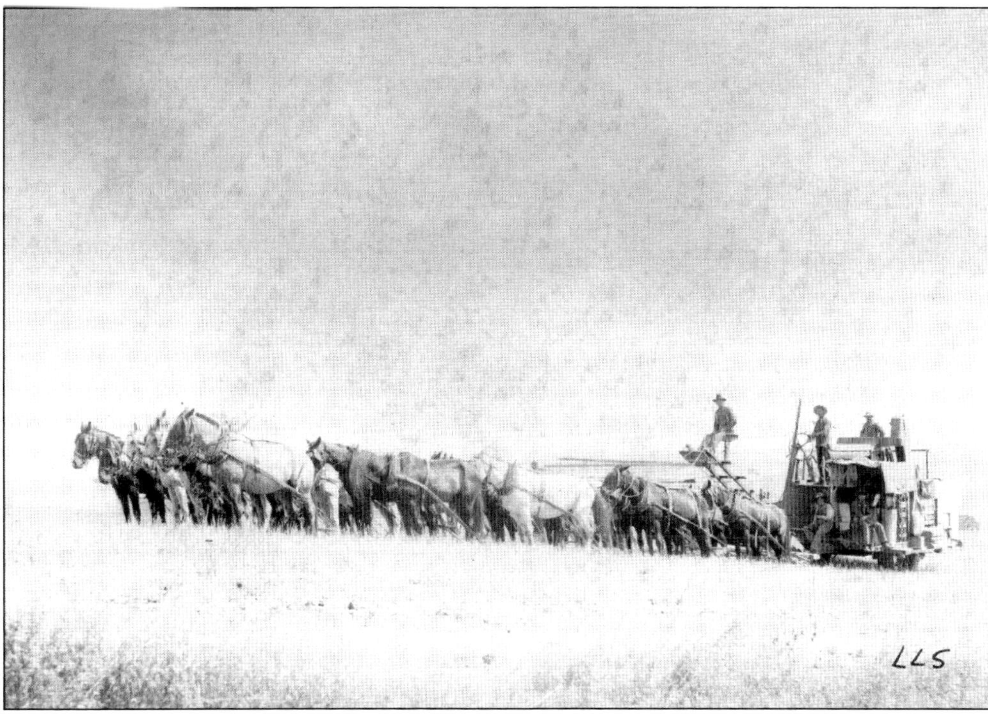

The Foskett and Elworthy crew are pictured here with a 25-mule team.

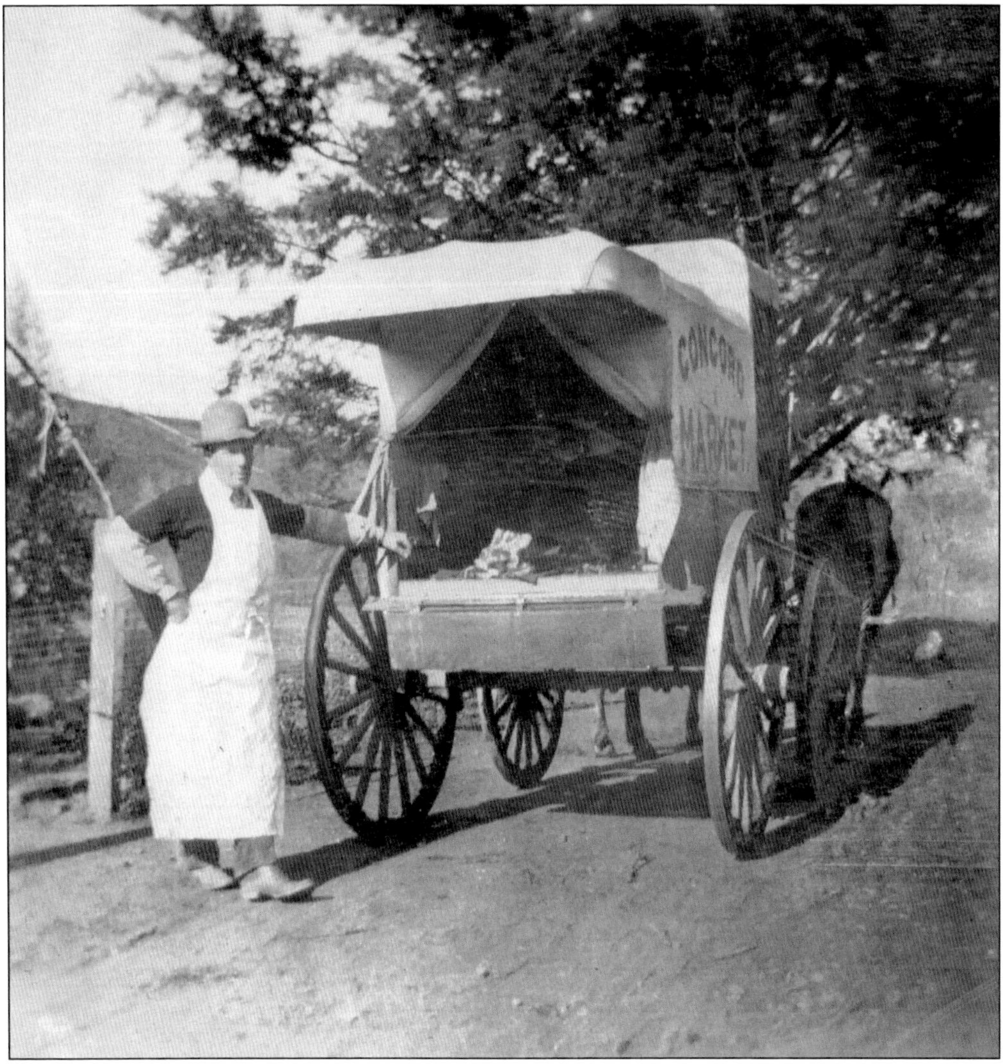

Charles Henry "Harry" Keller owned a butcher shop called the Concord Market. This picture of him was taken around 1900 standing by his cart. In those days, the butcher went to area ranches to slaughter livestock on site.

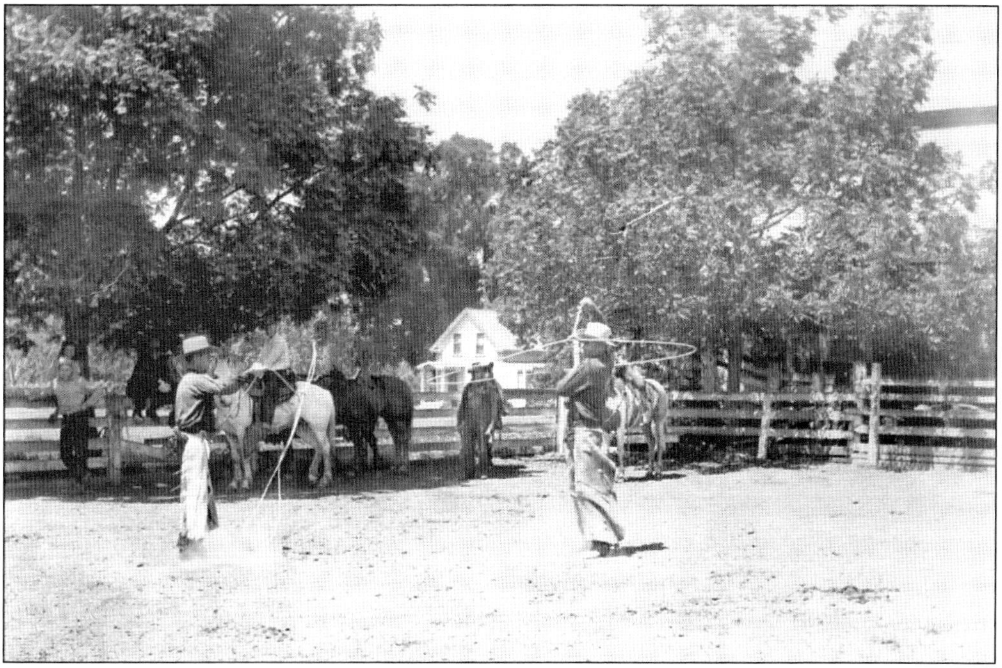

Around 1920, these ranch hands are working on the Keller ranch. Among the workers employed by the Kellers was Pete Brubeck, father of famous jazz musician Dave Brubeck.

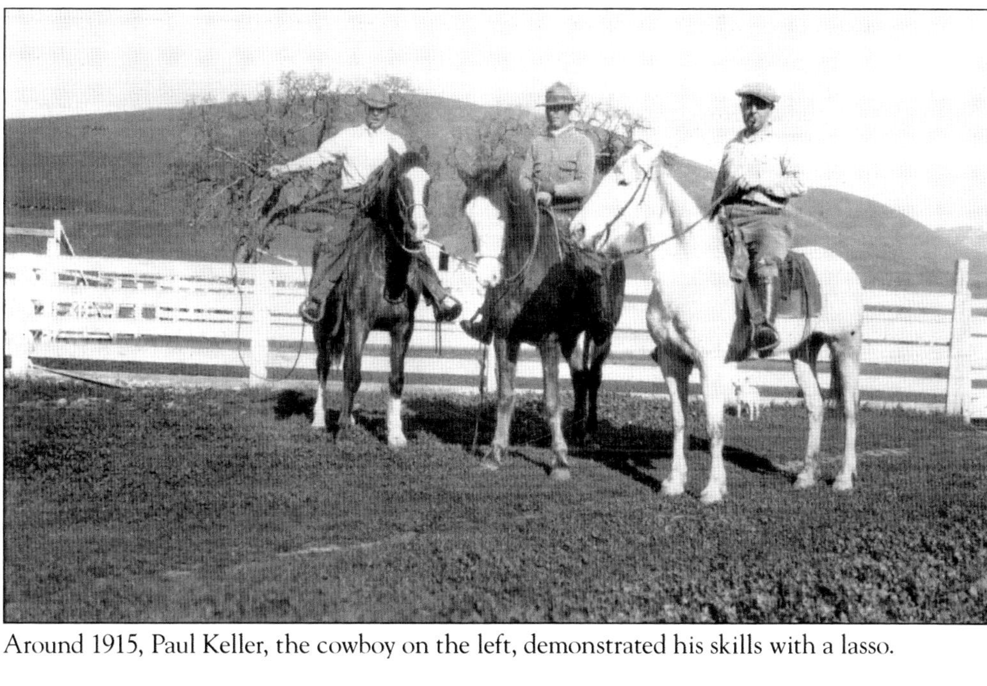

Around 1915, Paul Keller, the cowboy on the left, demonstrated his skills with a lasso.

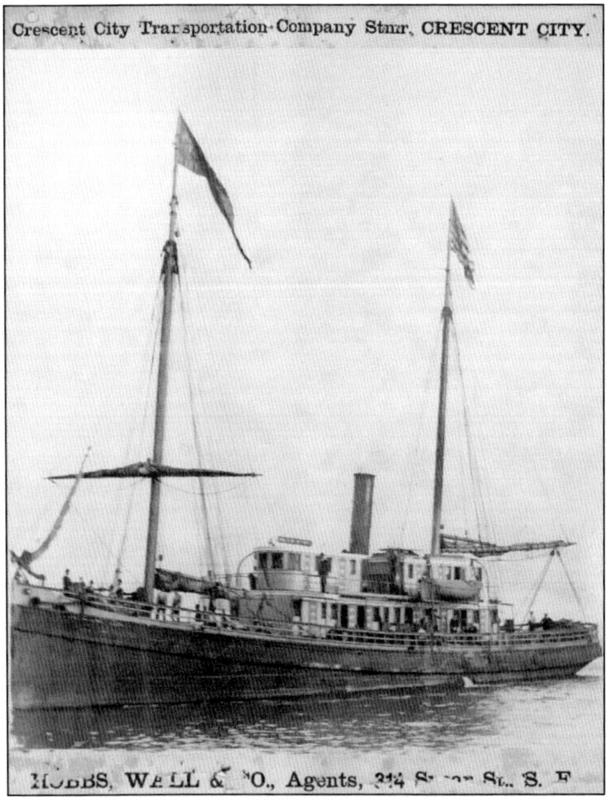

Capt. John Stockfleth is standing at the pilothouse of his schooner *Crescent City*, which was built in 1882. The 147-foot vessel hauled lumber from the north coast of California to the San Francisco Bay area. The Stockfleth family moved to Clayton from San Francisco around 1890. In 1900, Captain Stockfleth retired from sailing.

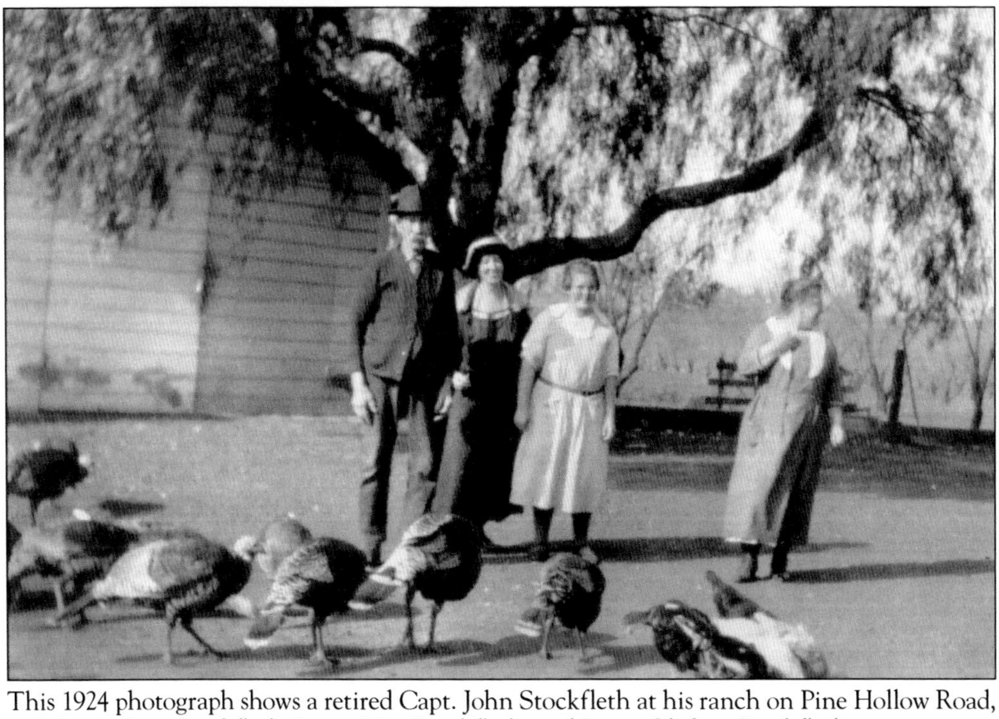

This 1924 photograph shows a retired Capt. John Stockfleth at his ranch on Pine Hollow Road, with Lucy Gray Stockfleth, Laura May Stockfleth, and Laura Olofson Stockfleth.

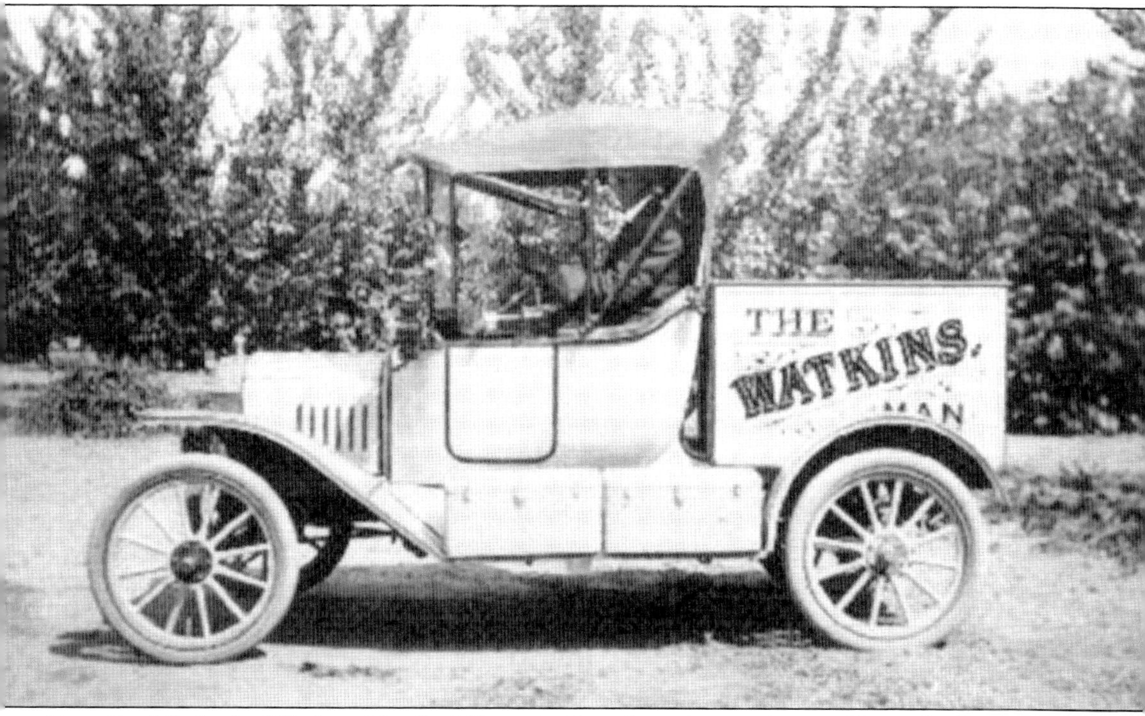

Dave Stockfleth, the "Watkins Man," sold household products door-to-door and began his business using a horse and buggy for transportation. In 1923, Dave married former Clayton schoolteacher Anna Jane O'Connell.

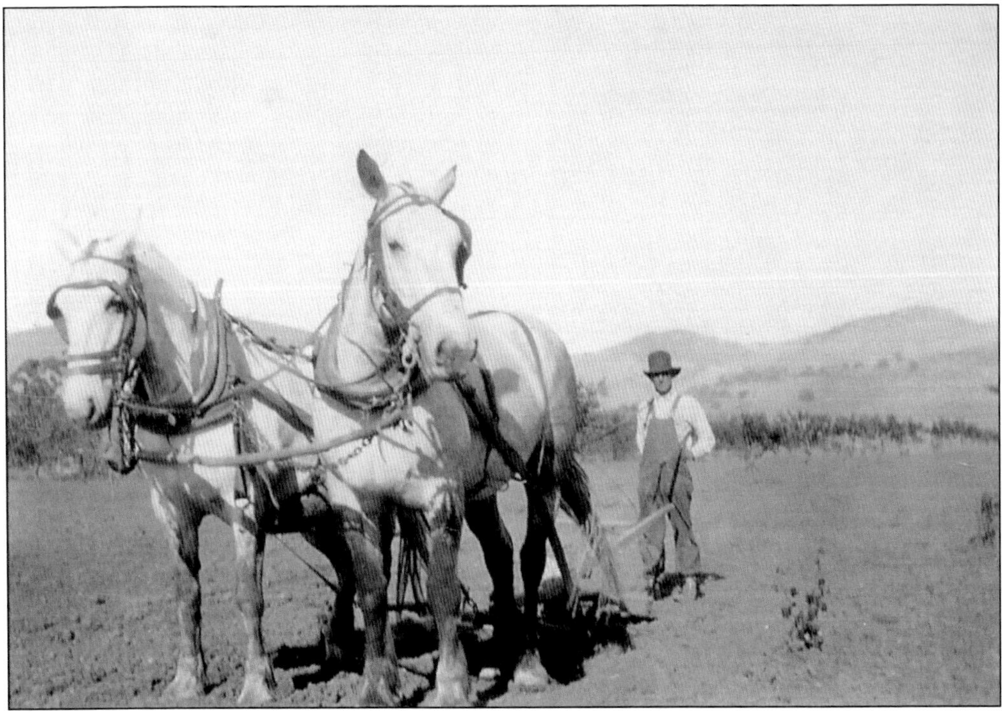

Will Frank is shown around 1920 with his workhorses. Will could make just about anything grow, and he was particularly good at grafting trees that produced several varieties of fruit.

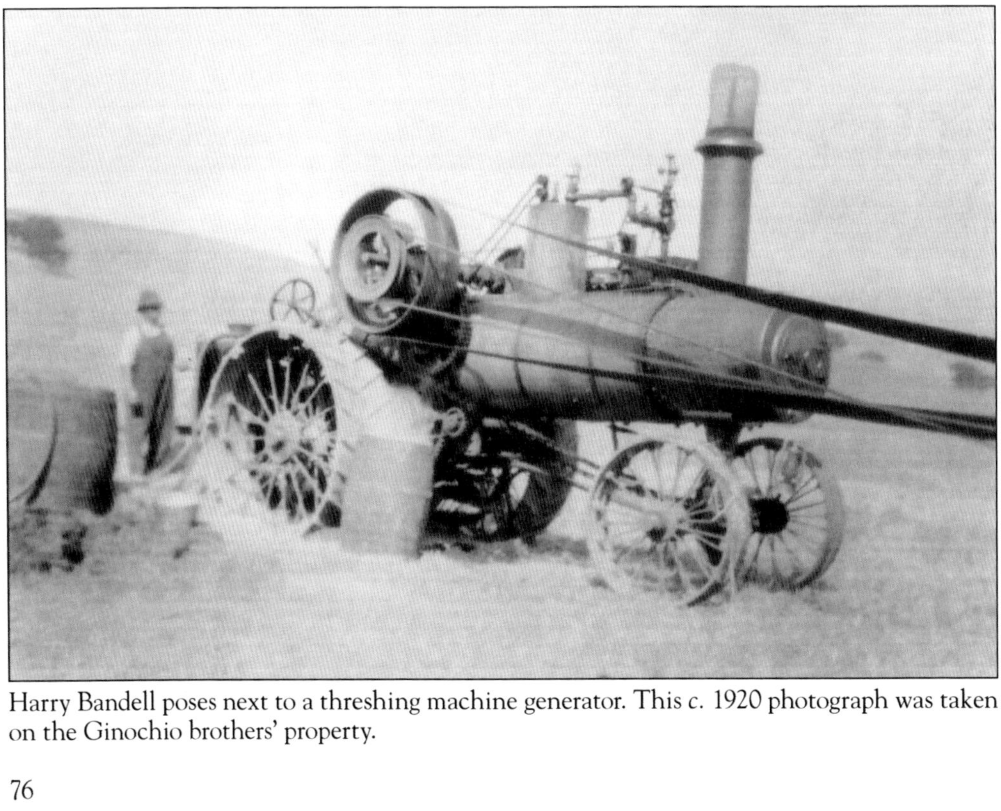

Harry Bandell poses next to a threshing machine generator. This *c.* 1920 photograph was taken on the Ginochio brothers' property.

Four

EVERYDAY LIFE

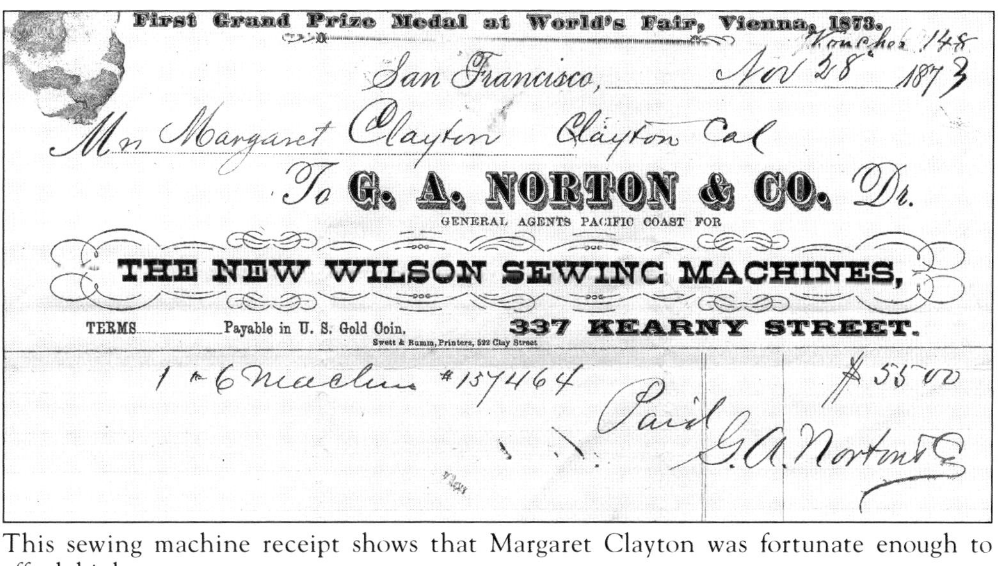
First Grand Prize Medal at World's Fair, Vienna, 1873.

Voucher 148

San Francisco, Nov 28 1873

Mrs Margaret Clayton Clayton Cal

To G. A. NORTON & CO. Dr.

GENERAL AGENTS PACIFIC COAST FOR

THE NEW WILSON SEWING MACHINES,

TERMS Payable in U. S. Gold Coin. 337 KEARNY STREET.

Swett & Bumm, Printers, 522 Clay Street

1 ~ 6 machine #157464 $55.00

Paid G. A. Norton & Co

This sewing machine receipt shows that Margaret Clayton was fortunate enough to afford this luxury.

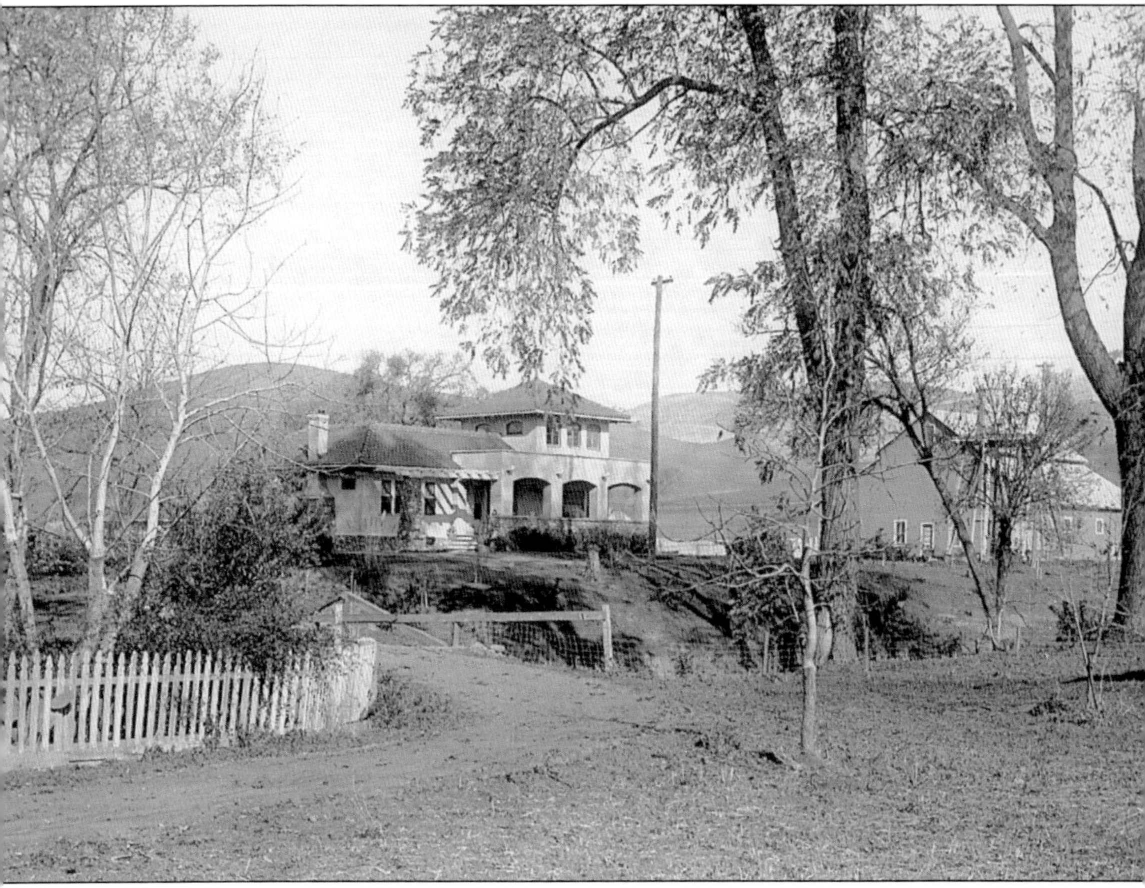

In 1912, the Keller house was built as a Mission-style home with Craftsman elements. "Casa del Sierra," the residence of Paul and Elodia Liberty Keller, was designed by Elodia. When this photograph was taken in 1912, the cement bridge had not yet been built.

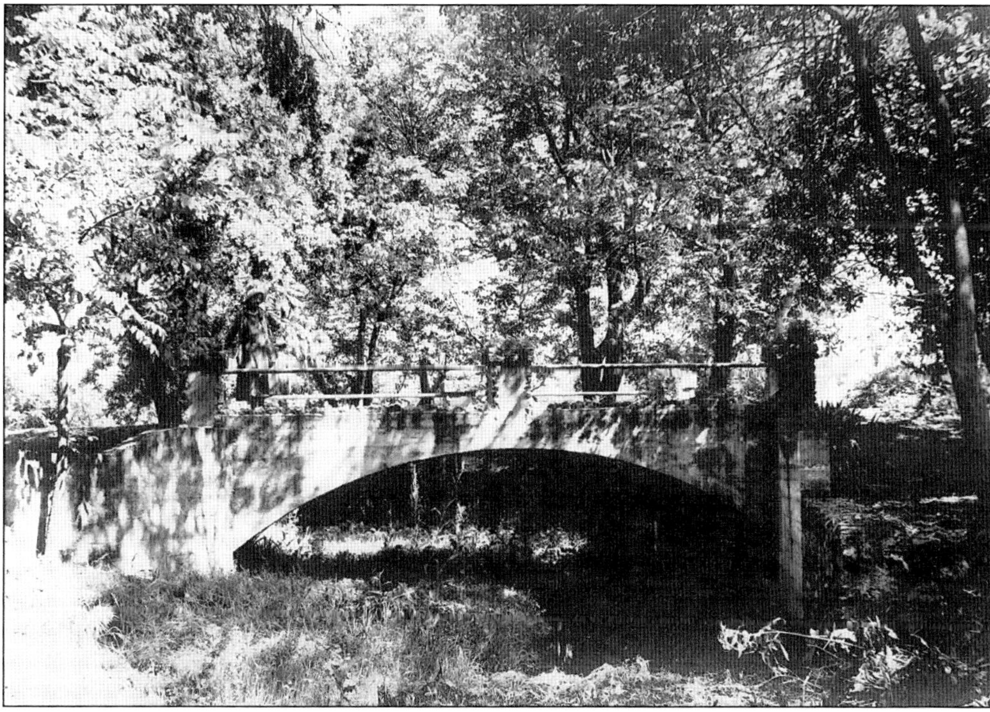
This 1925 photograph shows the Keller ranch bridge across Mitchell Creek.

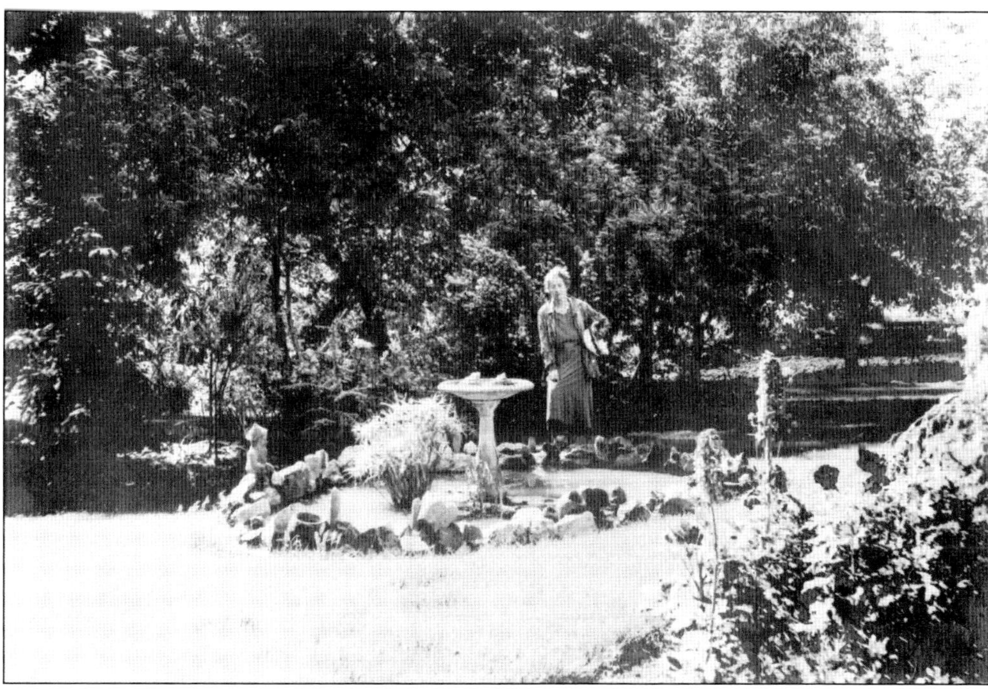
Around 1925, Elodia Liberty Keller, wife of Paul Keller, had this photograph taken in her garden. She was an artistic woman with an eye for beautiful things.

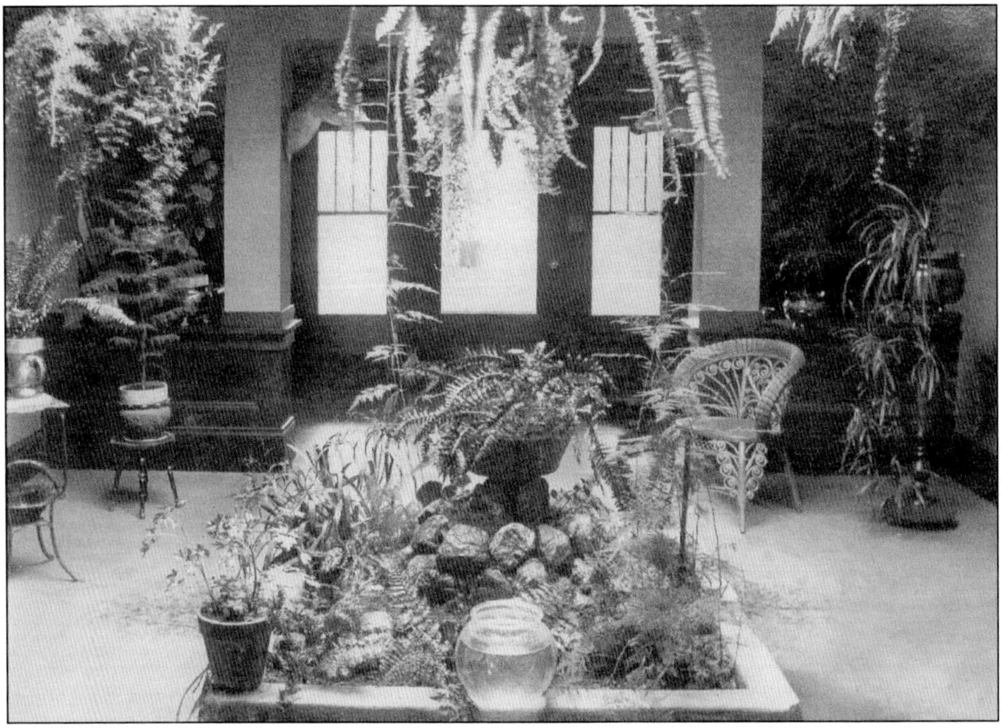

The Keller house atrium, or "fernery," was planted and tended by Elodia Liberty Keller. She had a natural flair for decorating.

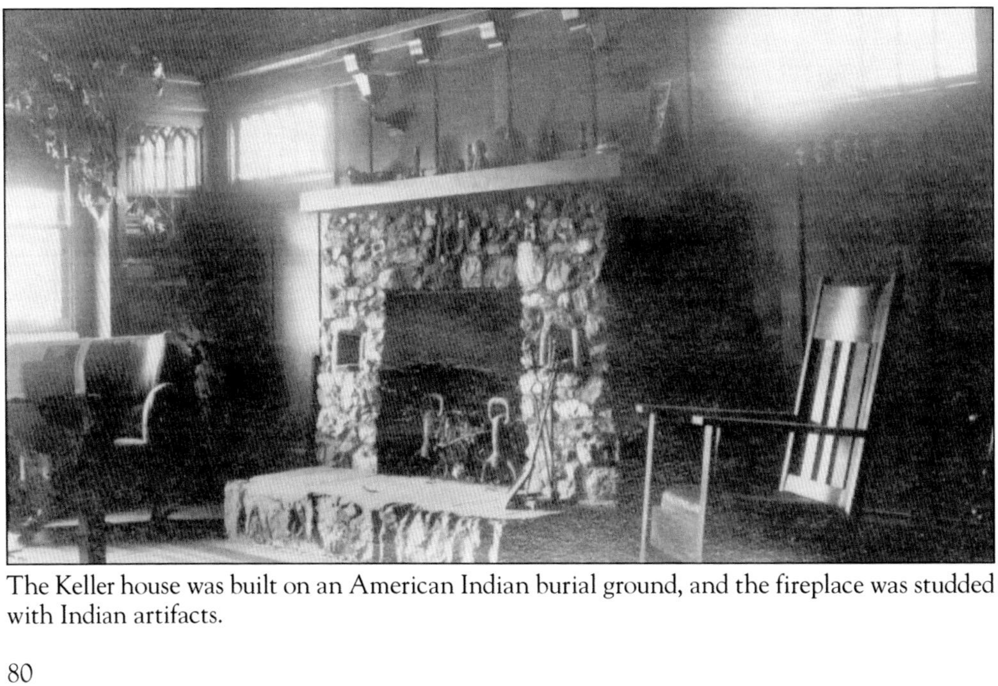

The Keller house was built on an American Indian burial ground, and the fireplace was studded with Indian artifacts.

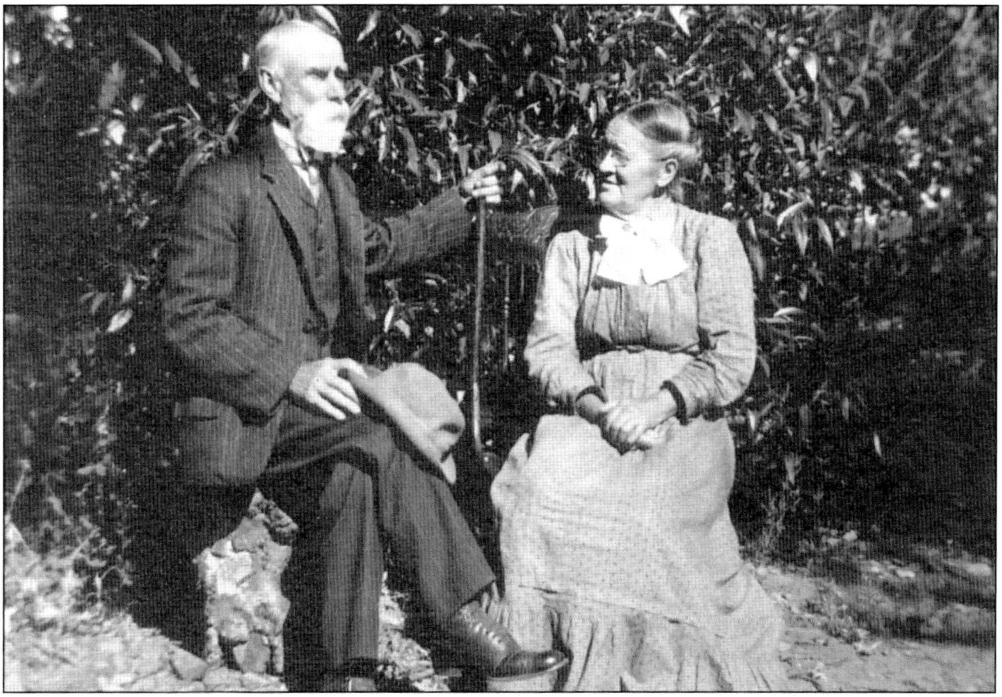

John Henry "Harry" Keller and Celestia Collins Keller are pictured here around 1915. Harry Keller's father died when he was only 12 years old. Forced to go to work, Harry became a stable boy and worked his way up to being a jockey. He owned the Concord Market, a butcher shop in Concord.

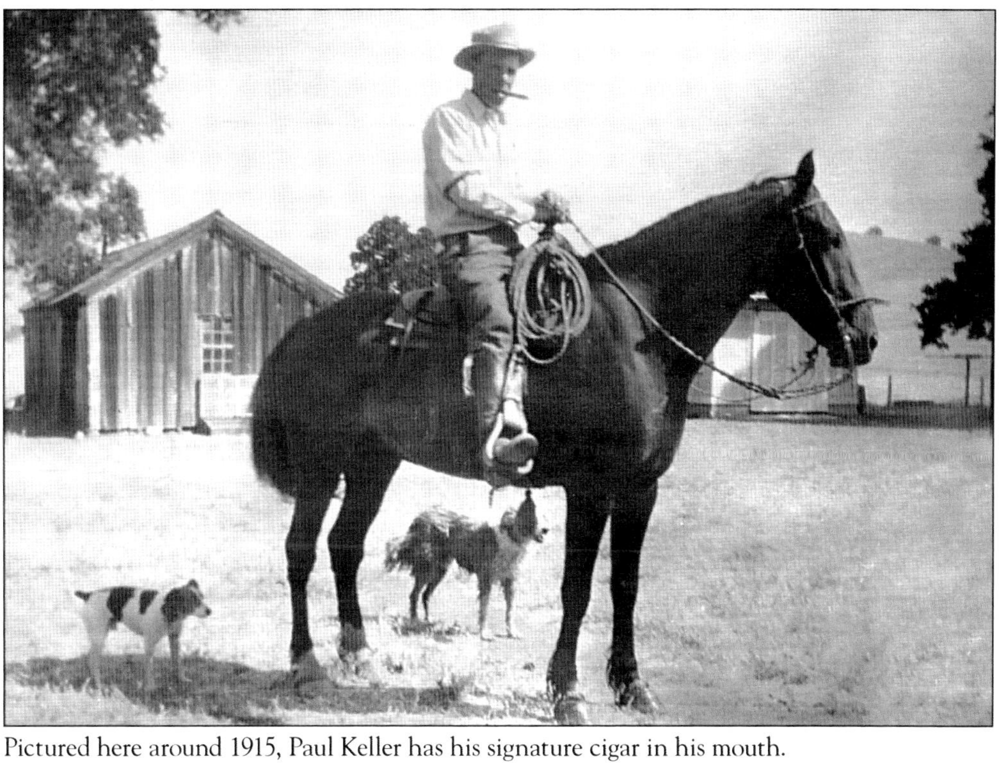

Pictured here around 1915, Paul Keller has his signature cigar in his mouth.

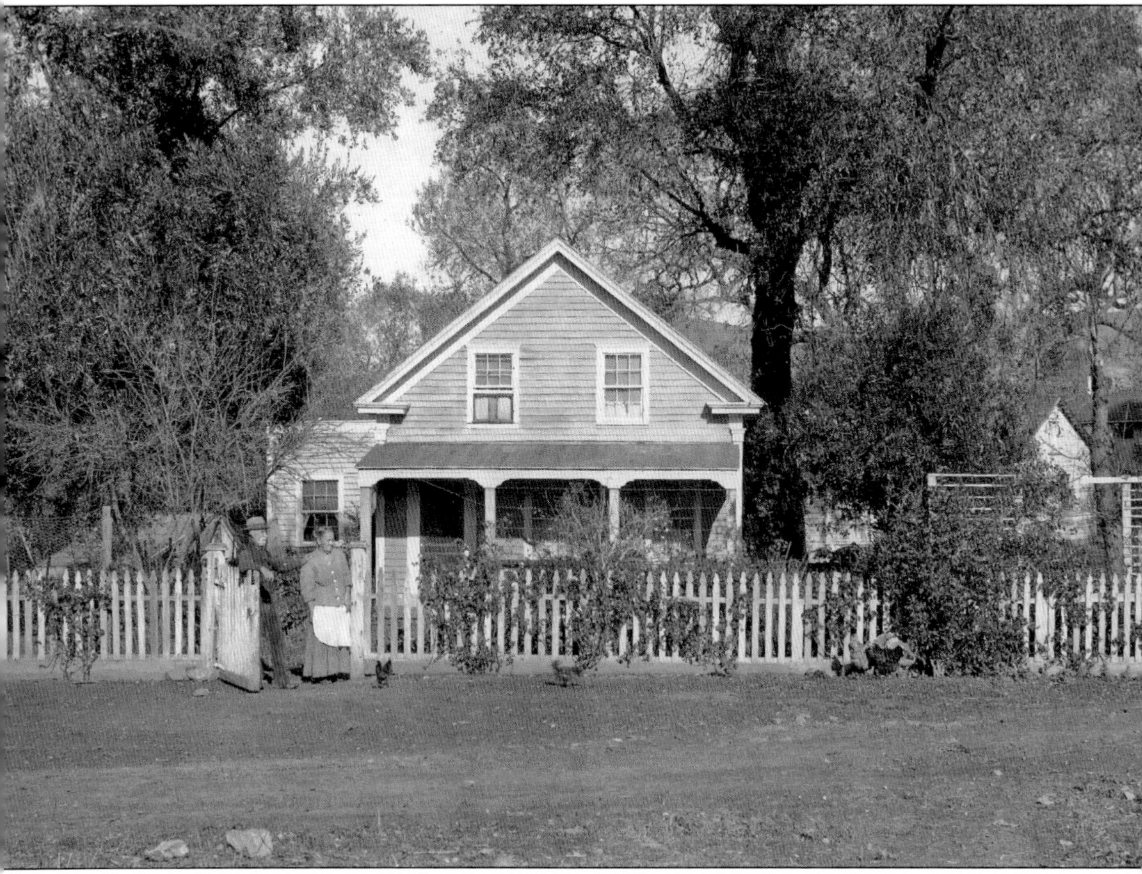

Around 1915, John Henry Keller and Celestia Keller are standing at the gate of the Clayton house. The house is believed to have been the second residence of Joel and Margaret Clayton. The Kellers later used the home as a bunkhouse for workers on the Keller ranch.

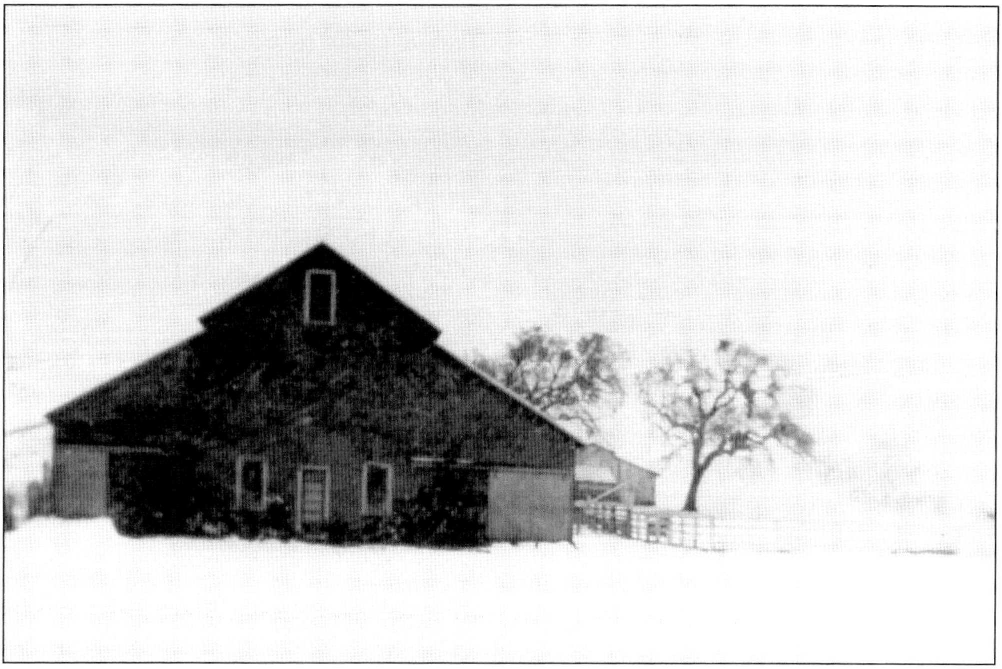

In 1937, the Keller barn is shown with a layer of snow on the ground.

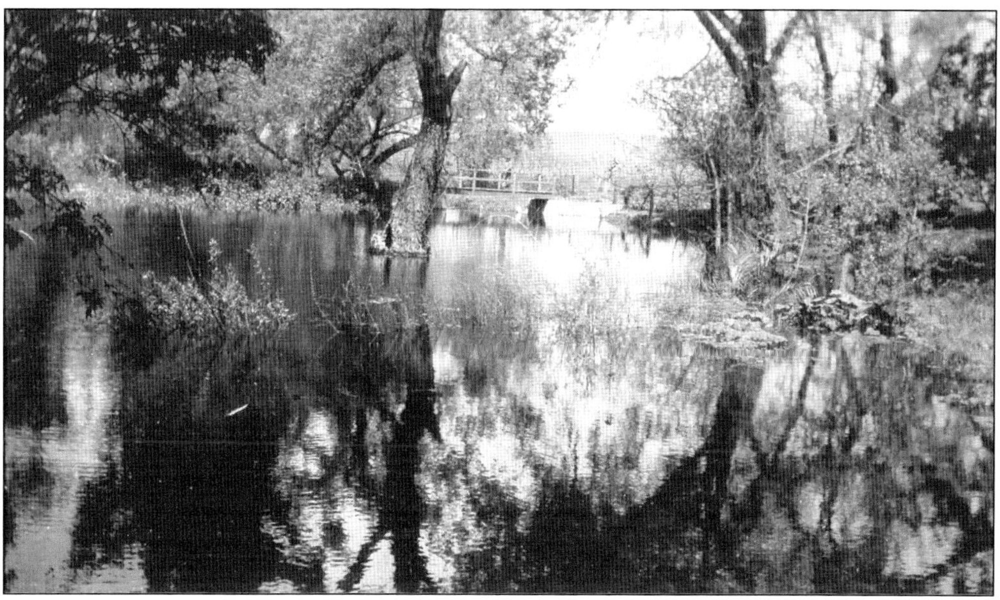

Mount Diablo Creek was dammed below the Keller Bridge when this 1930s photograph was taken. There was a picnic area nearby.

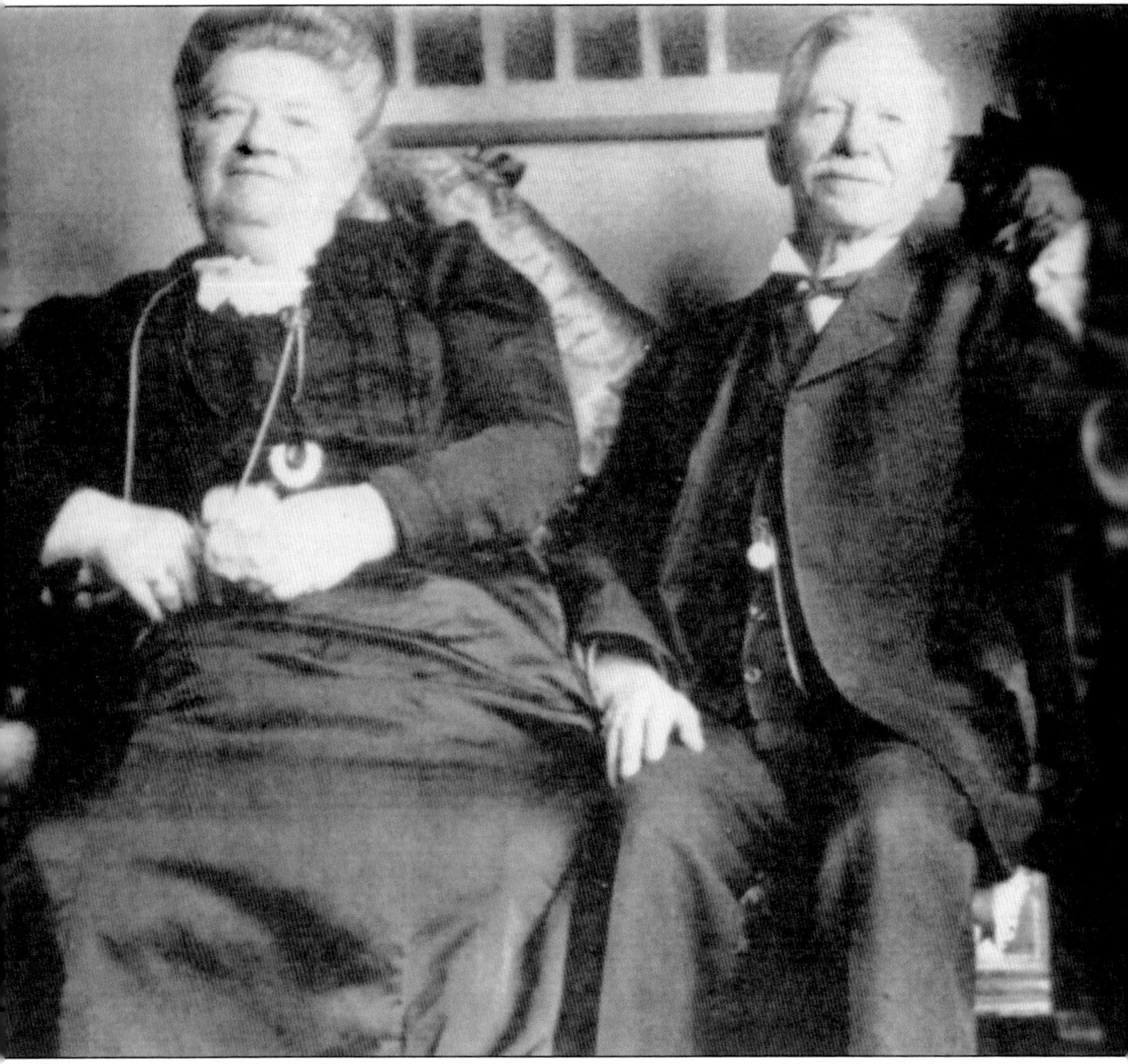

This 1920 photograph shows Charles and Cecelia Lobree Rhine. Charles owned Rhine's Store on Main Street.

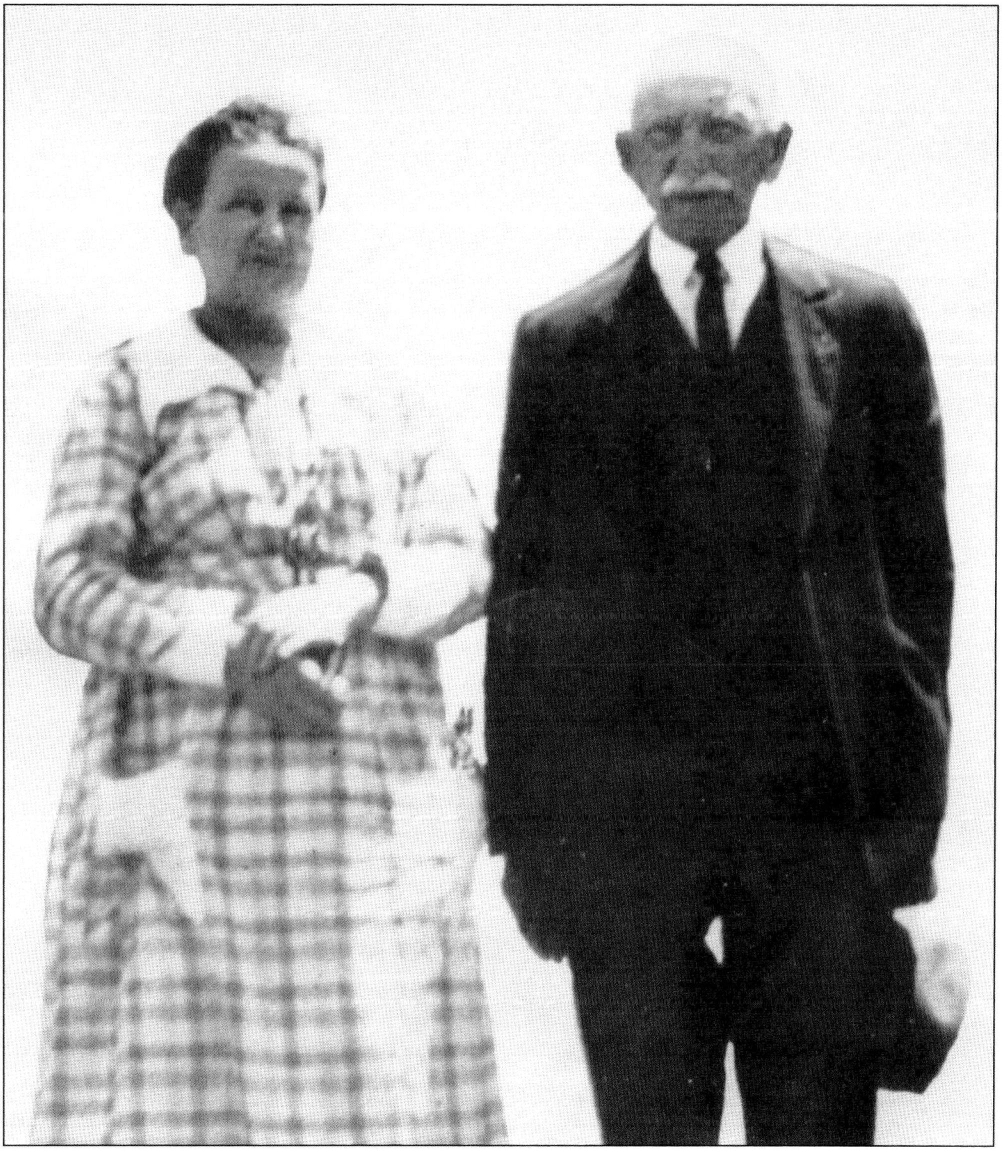

Jacob "Jake" Rhine and Dina Rhine posed for this photograph around 1920. Jacob owned the Rhine Hotel and Saloon on Main Street.

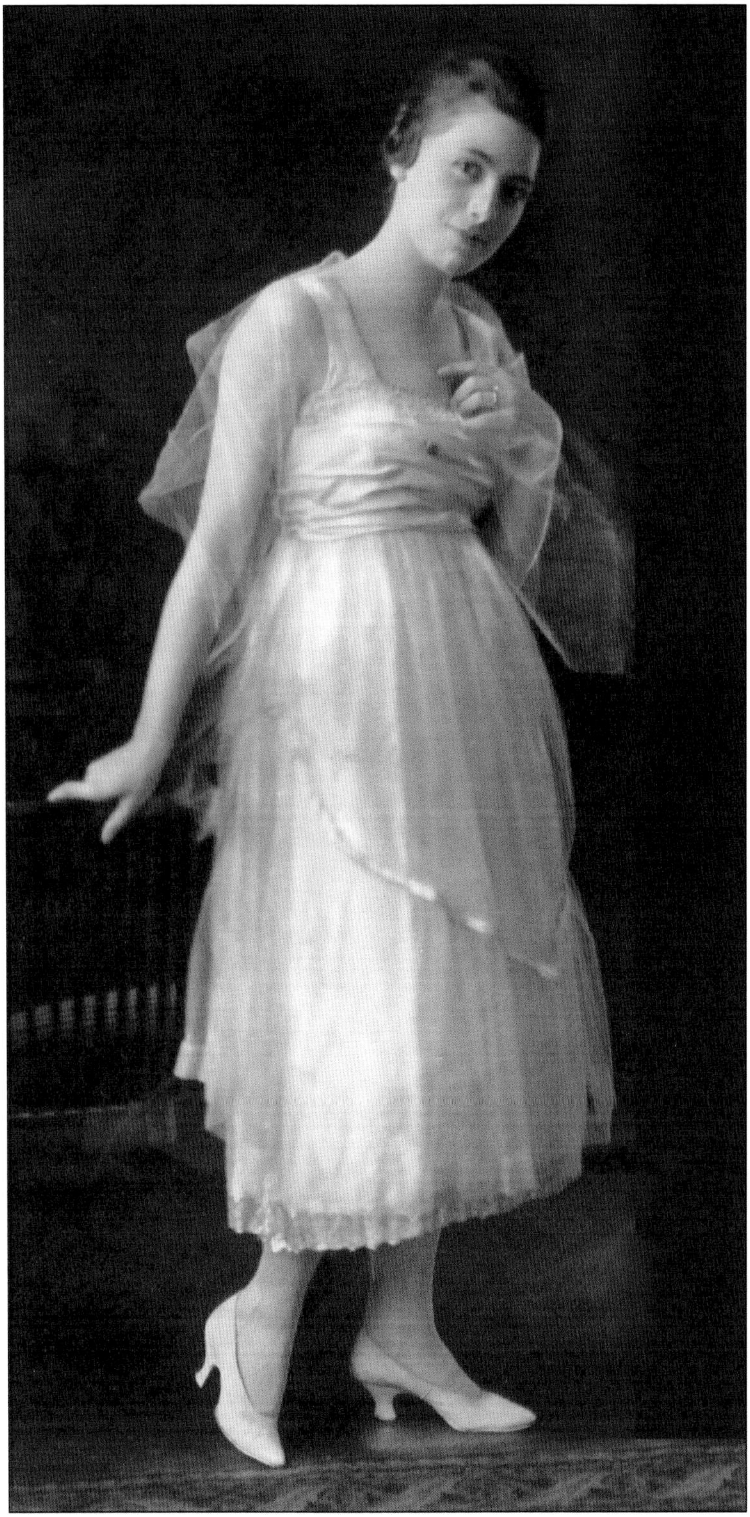

This engagement photograph of Miss Yetta Rhine, daughter of Jacob Rhine, was taken in 1919.

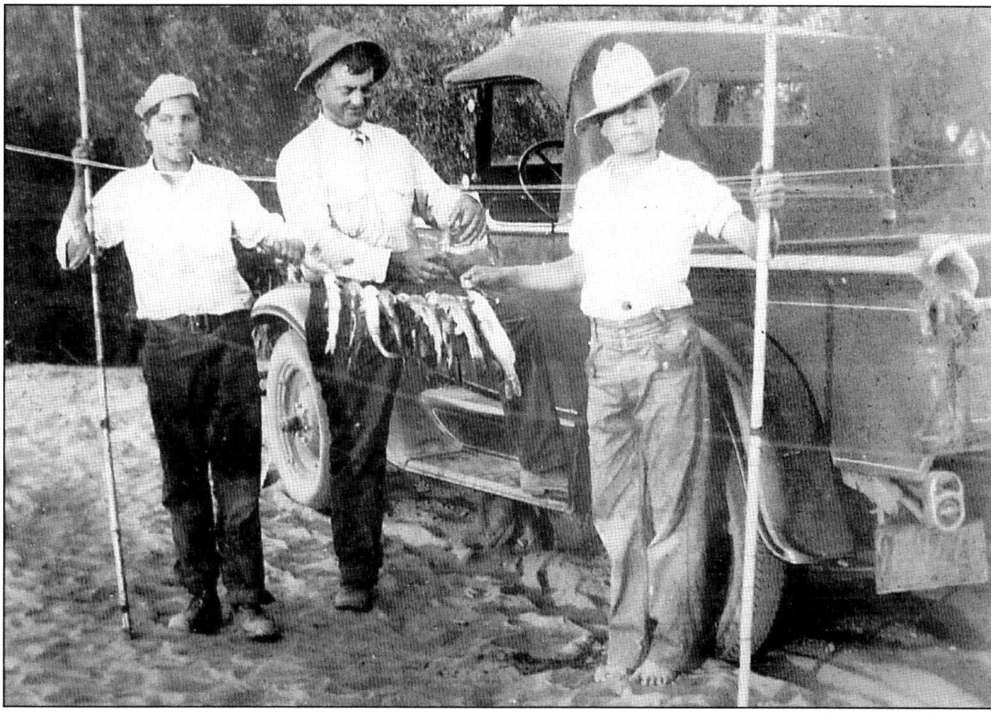

Members of the Gomez and Joaquin families loved to fish. Proudly posing around 1920 with their catch are Alvin Joaquin, Tony Joaquin, and Ed Gomez.

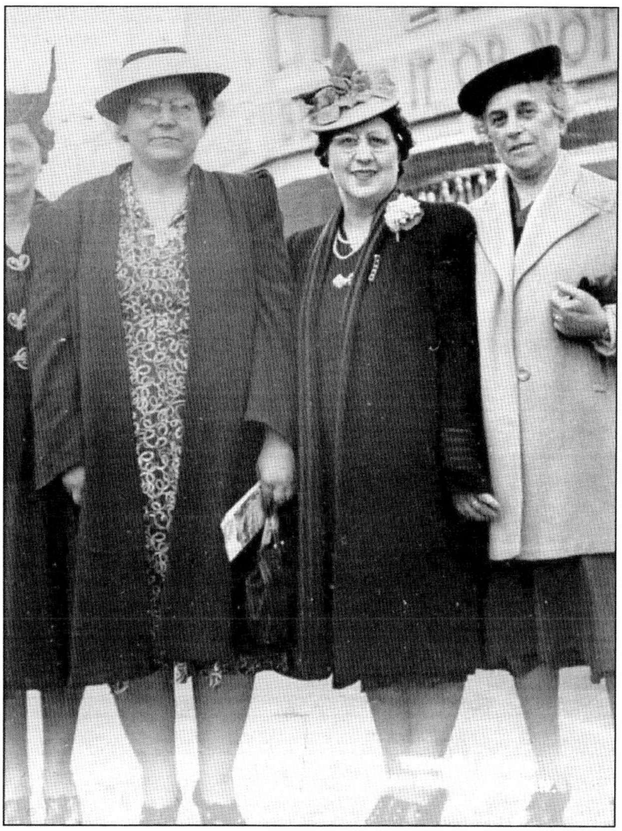

Many Clayton residents visited Treasure Island for the World's Fair Golden Gate International Exposition. Pictured here in 1940, from left to right, are Mabel Schwartz, Mary Matz, Mary Bloching, and Mrs. LeClaire.

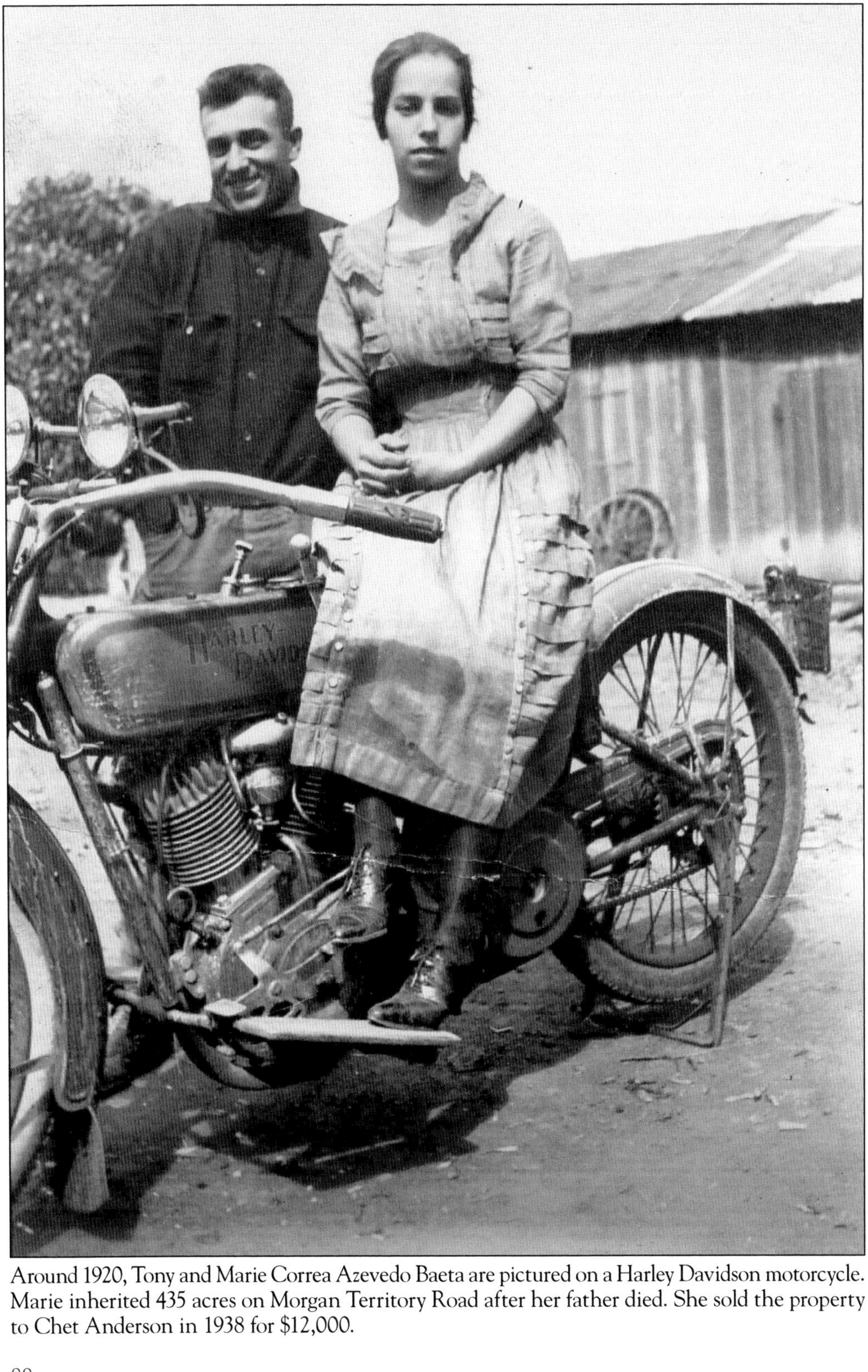

Around 1920, Tony and Marie Correa Azevedo Baeta are pictured on a Harley Davidson motorcycle. Marie inherited 435 acres on Morgan Territory Road after her father died. She sold the property to Chet Anderson in 1938 for $12,000.

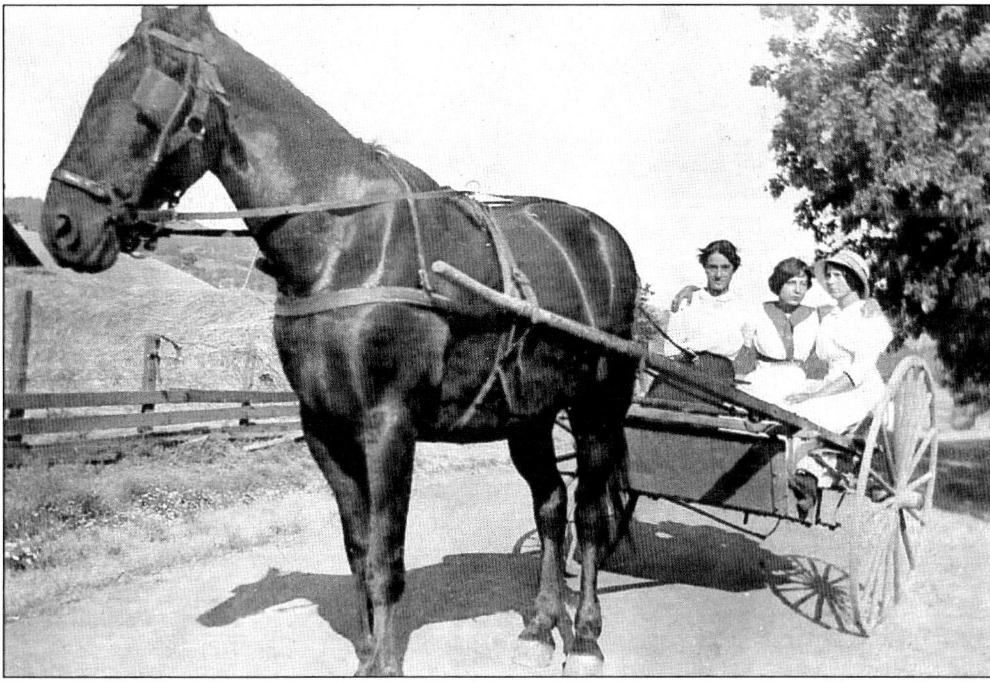

These three young women take a buggy ride around 1916. Pictured, from left to right, are Mary Joaquin, Rose Correa Azevedo, and Annie Correa Azevedo.

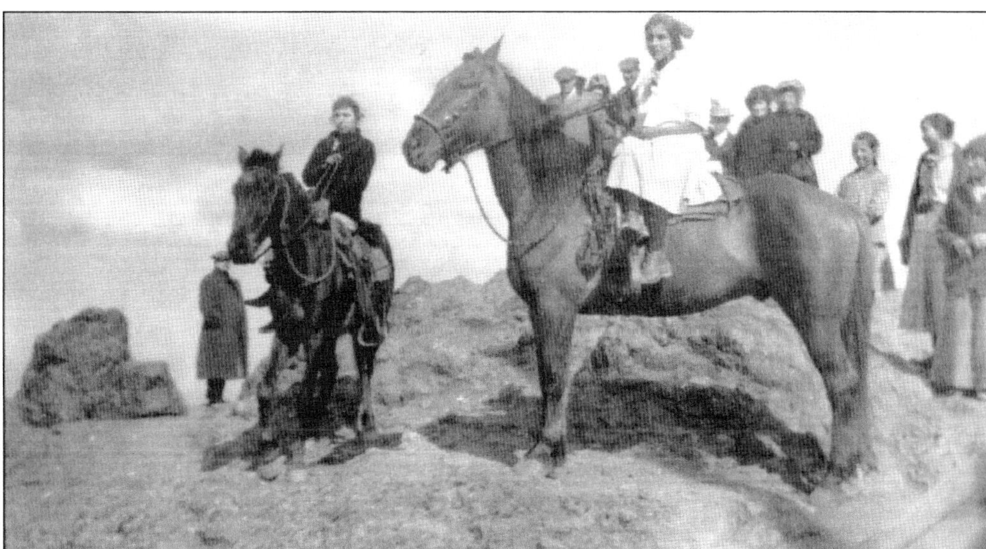

Lucy Correa, pictured in the center riding sidesaddle, was an avid horsewoman from an early age. This 1914 photograph was taken on top of Mount Diablo.

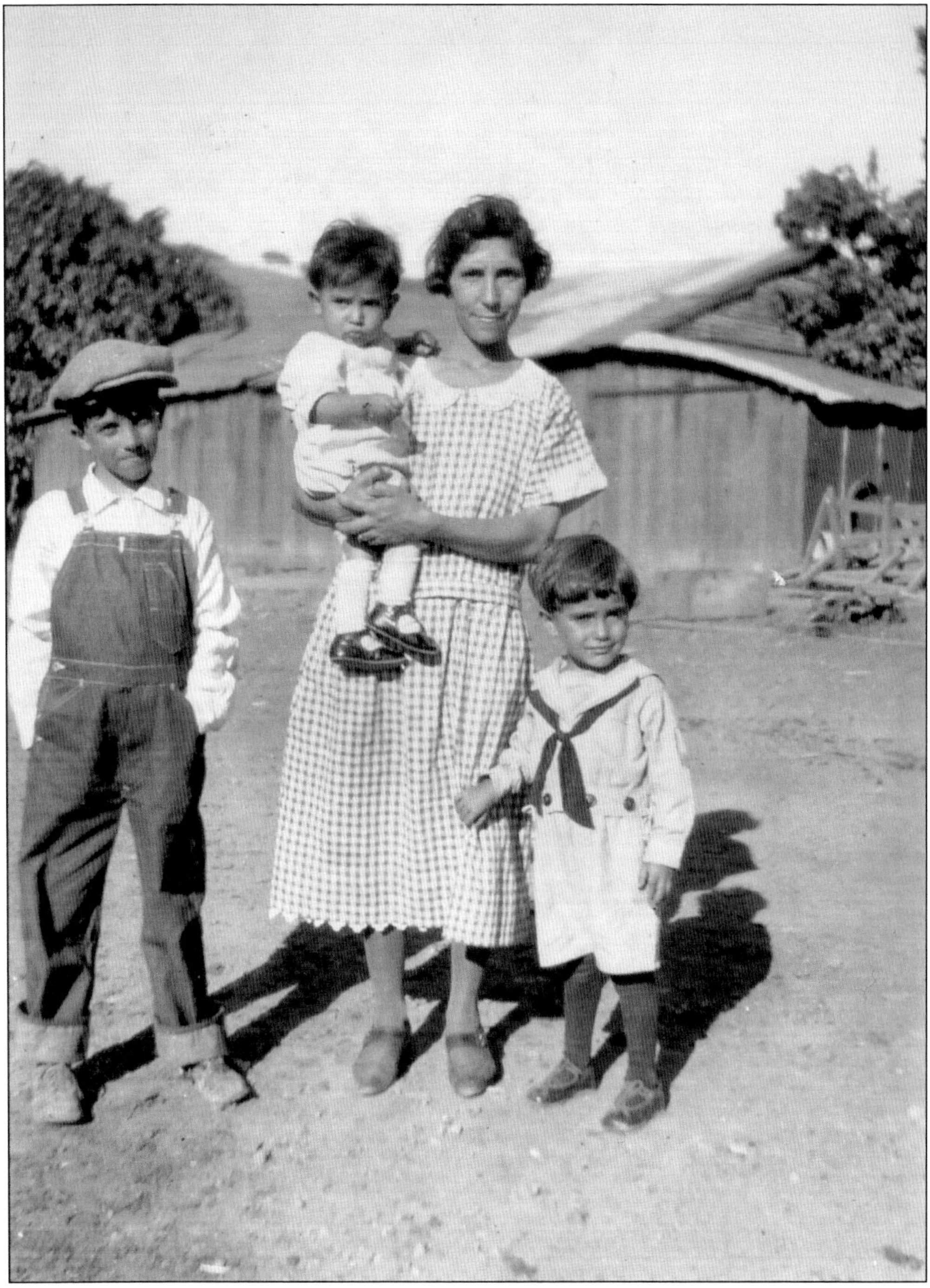

Around 1923, Libby Joaquin proudly displayed her growing family. The children pictured, from left to right, are Alvin, Johnny, and Artie.

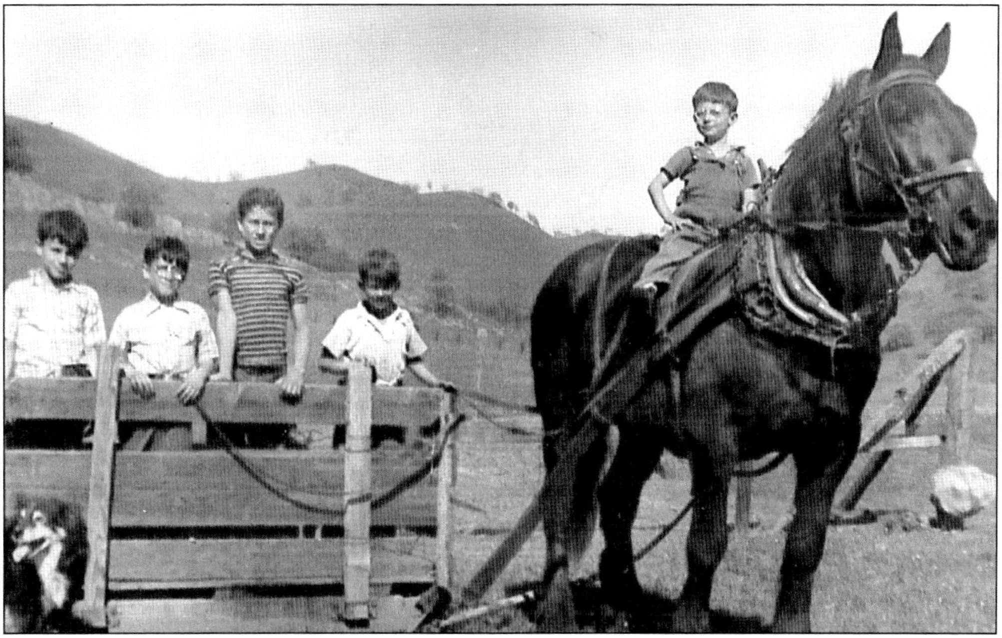

In 1939, five little boys were having fun with a workhorse. Pictured, from left to right, are Elmer Gomez, Enroy Gomez, Melvin Gomez, Joe Joaquin, and Don Joaquin.

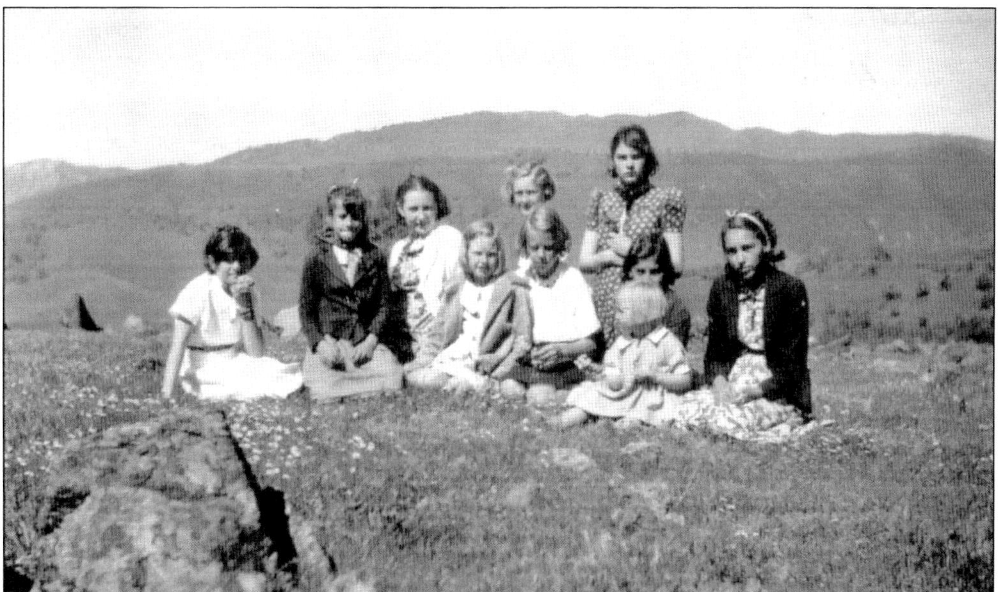

In 1938, a group of little girls hiked to Rocky Point. Pictured, from left to right, are Jackie ?, Phyllis Frank, Florence McKean, Bobbie ?, Barbara Duncan, Yvonne Chisholm?, Betty Arnold, Virginia Joaquin, and Audrey ?.

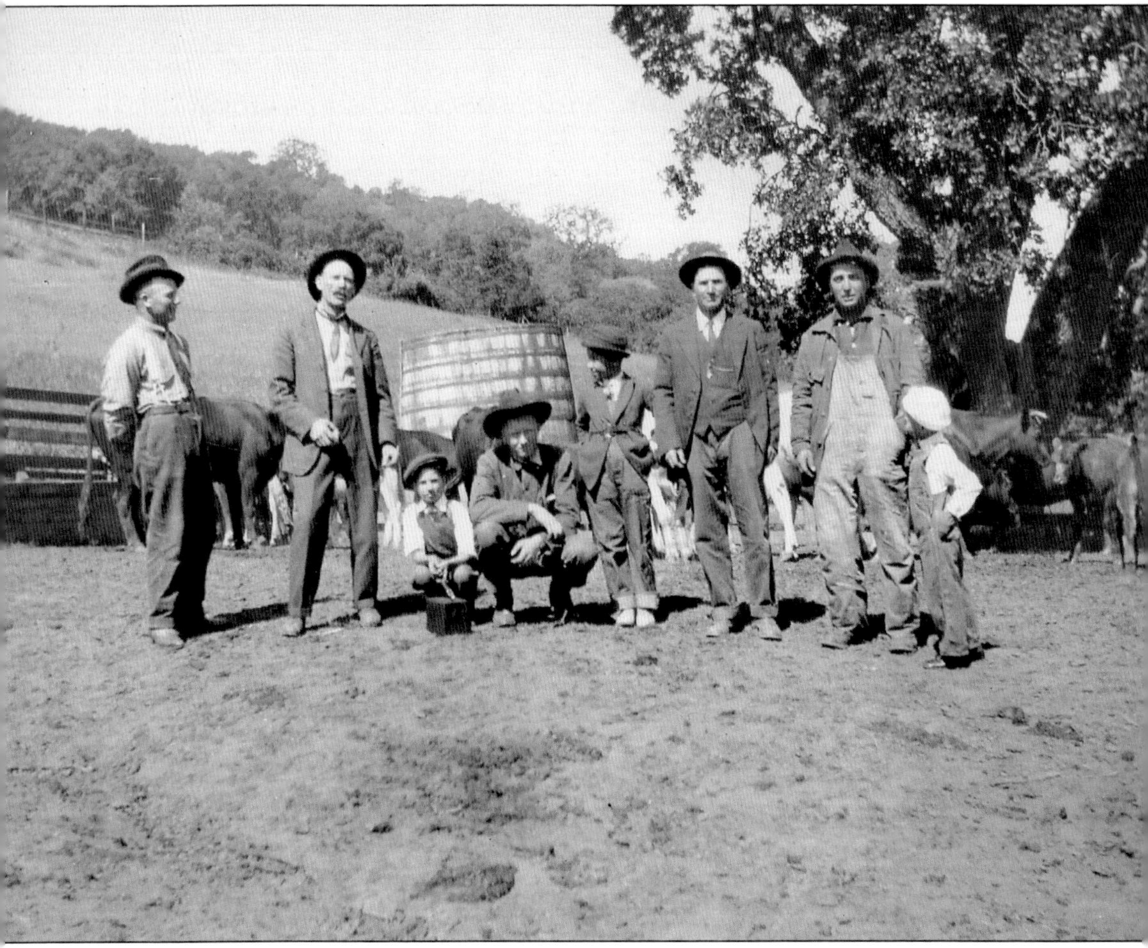

These men paused for a photograph in 1924 on the ranch of Manuel B. Nunez on section 14 in Morgan Territory. Pictured, from left to right, are Benjamin Guirado, Jack Duncan, unidentified, Bernie Duncan, unidentified, William R. Bloching, Marcos Guirado, and unidentified.

Rose Galvin is holding her son Everett in 1921 in the Joaquin front yard on Marsh Creek Road. The road runs between the picket fence and the barn in the background.

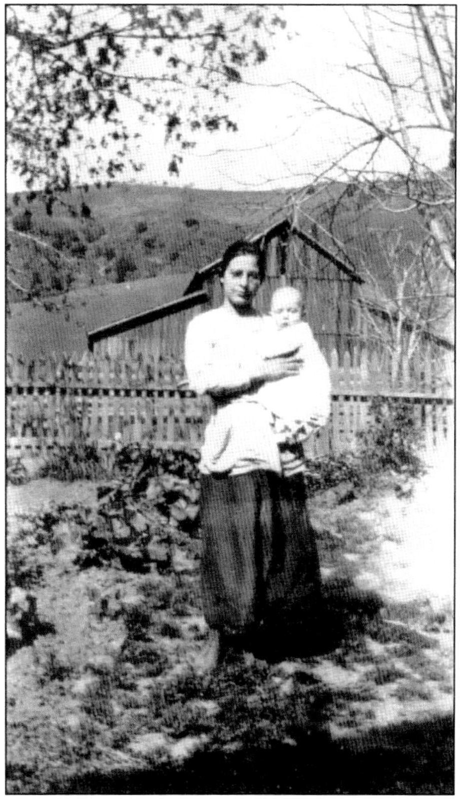

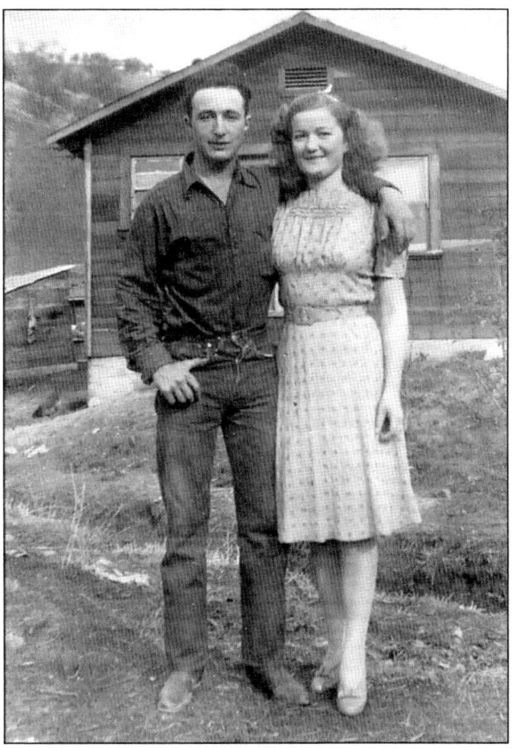

In 1944, a newly married Everett Galvin poses for this picture with his bride, Dorothy Horn.

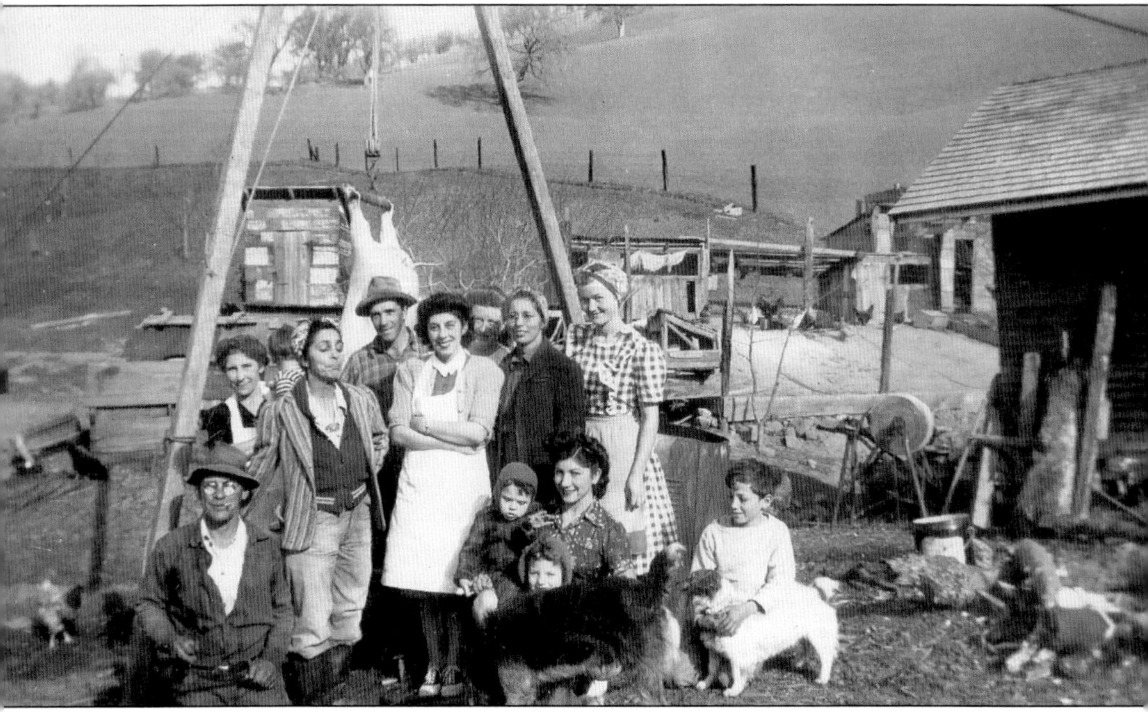

It was a bad day for the pig when this "butcher time" photograph was taken in the 1940s. Pictured, from left to right, are (first row) Ben Azevedo, two children, Virginia Joaquin Thomas, and Jerry Galvin; (second row) Libby Joaquin, Lucy Correa Viera, Alvin Joaquin, Margaret Lavera (a cousin from Oregon), Edith Joaquin, Annie Morgan, and Dorothy Galvin.

Tony and Mary Gomez owned and lived with their many children in what was later referred to as the "Pape House" on Oak Street. When they moved across the street, they rented out their former home. This rental agreement from 1942 shows the rent as $12 per month, with a disclosure that there was no indoor plumbing.

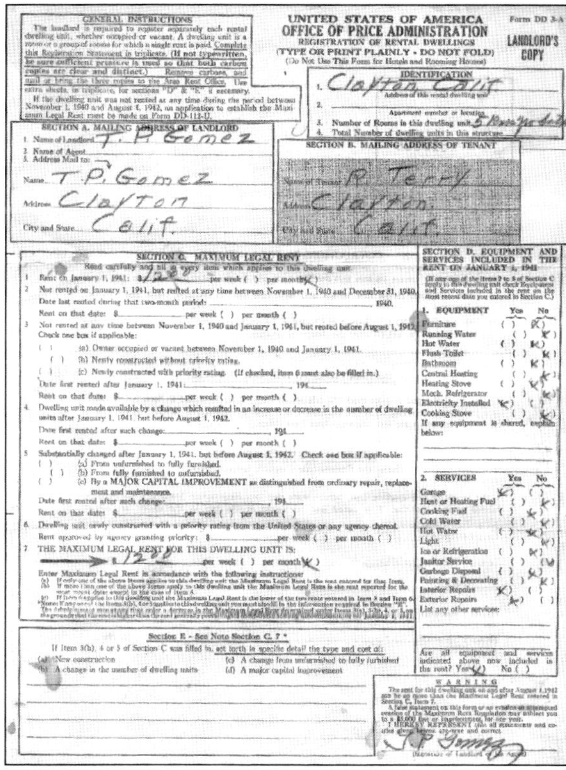

GENERAL INSTRUCTIONS

The landlord is required to register separately each rental dwelling unit, whether occupied or vacant. A dwelling unit is a room or a group of rooms for which a single rent is paid. Complete this Registration Statement in triplicate. (If not typewritten, be sure sufficient pressure is used so that both carbon copies are clear and distinct.) Remove carbons, and mail or bring the three copies to the Area Rent Office. Use extra sheets, in triplicate, for sections "D" & "E" if necessary.

If the dwelling unit was not rented at any time during the period between November 1, 1940 and August 1, 1942, an application to establish the Maximum Legal Rent must be made on Form DD-112-U.

UNITED STATES OF AMERICA
OFFICE OF PRICE ADMINISTRATION
REGISTRATION OF RENTAL DWELLINGS
(TYPE OR PRINT PLAINLY - DO NOT FOLD)
(Do Not Use This Form for Hotels and Rooming Houses)

Form DD 3-A

LANDLORD'S COPY

IDENTIFICATION
1. Clayton, Calif.
Address of this rental dwelling unit
2. ______
Apartment number or location
3. Number of Rooms in this dwelling unit 5 Rooms
4. Total Number of dwelling units in this structure 1

SECTION A. MAILING ADDRESS OF LANDLORD
1. Name of Landlord T. P. Gomez
2. Name of Agent
3. Address Mail to: →
Name T. P. Gomez
Address Clayton
City and State Calif.

SECTION B. MAILING ADDRESS OF TENANT
Name of Tenant R. Terry
Address Clayton.
City and State Calif.

SECTION C. MAXIMUM LEGAL RENT
Read carefully and fill in every item which applies to this dwelling unit.

1 Rent on January 1, 1941: $12.00 per week ( ) per month (X)
2 Not rented on January 1, 1941, but rented at any time between November 1, 1940 and December 31, 1940.
Date last rented during that two-month period: ______ 1940.
Rent on that date: $______ per week ( ) per month ( )
3 Not rented at any time between November 1, 1940 and January 1, 1941, but rented before August 1, 1942.
Check one box if applicable:
( ) (a) Owner occupied or vacant between November 1, 1940 and January 1, 1941.
( ) (b) Newly constructed without priority rating.
( ) (c) Newly constructed with priority rating. (If checked, item 6 must also be filled in.)
Date first rented after January 1, 1941: ______ 194__
Rent on that date: $______ per week ( ) per month ( )
4 Dwelling unit made available by a change which resulted in an increase or decrease in the number of dwelling units after January 1, 1941, but before August 1, 1942.
Date first rented after such change: ______ 194__
Rent on that date: $______ per week ( ) per month ( )
5 Substantially changed after January 1, 1941, but before August 1, 1942. Check one box if applicable:
( ) (a) From unfurnished to fully furnished.
( ) (b) From fully furnished to unfurnished.
( ) (c) By a MAJOR CAPITAL IMPROVEMENT as distinguished from ordinary repair, replacement and maintenance.
Date first rented after such change: ______ 194__
Rent on that date: $______ per week ( ) per month ( )
6 Dwelling unit newly constructed with a priority rating from the United States or any agency thereof.
Rent approved by agency granting priority: $______ per week ( ) per month ( )
7 THE MAXIMUM LEGAL RENT FOR THIS DWELLING UNIT IS:
→ $12.00 per week ( ) per month (X)
Enter Maximum Legal Rent in accordance with the following instructions:

SECTION D. EQUIPMENT AND SERVICES INCLUDED IN THE RENT ON JANUARY 1, 1941
(If any one of the items 2 to 5 of Section C apply to this dwelling unit check Equipment and Services included in the rent on the most recent date you entered in Section C.)

1. EQUIPMENT	Yes	No
Furniture	( )	(X)
Running Water	( )	(X)
Hot Water	( )	(X)
Flush Toilet	( )	(X)
Bathroom	( )	(X)
Central Heating	( )	(X)
Heating Stove	( )	(X)
Mech. Refrigerator	( )	(X)
Electricity Installed	(X)	( )
Cooking Stove	( )	(X)

If any equipment is shared, explain below:

2. SERVICES	Yes	No
Garage	(X)	( )
Heat or Heating Fuel	( )	(X)
Cooking Fuel	( )	(X)
Cold Water	( )	(X)
Hot Water	( )	(X)
Light	( )	(X)
Ice or Refrigeration	( )	(X)
Janitor Service	( )	(X)
Garbage Disposal	( )	(X)
Painting & Decorating	( )	(X)
Interior Repairs	(X)	( )
Exterior Repairs	(X)	( )

List any other services:

Are all equipment and services indicated above now included in the rent? Yes (X) No ( )

Section E - See Note Section C. 7 *
If Item 3(b), 4 or 5 of Section C was filled in, set forth in specific detail the type and cost of:
(a) New construction
(b) A change in the number of dwelling units
(c) A change from unfurnished to fully furnished
(d) A major capital improvement

WARNING
The rent for this dwelling unit on and after August 1, 1942 can be no more than the Maximum Legal Rent entered in Section C, Item 7.
A false statement on this form or an evasion or attempted evasion of the Maximum Rent Regulation may subject you to a $5,000 fine or imprisonment for one year.
I HEREBY REPRESENT that all statements and entries given herein are true and correct.
T. P. Gomez
(Signature of Landlord or his Agent)

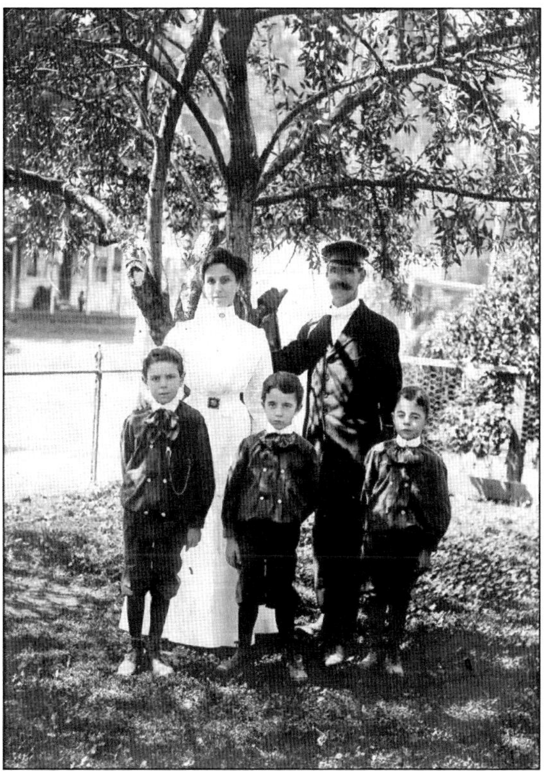

Clayton did not have a resident doctor, so Concord's Doctor Neff was one of the doctors who made house calls to Clayton to tend to the ill. Pictured here in 1908 are Dr. and Annie Neff with their three sons Francis, Ben, and Jack. Annie Neff was a teacher in Concord.

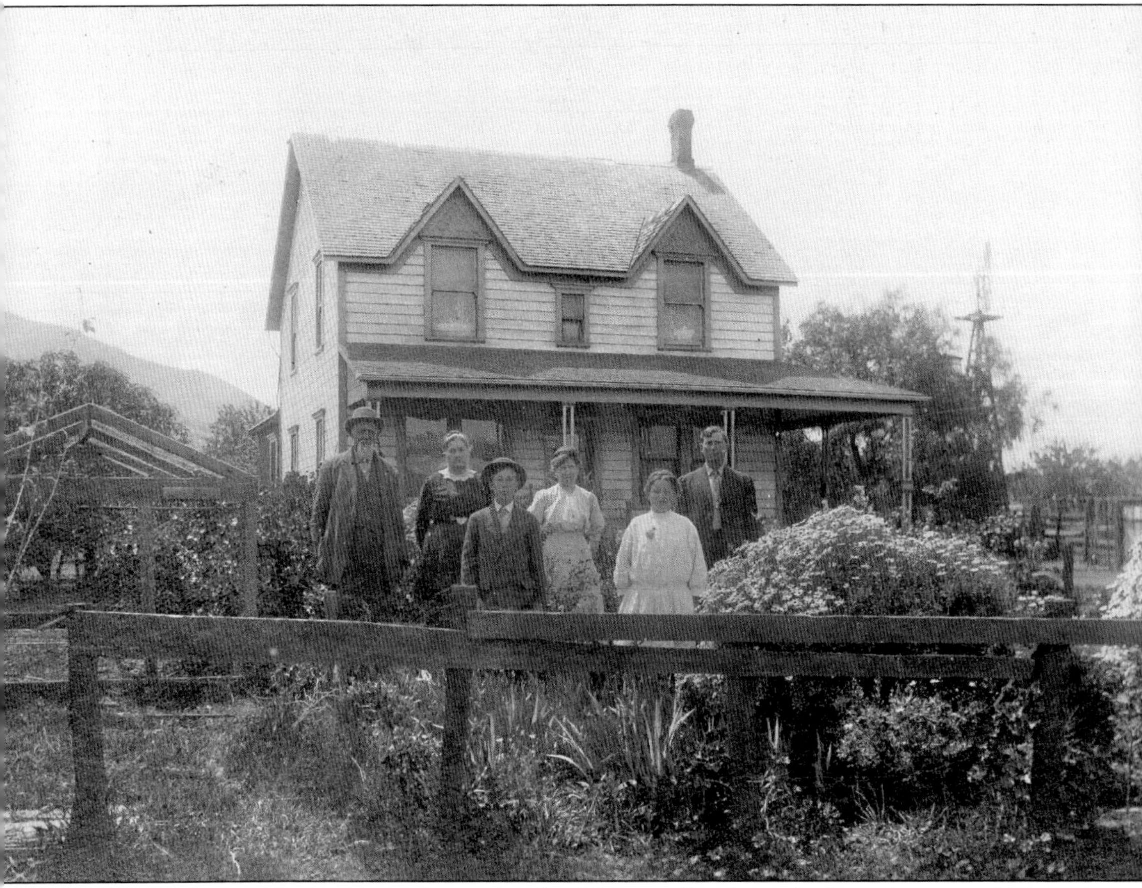

The Atchinson home was on the south side of Clayton Road, not far from the town of Clayton. This 1913 photograph shows, from left to right, George W. Atchinson, Elizabeth Butler, Wilbur Atchinson, Hilda Rhine Atchinson, Mildred Fern Atchinson, and Jack W. Atchinson. Jack and George Atchinson ran stages from Clayton carrying mail, money, and passengers. They traveled to and from Martinez, Pacheco, Concord, Nortonville, Somersville, and Antioch.

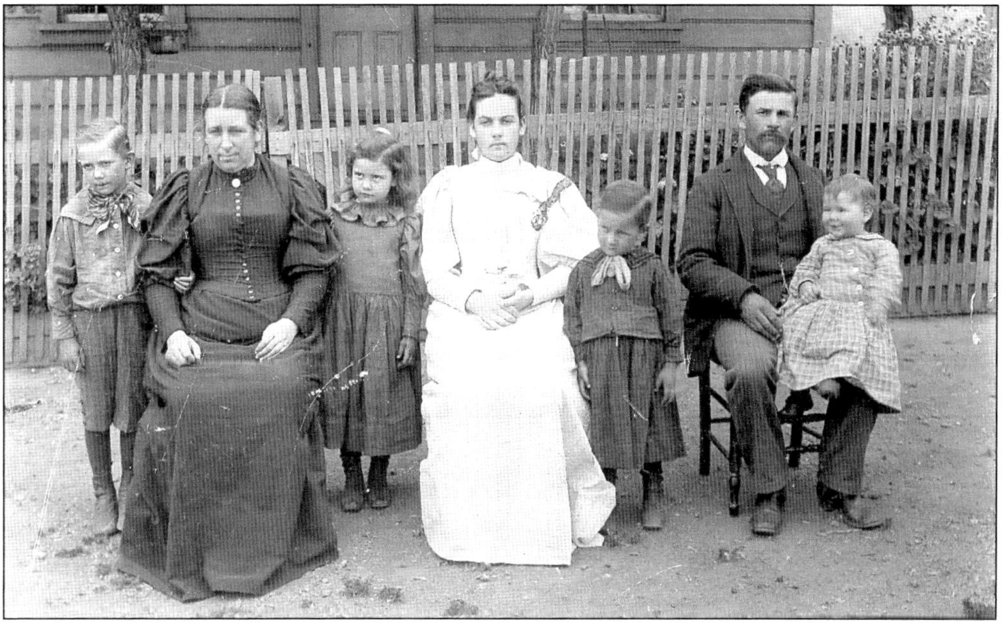

The Matheron family lived on the north side of Clayton Road about a half-mile east of Kirker Pass, down by Mitchell Creek. Individual names of the people in this photograph are unknown, but the Congregational church records from the 1890s indicated that the family consisted of adults Frank and Annie Matheron and children Elie Soring, Annie True, Joseph Frederick, Leona Adella, Frank Charles, and Percy Raymond.

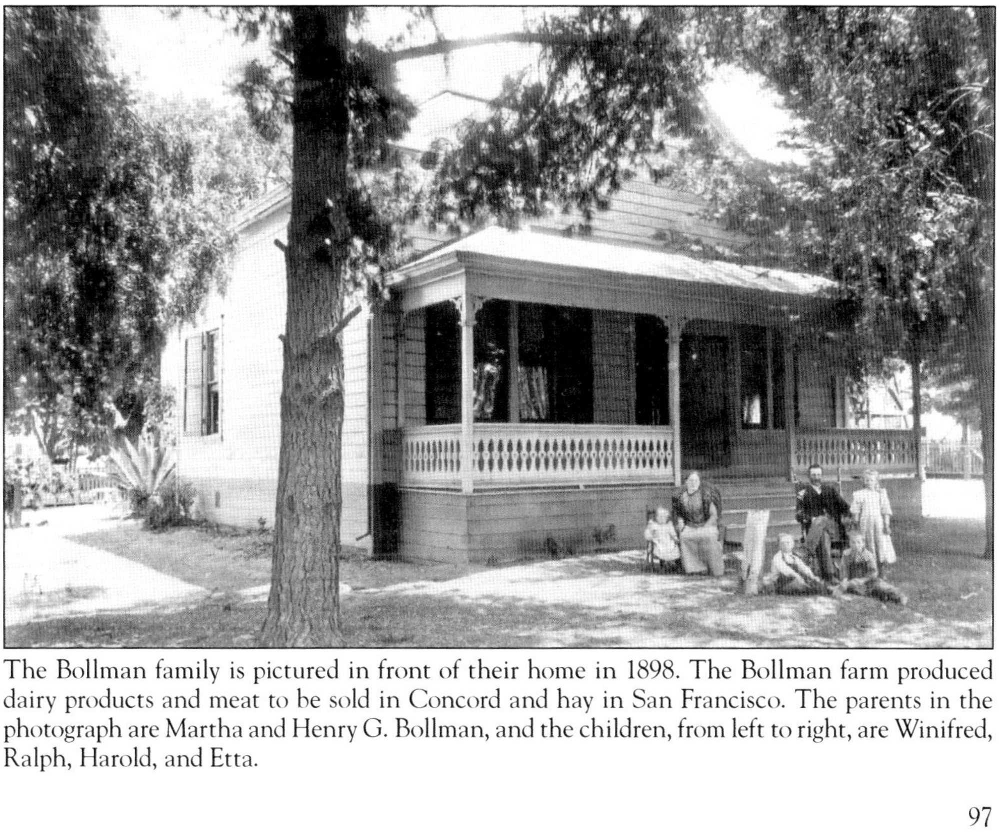

The Bollman family is pictured in front of their home in 1898. The Bollman farm produced dairy products and meat to be sold in Concord and hay in San Francisco. The parents in the photograph are Martha and Henry G. Bollman, and the children, from left to right, are Winifred, Ralph, Harold, and Etta.

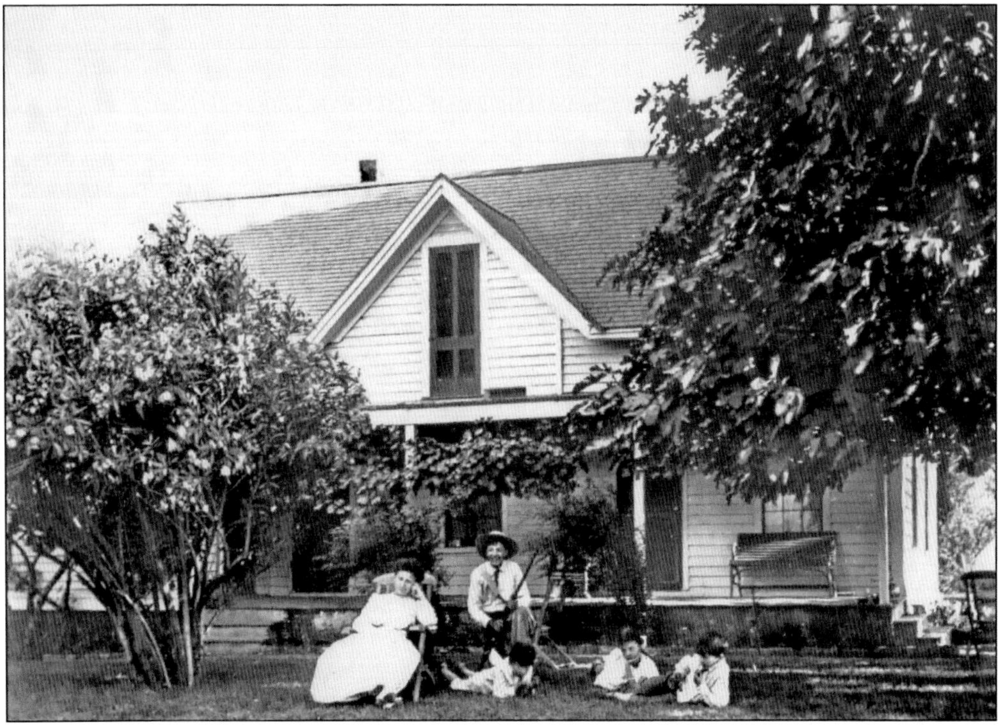

This 1911 photograph shows the Salazar home, with the Salazar family in the front yard. Mr. Salazar was the manager of the Mount Diablo Winery.

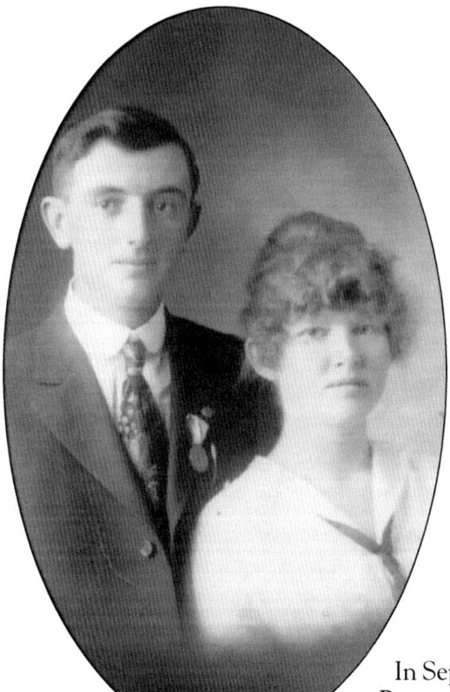

In September 1917, John Howard Morgan married Lili von Buren. John was the son of Isaac Morgan and the grandson of Morgan Territory pioneer Jeremiah Morgan.

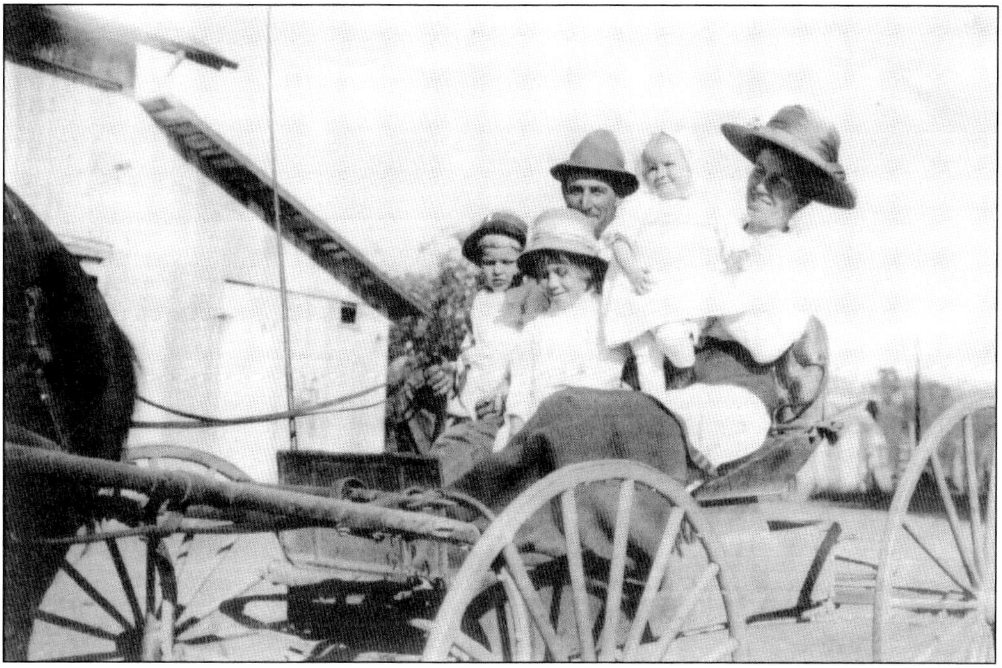

In 1914, the Will Frank family is taking a buggy ride. Pictured, from left to right, are George, Dorothy, Will, Willmetta, and Metta.

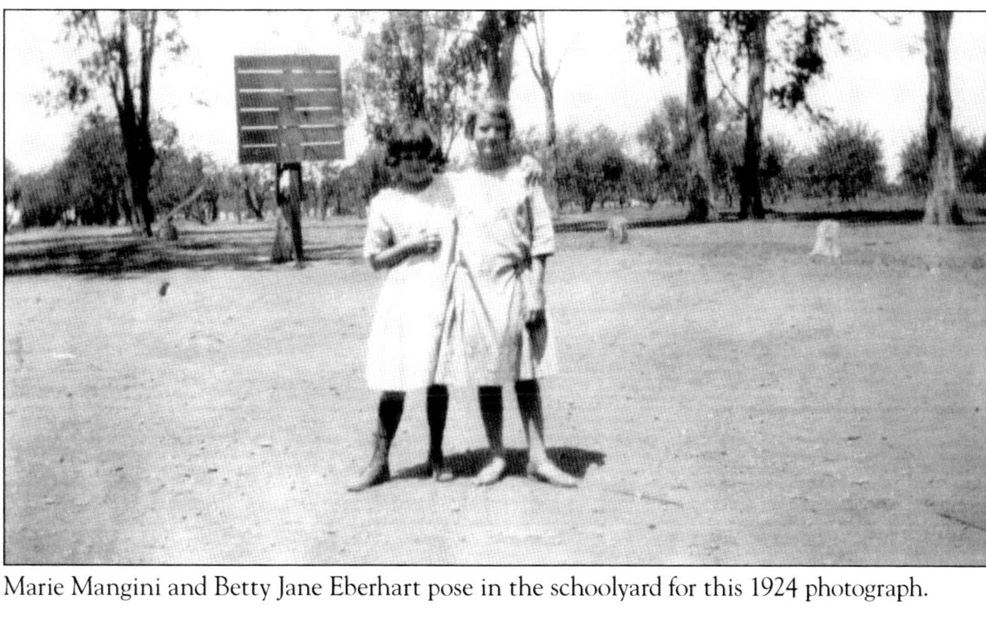

Marie Mangini and Betty Jane Eberhart pose in the schoolyard for this 1924 photograph.

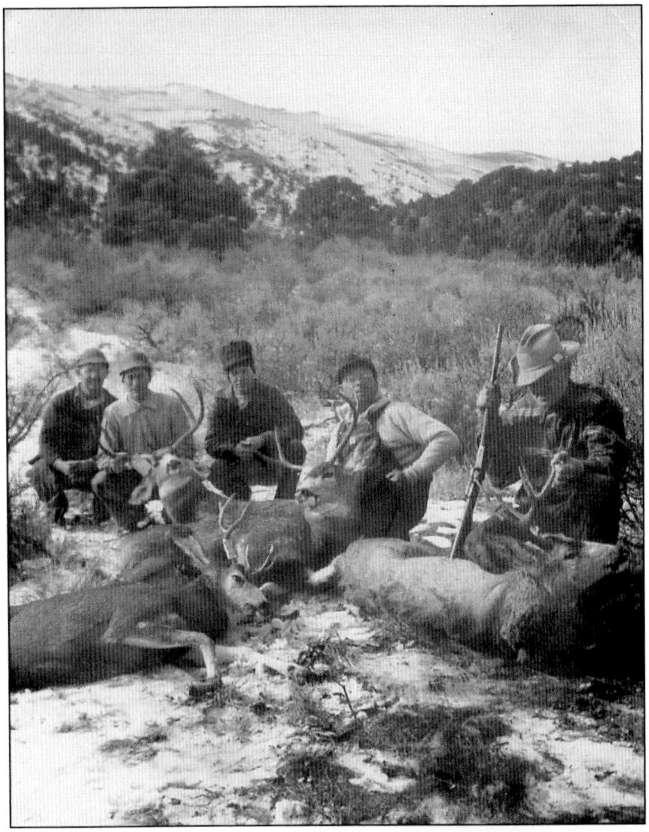

The results of a successful deer-hunting expedition are evident in this picture. Hunting trips were important to the men of Clayton. Pictured, from left to right, are three unidentified men, Pete Garcia, and Bernie Duncan.

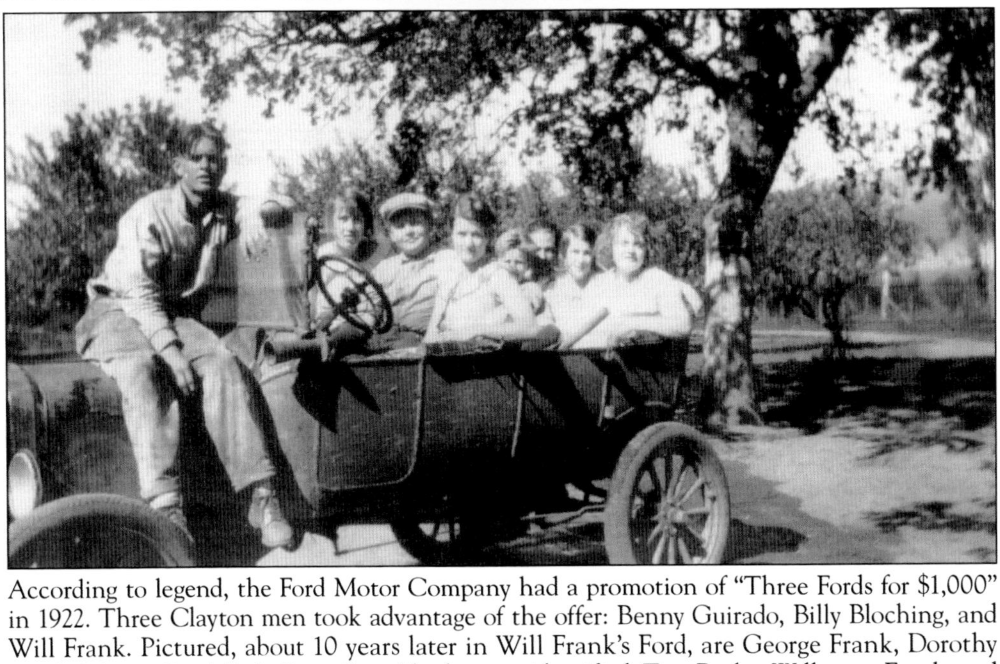

According to legend, the Ford Motor Company had a promotion of "Three Fords for $1,000" in 1922. Three Clayton men took advantage of the offer: Benny Guirado, Billy Bloching, and Will Frank. Pictured, about 10 years later in Will Frank's Ford, are George Frank, Dorothy Frank, Johnny Stockfleth, Betty Jane Eberhart, unidentified, Tom Butler, Willmetta Frank, and Laura May Stockfleth.

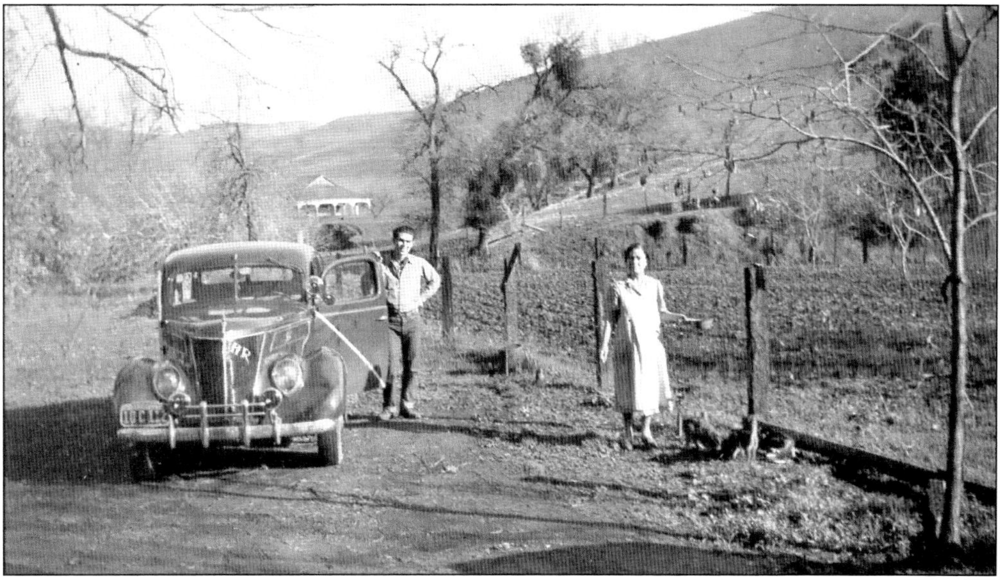

In 1940, Harold Russell (left) was proud of his 1937 Ford—he had his initials installed on the grille. Mrs. Russell, his mother, is on the right. The Russells lived on Main Street.

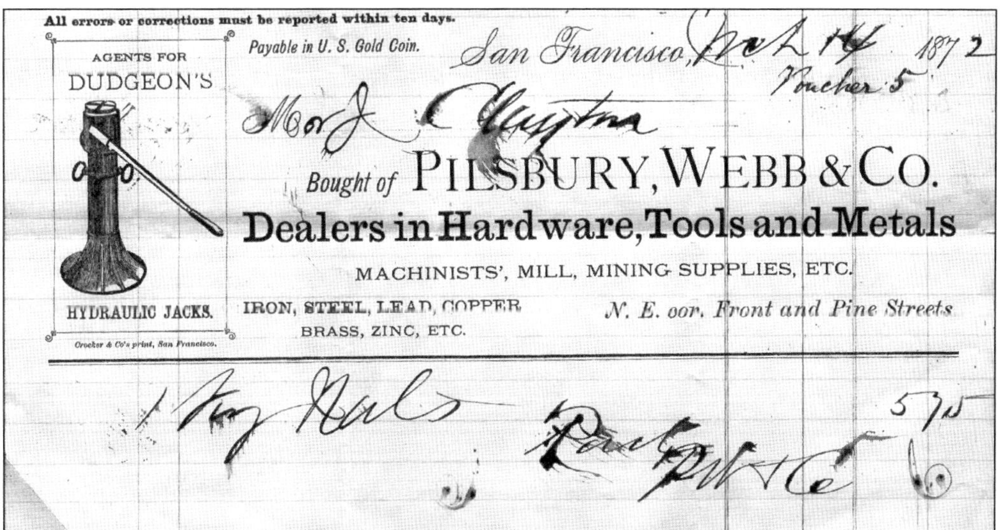

All errors or corrections must be reported within ten days.

AGENTS FOR
DUDGEON'S
HYDRAULIC JACKS.
Crocker & Co's print, San Francisco.

Payable in U. S. Gold Coin. San Francisco, 1872
Voucher 5

Bought of PILSBURY, WEBB & CO.
Dealers in Hardware, Tools and Metals
MACHINISTS', MILL, MINING SUPPLIES, ETC.
IRON, STEEL, LEAD, COPPER
BRASS, ZINC, ETC.
N. E. cor. Front and Pine Streets

Not all goods and supplies were available in early Clayton. Here is a receipt that shows Joel Clayton purchased a keg of nails in San Francisco.

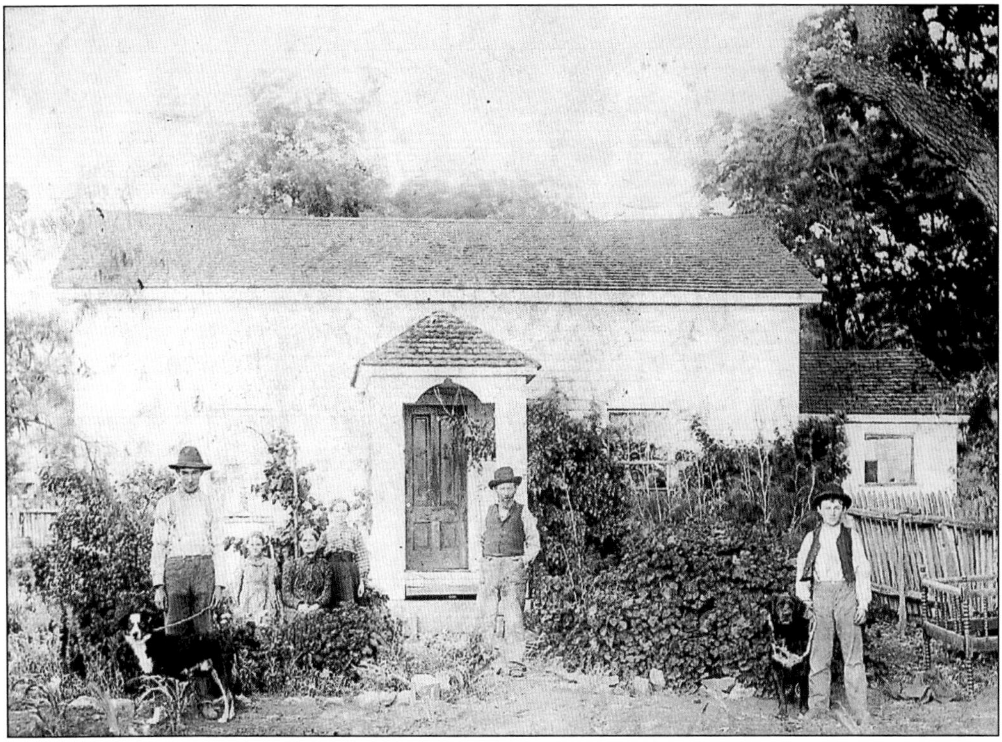

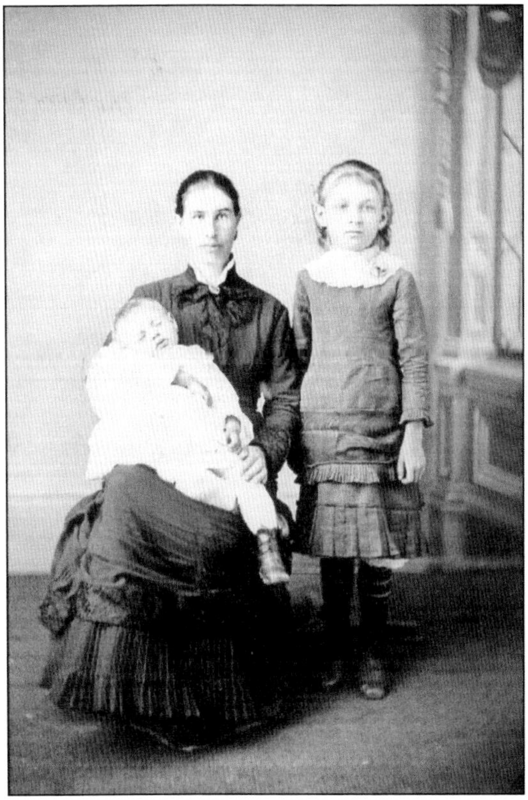

In the late 1890s, Fred and Elizabeth Frank and some of their children stand in front of their home. They first rented the house before purchasing it in 1900 with money their eldest son Frederick Jr. earned in the Yukon gold rush.

Elizabeth Bisber Frank was holding her son Bartholomes "Bart," with daughter Elizabeth "Lizzie" standing by, when this photograph was taken around 1882.

Pictured here in the mid-1890s, from left to right, are Gesine Kruse Russelmann, daughter Lillien, and Gesine's husband, Capt. H. Friedrich Russelmann.

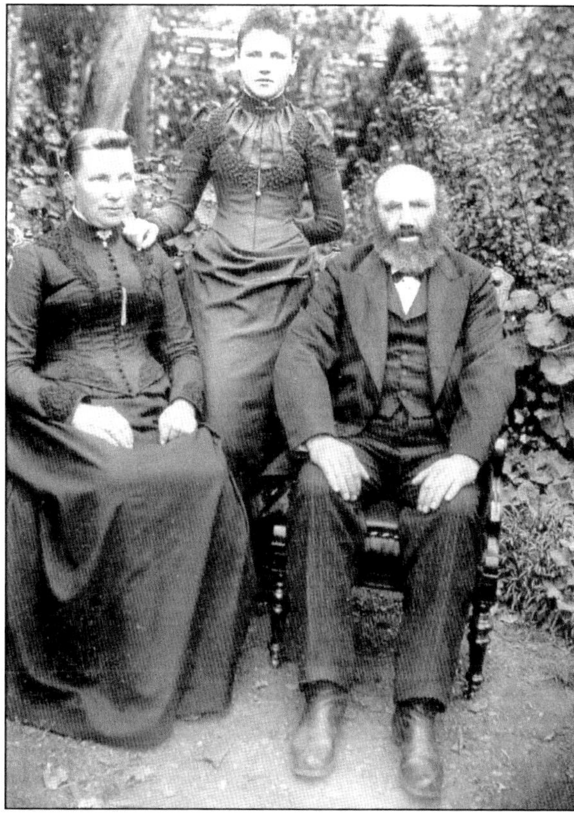

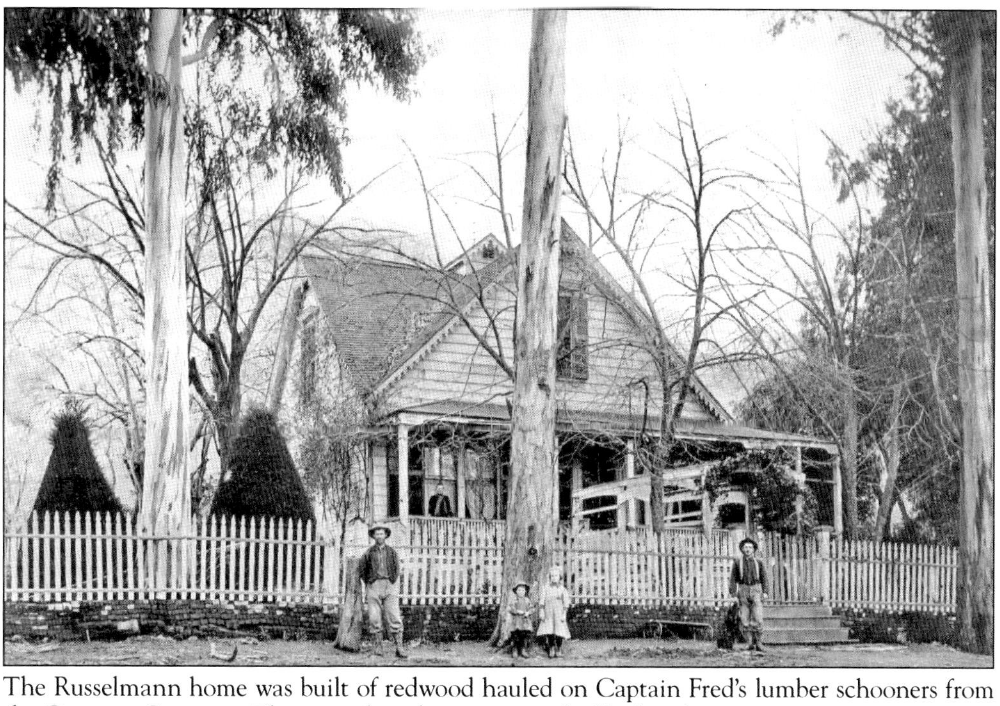

The Russelmann home was built of redwood hauled on Captain Fred's lumber schooners from the Crescent City area. The gingerbread trim was crafted by hand.

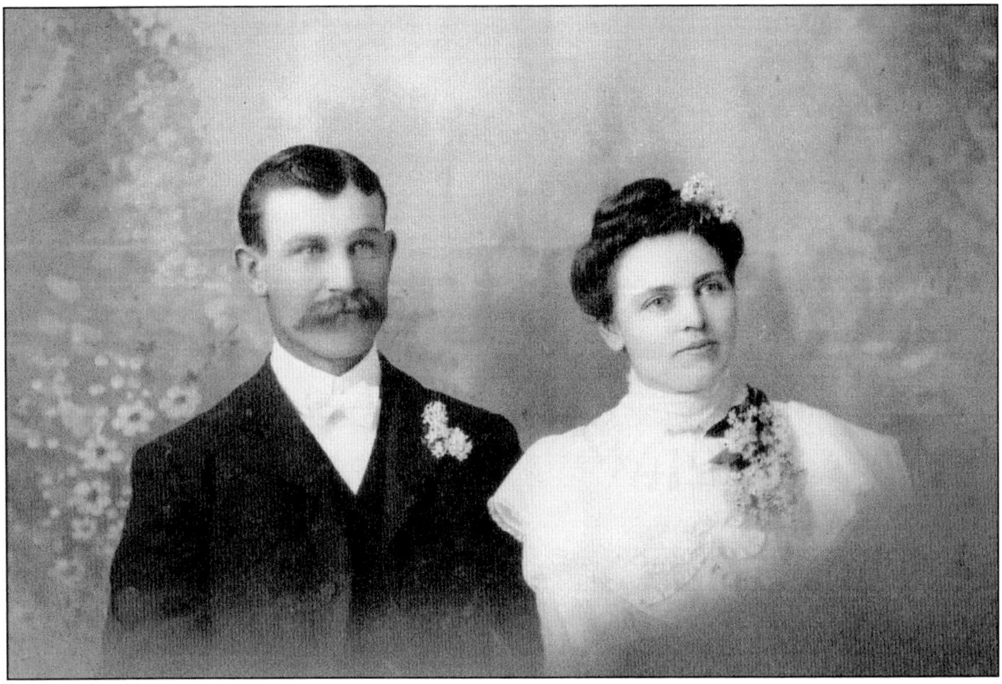

In April 1903, Henry Frank married Lillien Mathilda Russelmann. Lillien taught Sunday school at the Congregational church and Henry worked as a ranch hand for Captain Russelmann.

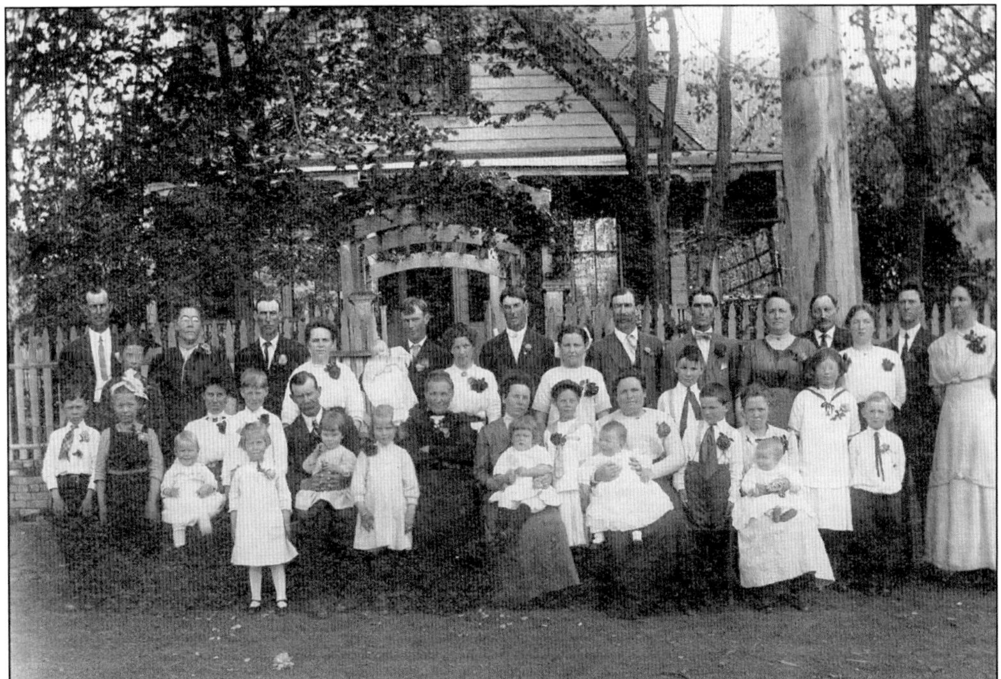

In 1913, all of Henry Frank's brothers and sisters and their spouses and children joined him and his wife, Lillien, as they celebrated their 10th wedding anniversary. Lillien is the fourth person in the top row, and Henry is seated in front of her.

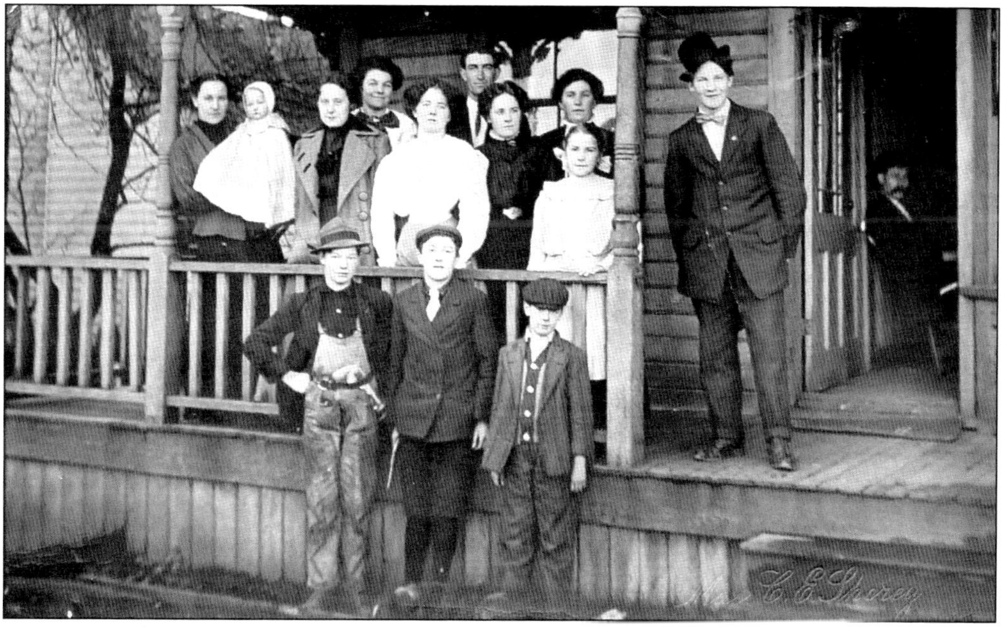

This postcard was sent in December 1910 to Lillian Frank by her brother Albert, after he had gone to work at the Black Diamond Mine. From the left, Albert is the sixth person in the top row. The seventh person is referred to by him as "my steady one up here." It is Terry Weston, whom he later married.

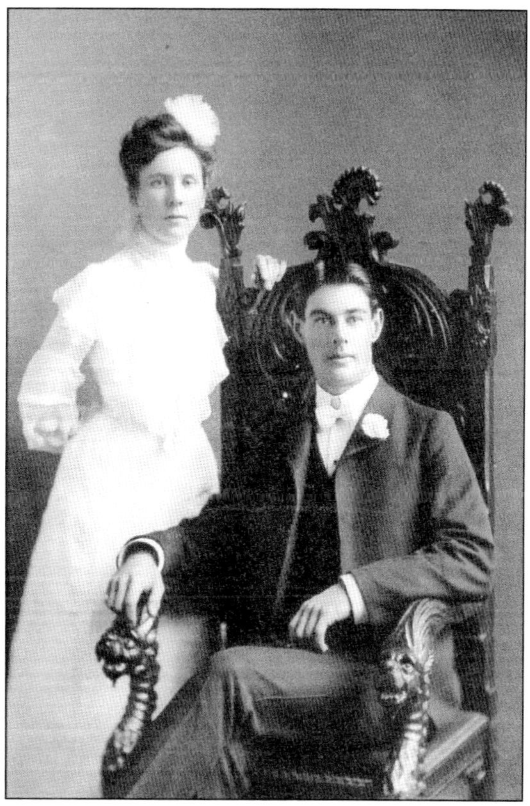

In October 1903, Alexander Bartholomes "Bart" Frank married Evelyn Alice Brown. Bart worked at the Cowell Cement Company, and Evelyn was a Sunday school teacher at the Congregational church.

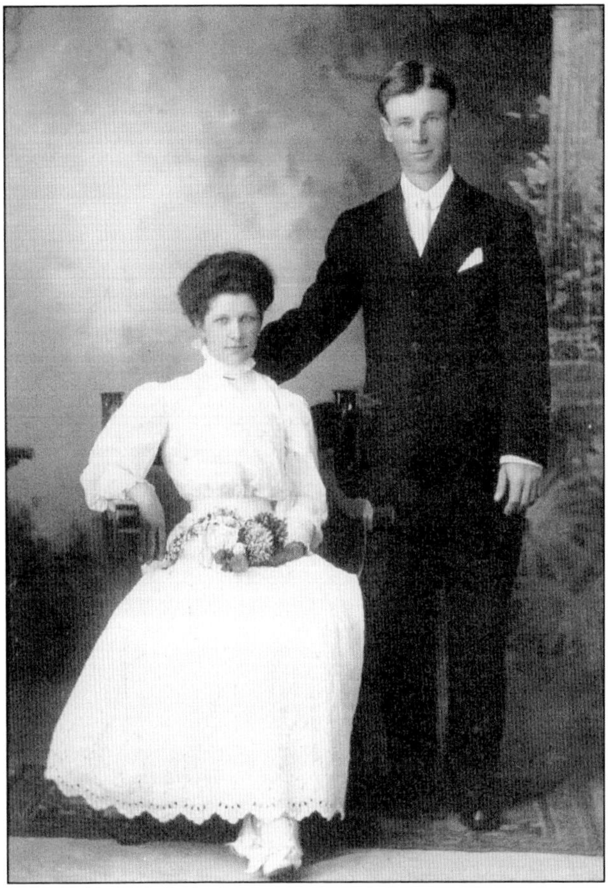

In October 1908, Charles "Charley" Frank married Agnes Louise Duncan. Agnes was the daughter of John and Maria Weaver Duncan. Charley was a talented horse trainer.

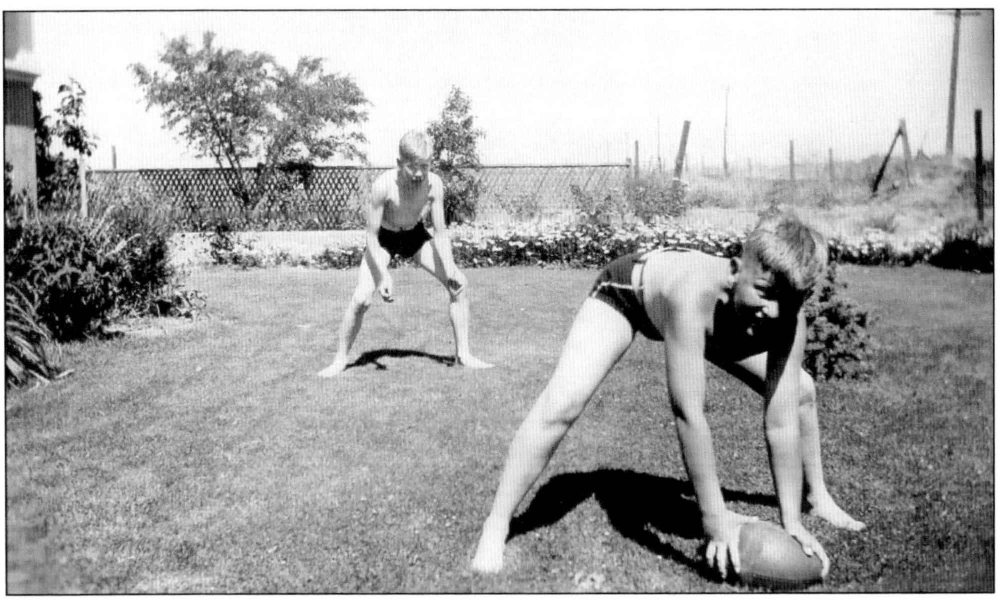

Billy Duncan (left) and Earl Duncan envisioned themselves to be future football stars when this picture was taken in 1934.

In January 1912, Lillian "Lily" Frank married George Rudolph "Dutch" Trette. Lily was a nurse, and Dutch was a blacksmith.

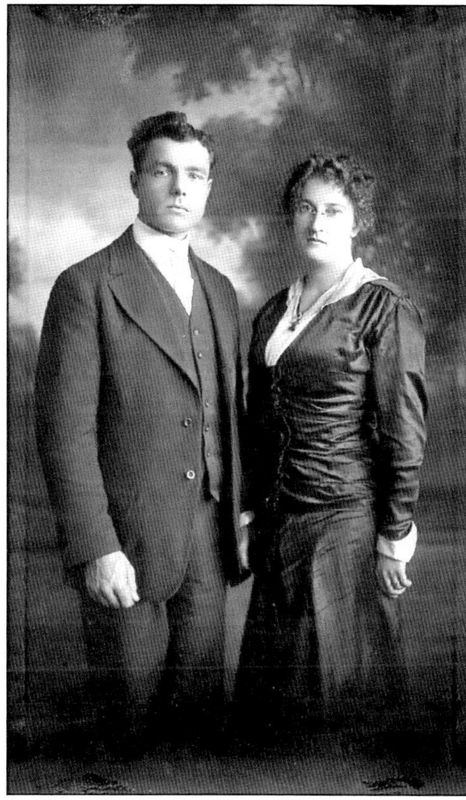

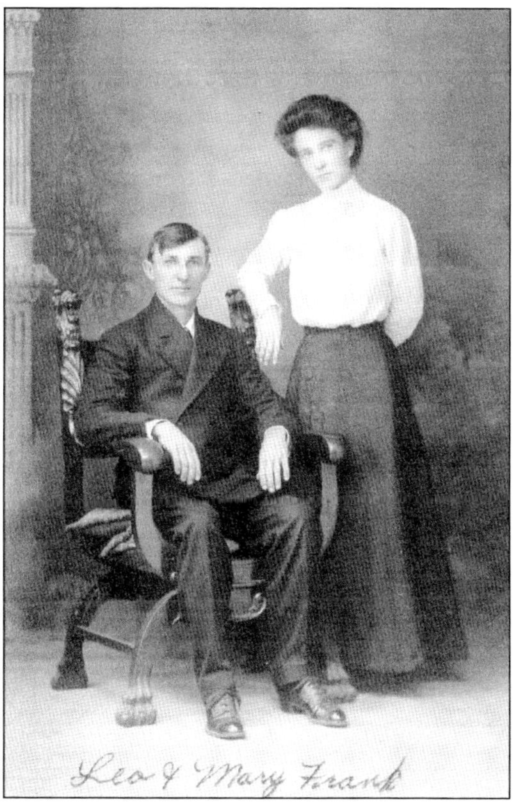

In April 1907, Vincent "Leo" Frank married Mary Mitchell, the daughter of "Buck" and Margaret Mitchell.

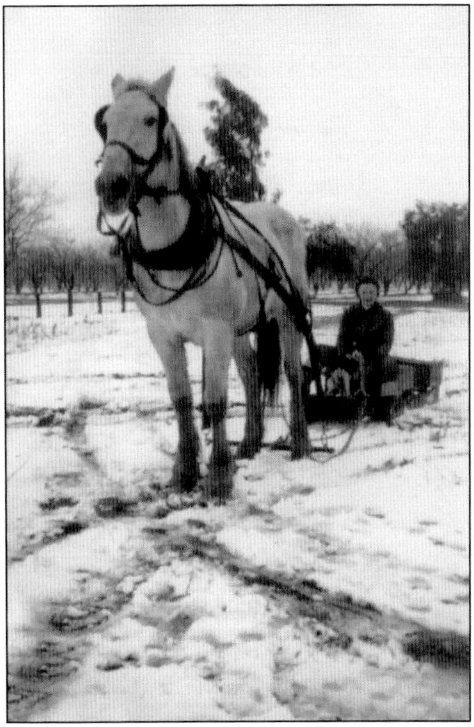

In January 1937, a considerable amount of snow fell in Clayton. Carmen Dobbel, future wife of George Frank, was pulled on this sled by a horse named Dolly.

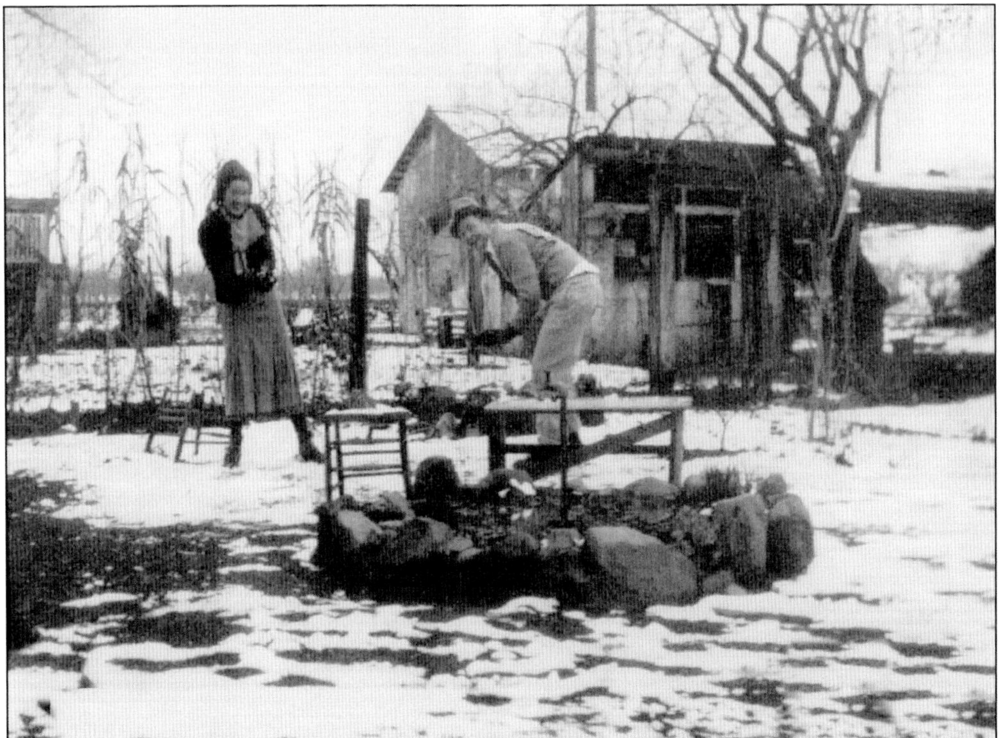

In January 1937, Willmetta Frank and her future husband, Charles Mann, have a snowball fight in the big snow.

Will Frank and his son George built a snowman by the barn on their farm on Pine Hollow Road.

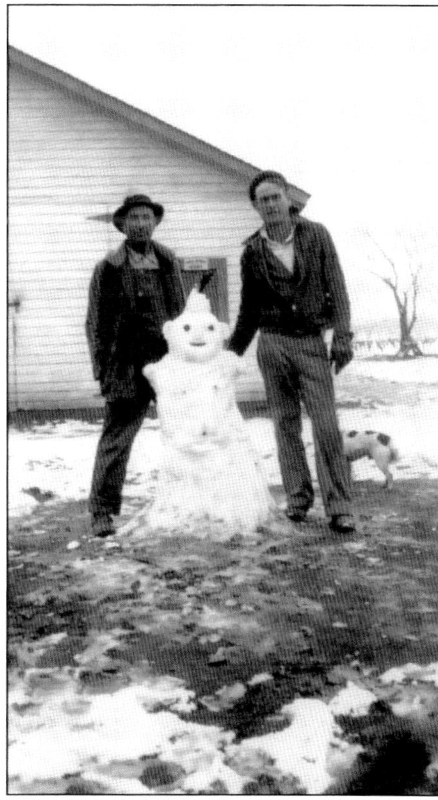

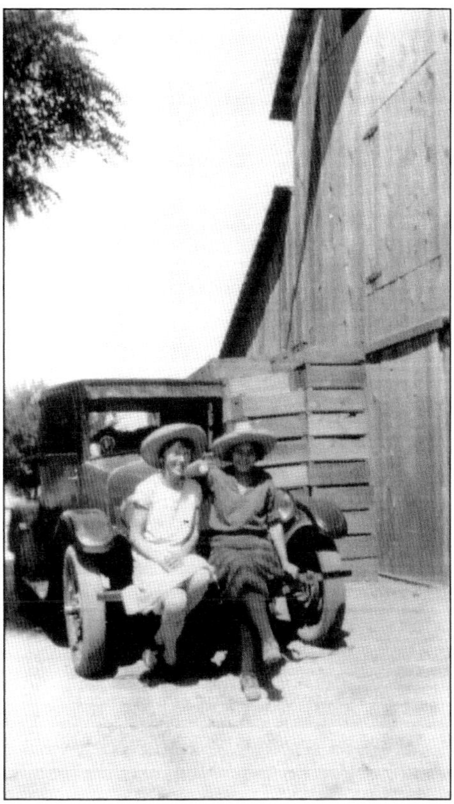

In the 1930s, Lois Bigelow and Mary Mitchell Frank pose on the front bumper of a car before heading out for a trip to Yosemite.

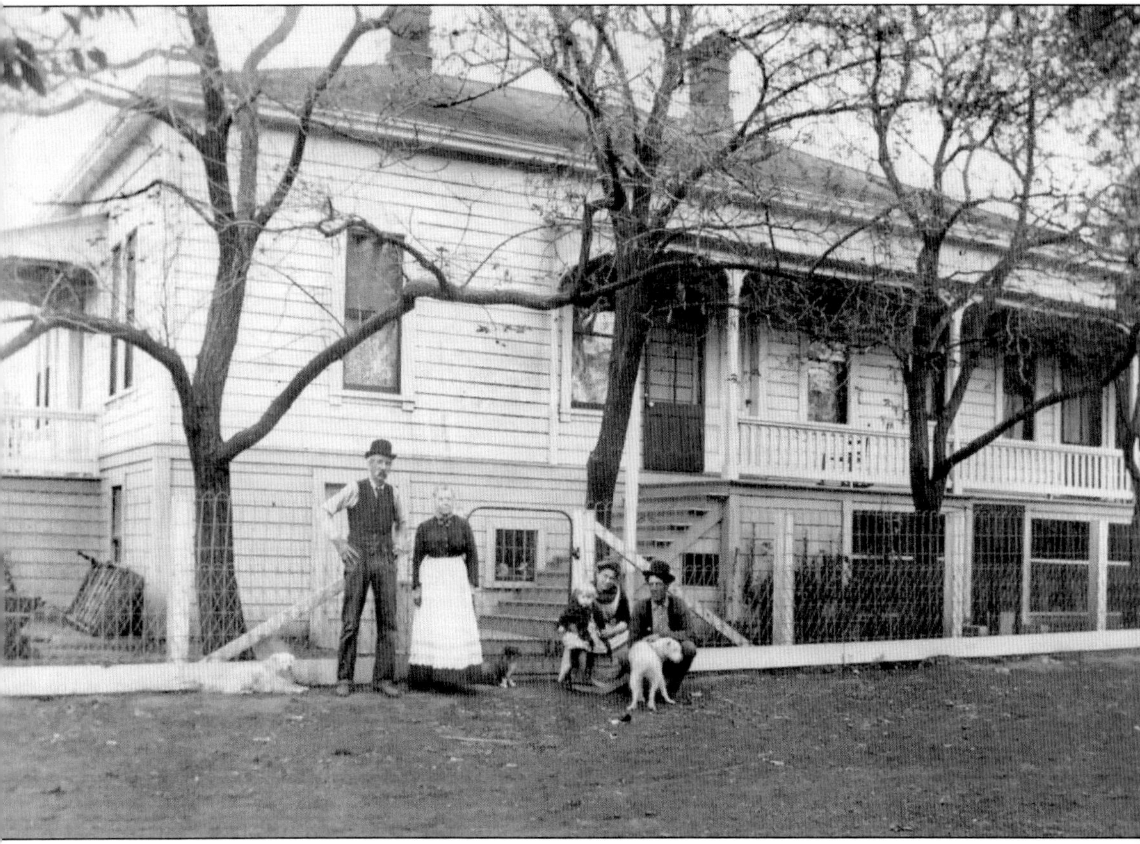

While the Stockfleth home was being built on Pine Hollow Road in the 1890s, the family stayed at the Kirkwood place. This 1914 photograph shows the Stockfleth house. Standing, from left to right, are Capt. John Stockfleth, Mrs. Olofson, Laura May Stockfleth, Laura Olofson Stockfleth, and Joe Stockfleth.

This tintype picture of Isabell Wilkie Stockfleth, wife of Capt. John Stockfleth, was taken around 1875. Isabell provided midwife services in Clayton and gave birth to 10 of her own children.

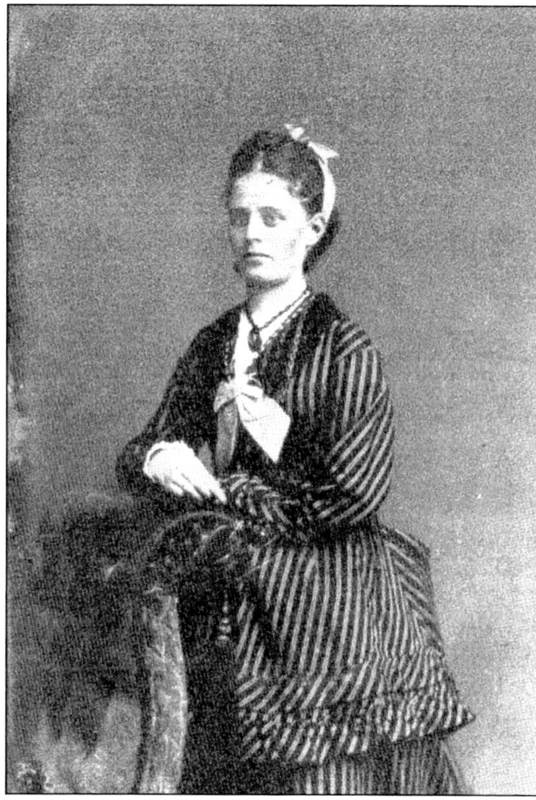

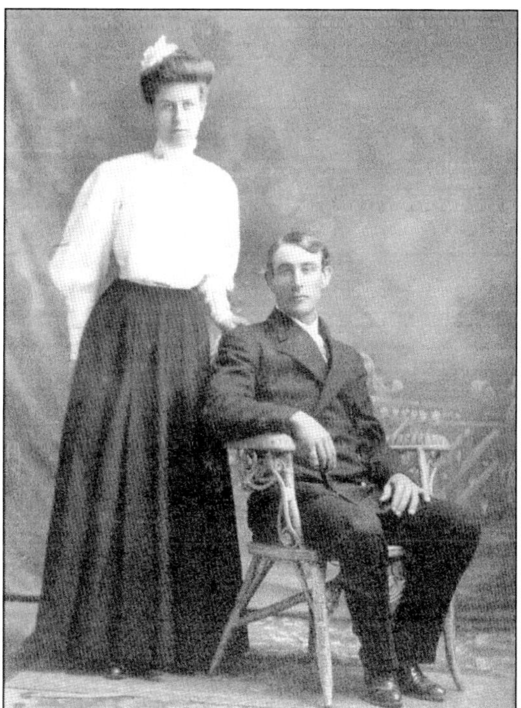

In August 1906, William "Will" Frank married Metta Isabel Stockfleth. Will was a farmer, and Metta was the daughter of Capt. John and Isabell Wilkie Stockfleth.

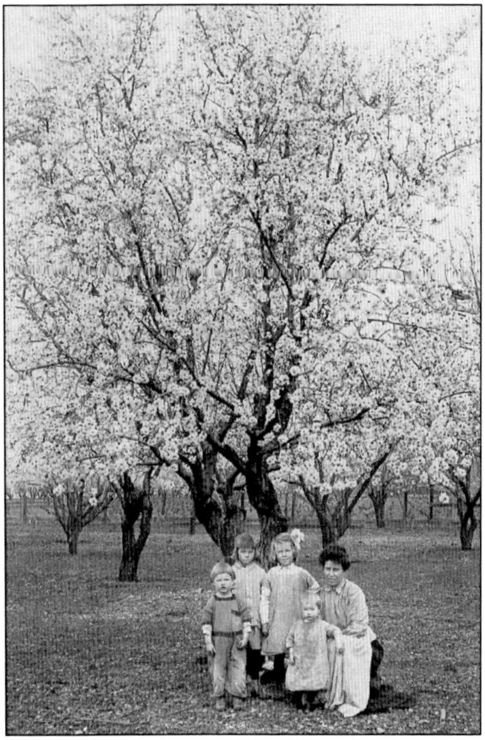

The blossoms on the almond trees created a beautiful background for this 1915 picture of George Frank, Ethel Henderson, Dorothy Frank, Willmetta Frank, and Metta Stockfleth Frank.

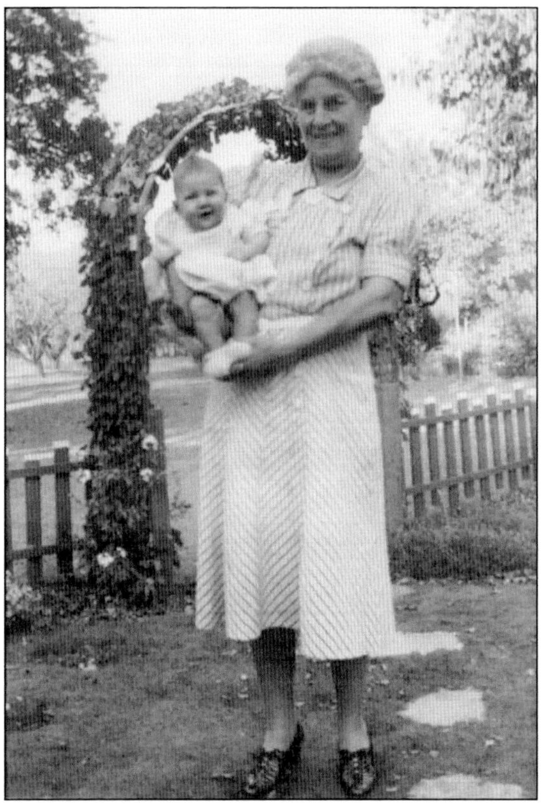

Metta Stockfleth Frank poses in her garden for this 1940 photograph while holding her first grandchild Charmetta Mann. Her home was near Clayton Grammar School, and if a child forgot his lunch or got sick during the school day, he was sent to Metta's house.

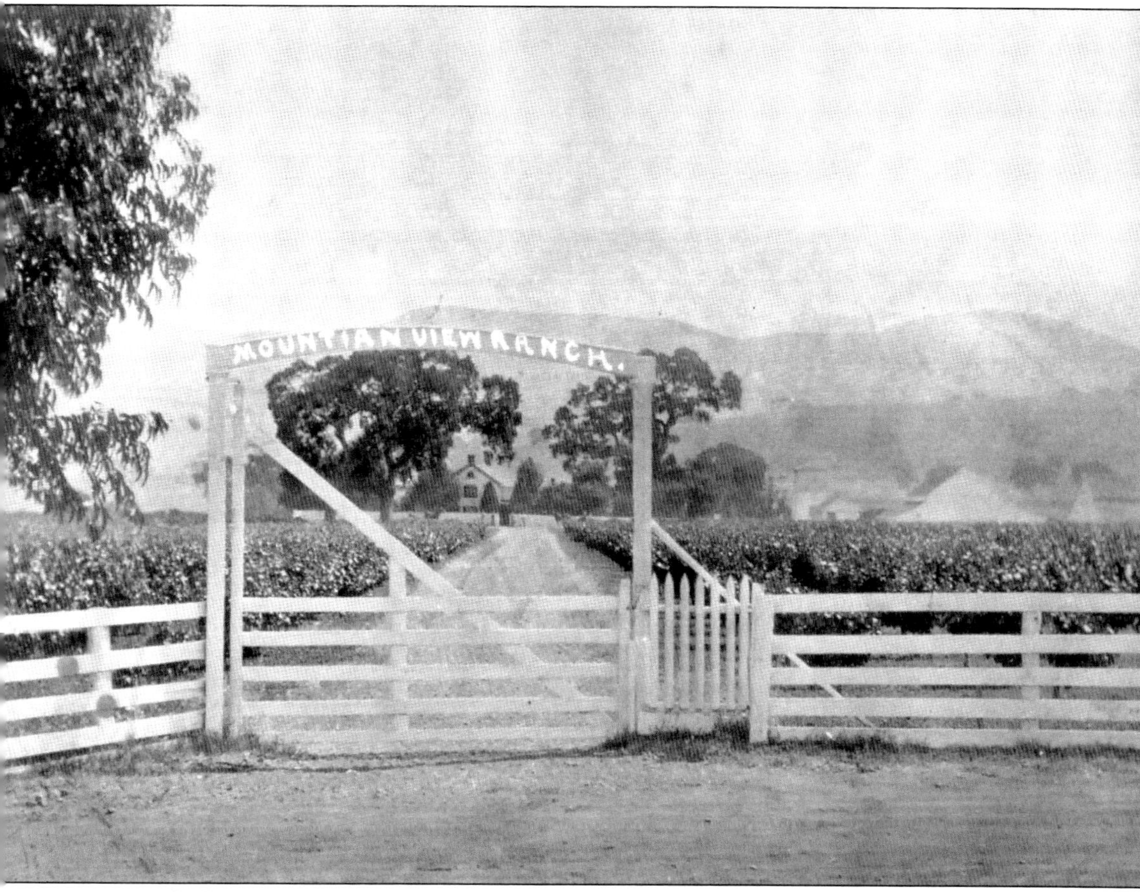

"Mountian [sic] View Ranch" was the name Isaac Smith gave his property at the intersection of Clayton Road and Kirker Pass. The house sat on the northeast corner. Smith was a farmer from New York who married Catherine Alice Sherman, the sister of Gen. William Tecumseh Sherman.

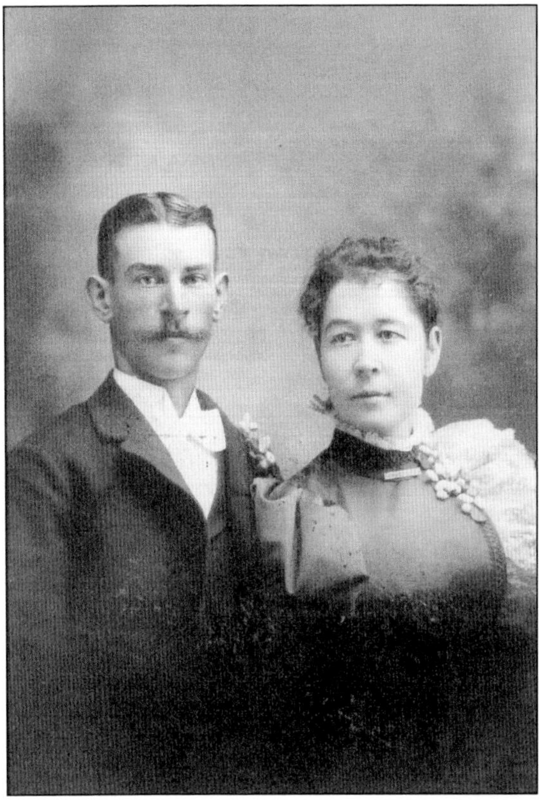

In 1899, Joseph "Joe" Frank married Nancy "Tib" Smith. Joe was a farmer and well driller, and Tib was the daughter of Isaac and Catherine Sherman Smith.

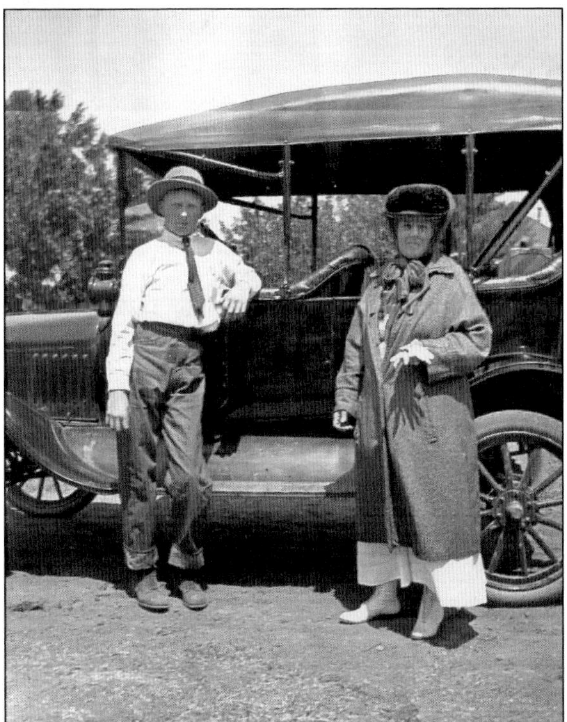

In April 1923, Helen Frank, daughter of Joseph and Nancy Smith Frank, married Bernard McKinley Duncan at the Mountain View Ranch.

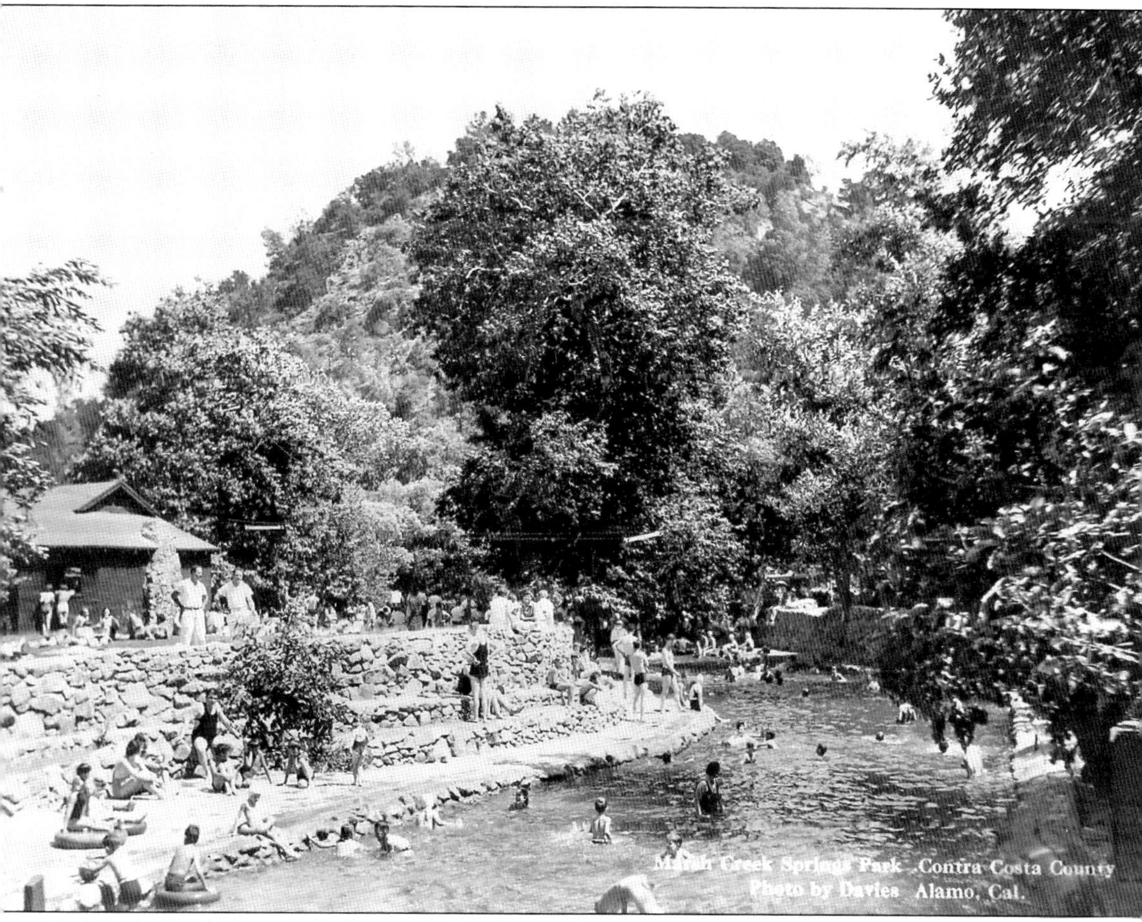

At Marsh Creek Springs Park, Marsh Creek was dammed to create a swimming pool. In 1927, this picnic ground began operation.

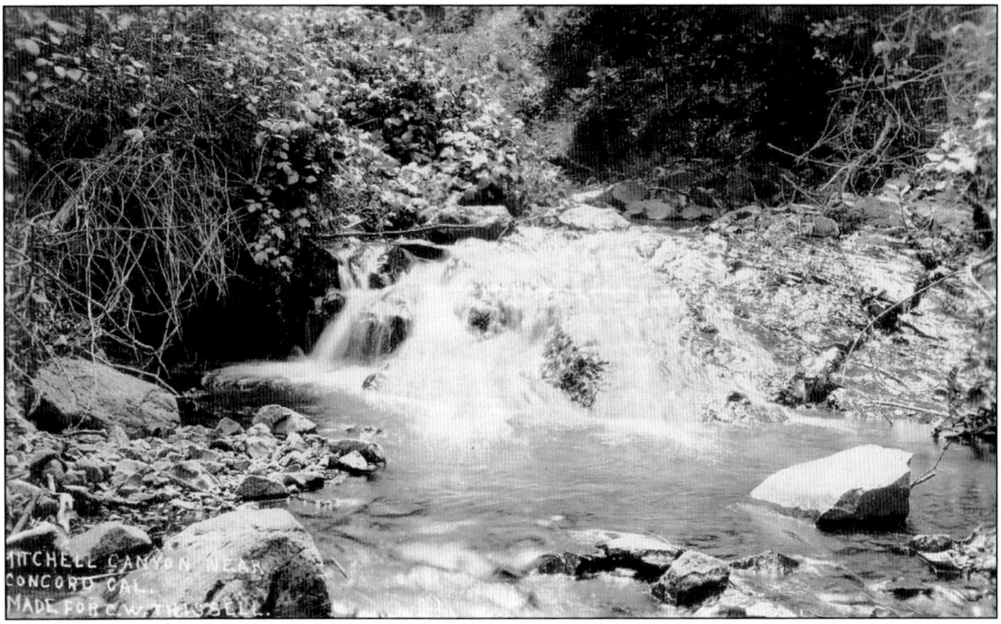

In the early days, townspeople rode in carriages and wagons to Mitchell Canyon Park. Its close proximity to town made it a popular picnic area.

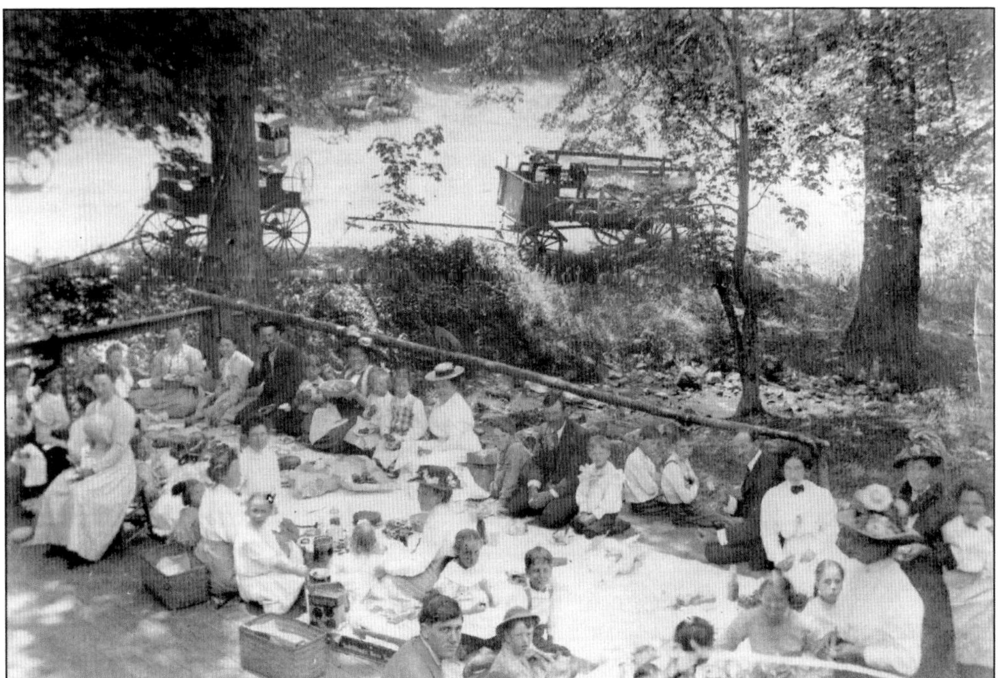

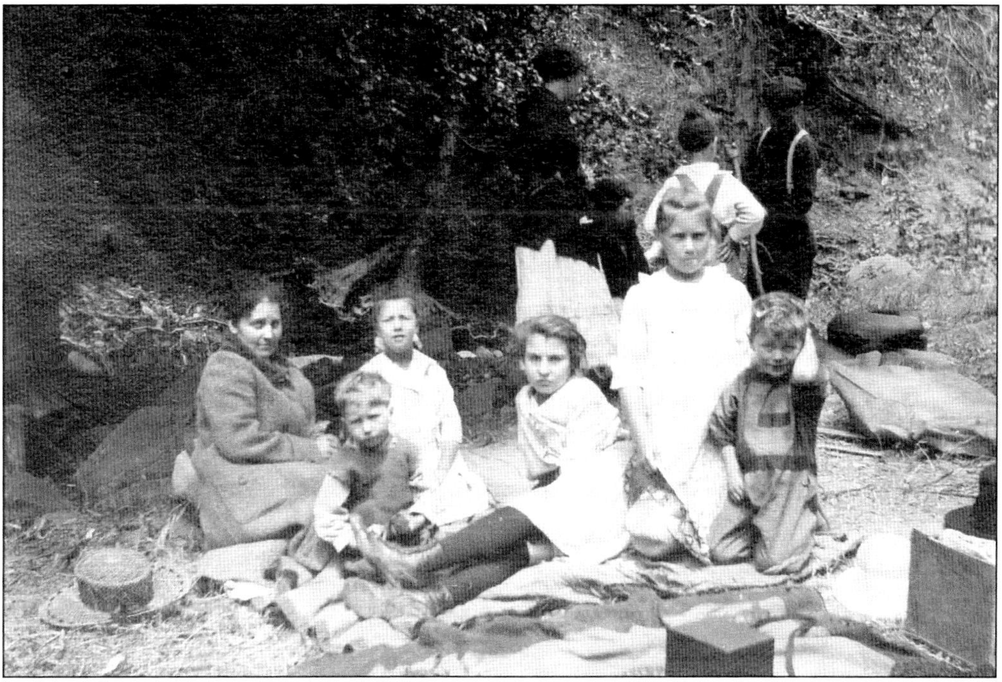

This 1918 photograph was taken at Mitchell Canyon Park. Facing the camera, from left to right, are Lena Tavaarossi, Norman Bloching, Irene Schwartz, Virginia Marshall, Madonna Schwartz, and Alfred Schwartz.

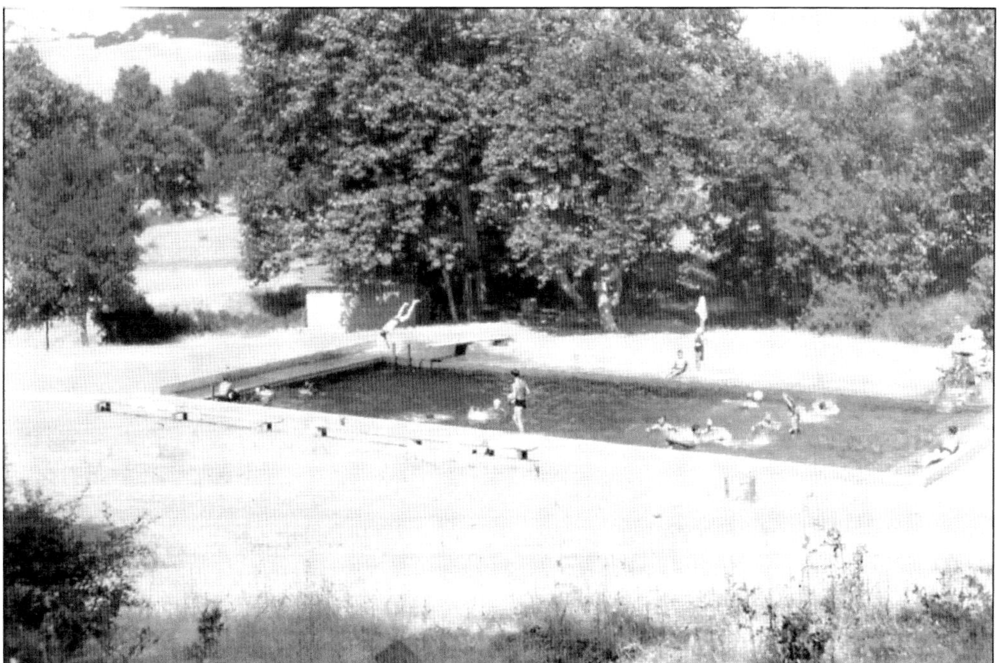

Curry Creek Park in Morgan Territory was a popular picnic ground, as shown in this 1937 photograph. Sylvester Olosfon founded the park in 1925, and the cement pool was constructed in 1933.

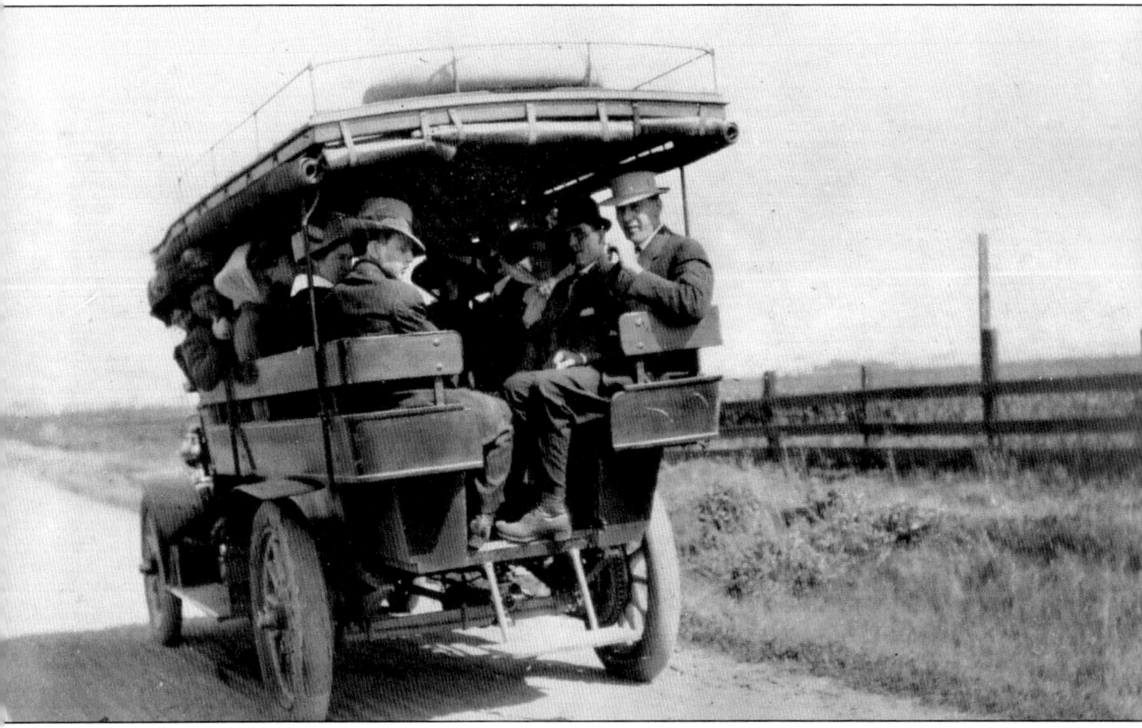

An early automobile "picnic stage" replaced horses and shank's mare as the preferred mode of transportation for picnickers.

Five

CHARACTERS AND ODDITIES

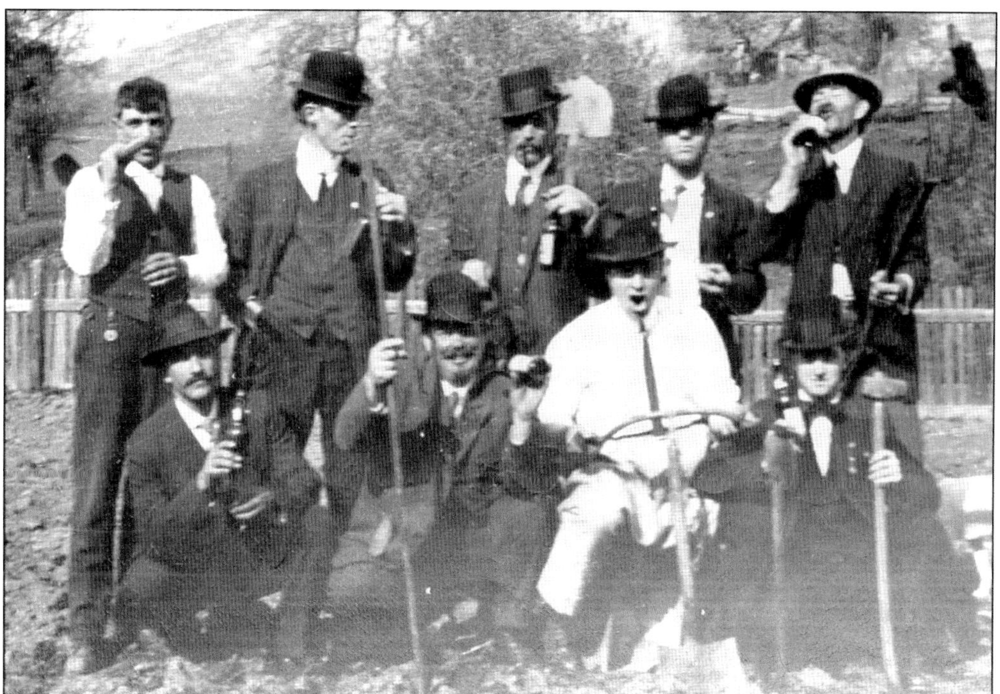

Clayton attracted its share of characters. They were fun-loving people not afraid to be themselves. Dramatic events were big news.

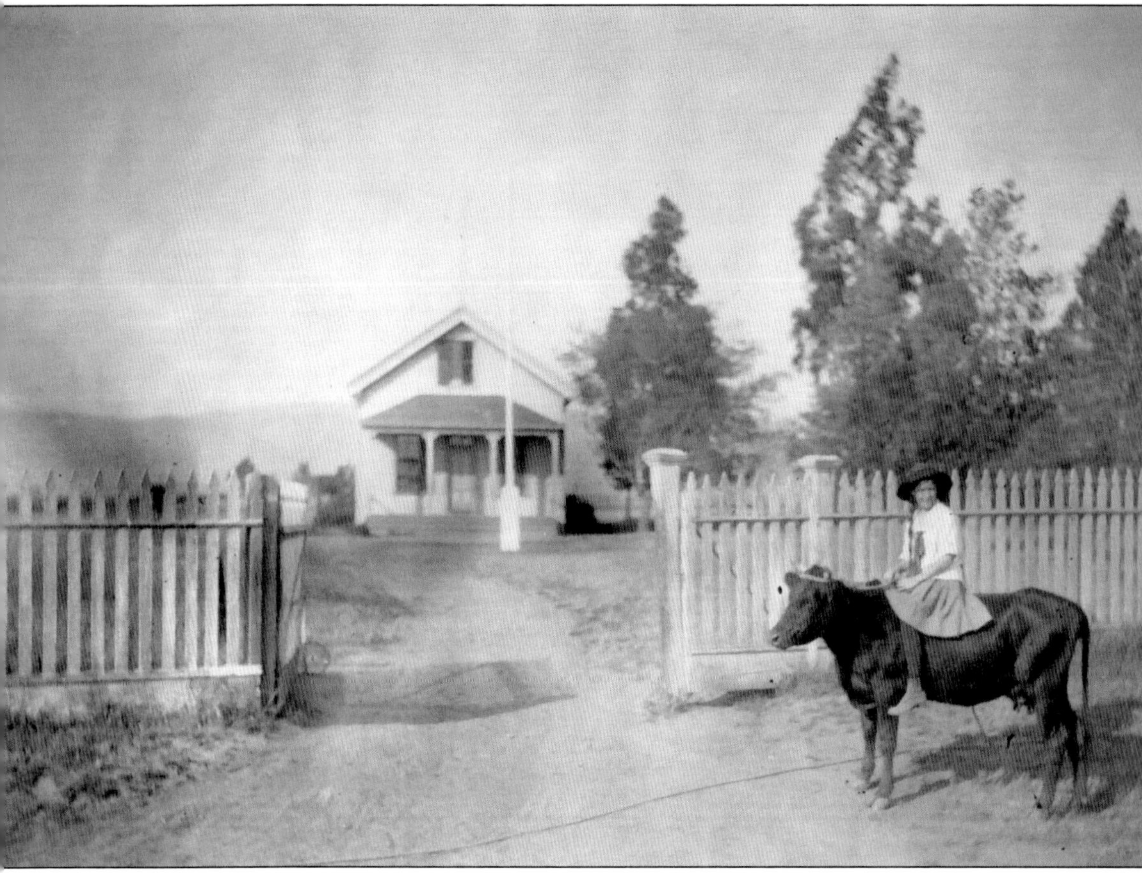

Marjorie Claire Matheson rode a cow to Lime Quarry School. Visitors to the Clayton area from New York took this picture around 1912. They promised to send her a photograph and when Marjorie's long awaited package arrived, it was addressed only to "The Little Girl Who Rides the Cow, Contra Costa County, California." That scant address was enough to reach her.

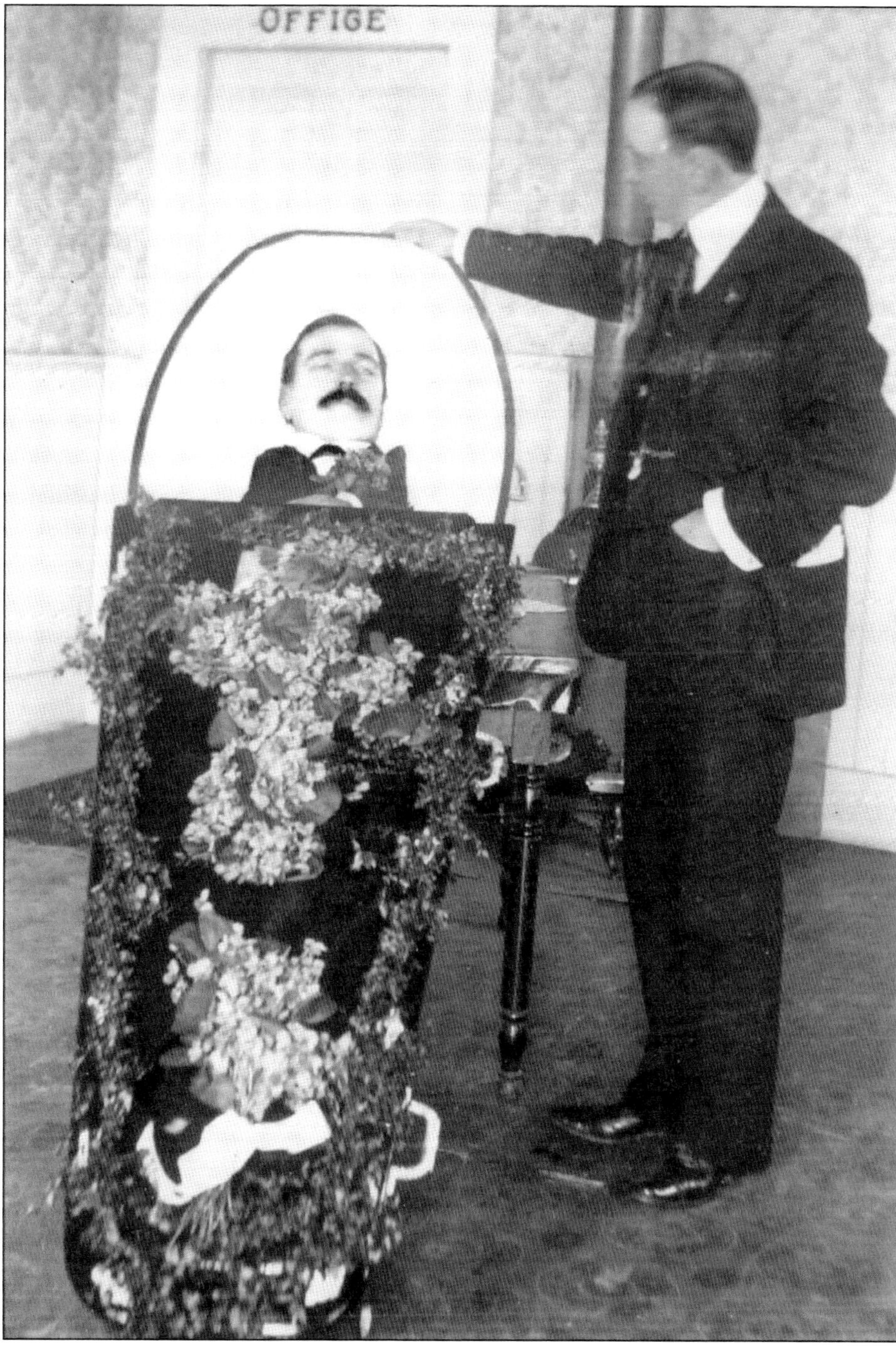

Albert Crandall is pictured in his coffin with undertaker Henry Curry standing near. Crandall was killed by "Doc" William Ryder Powell, an eccentric who lived in a San Francisco streetcar on section 29 on the Marsh Creek divide. In an altercation, Powell accused Crandall of trespassing, even though the land involved did not belong to Powell. Crandall was fatally shot. One month later, in June 1904, a similar trespassing incident occurred between Powell and M. P. Cardoza. Powell was the loser in that exchange of gunfire.

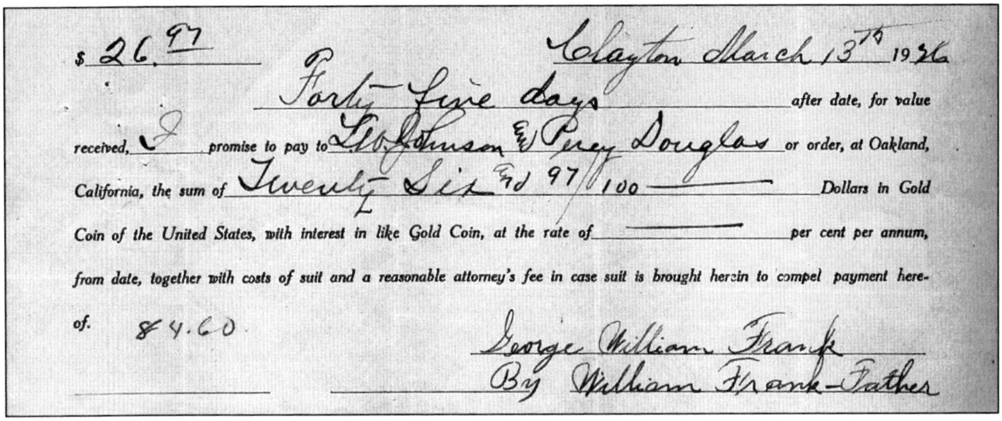

$ 26.97 Clayton March 13th 1926

Forty five days after date, for value received, I promise to pay to L. O. Johnson & Percy Douglas or order, at Oakland, California, the sum of Twenty Six and 97/100 Dollars in Gold Coin of the United States, with interest in like Gold Coin, at the rate of —— per cent per annum, from date, together with costs of suit and a reasonable attorney's fee in case suit is brought herein to compel payment hereof.

84.60

George William Frank
By William Frank–Father

In 1926, when he was 14 years old, George Frank was fined $26.97 for illegal hunting. The game warden caught him shooting a cottontail rabbit and George's father had to sign the promissory note for him.

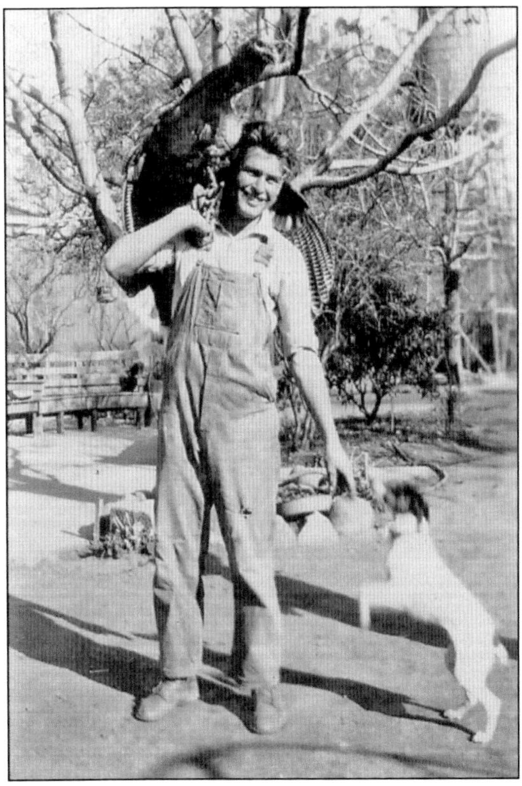

George Frank poses for the camera with a turkey on his shoulder and a dog at his hand.

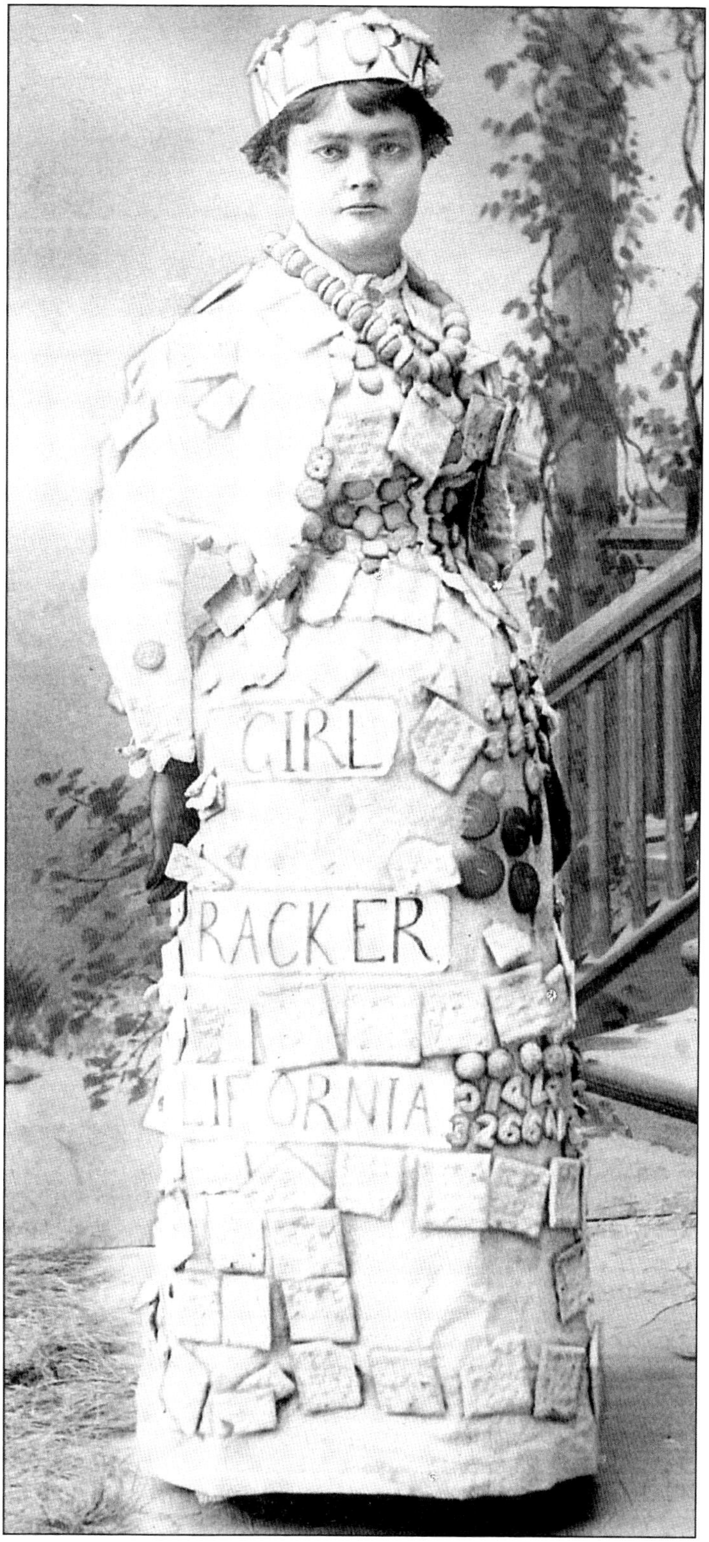

Mabel Trette, daughter of blacksmith Charles H. Trette, was photographed in her California Cracker Girl dress. Note the lovely cracker detail at the waistline and the stunning cracker necklace.

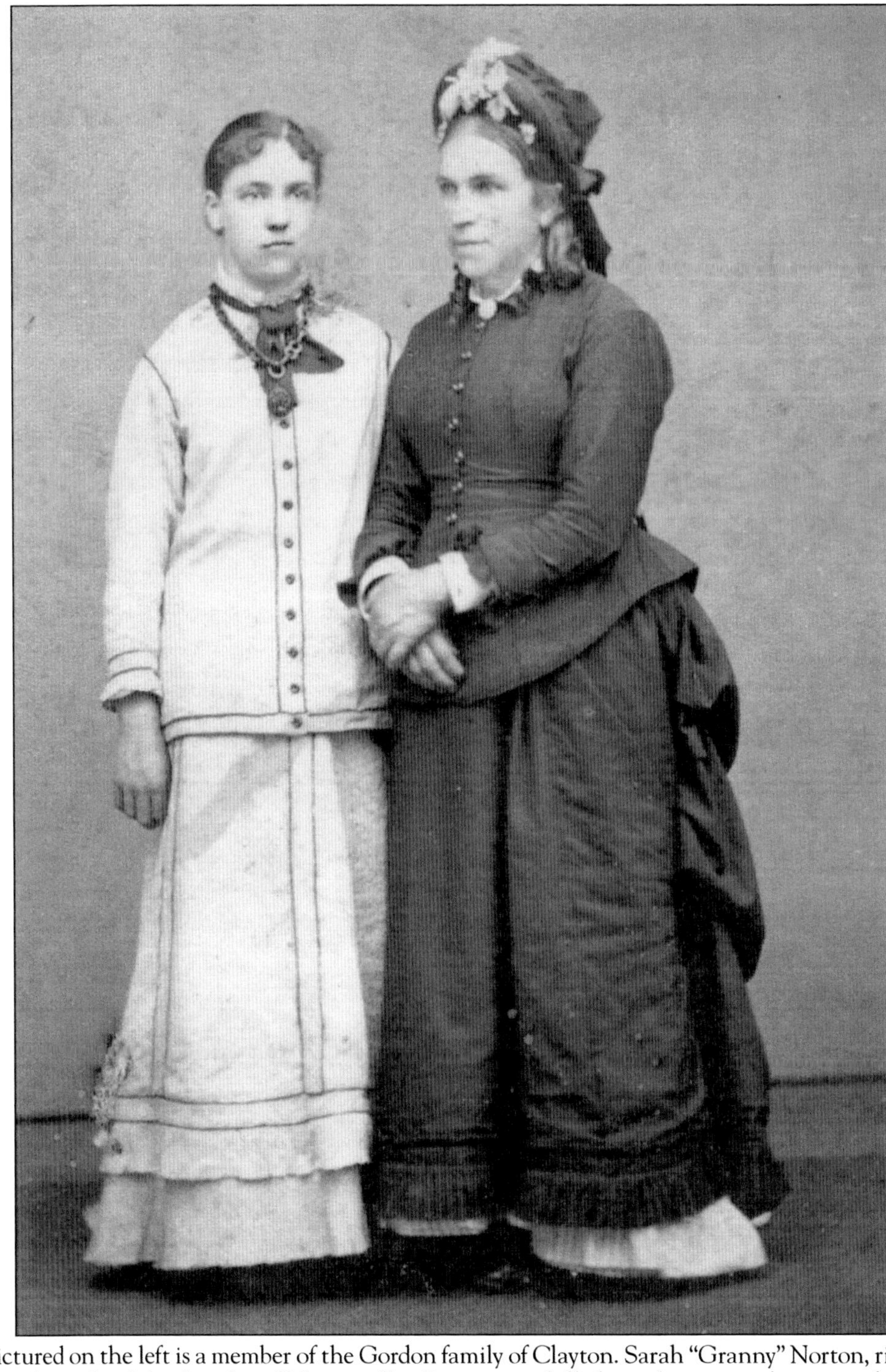

Pictured on the left is a member of the Gordon family of Clayton. Sarah "Granny" Norton, right, was the wife of the founder of Nortonville. Granny was killed in a buggy accident caused by a runaway horse in 1879 when she had been summoned to Clayton to perform midwife services. Morgan E. James was held responsible for her death for allowing the use of a horse that could not be trusted in harness.

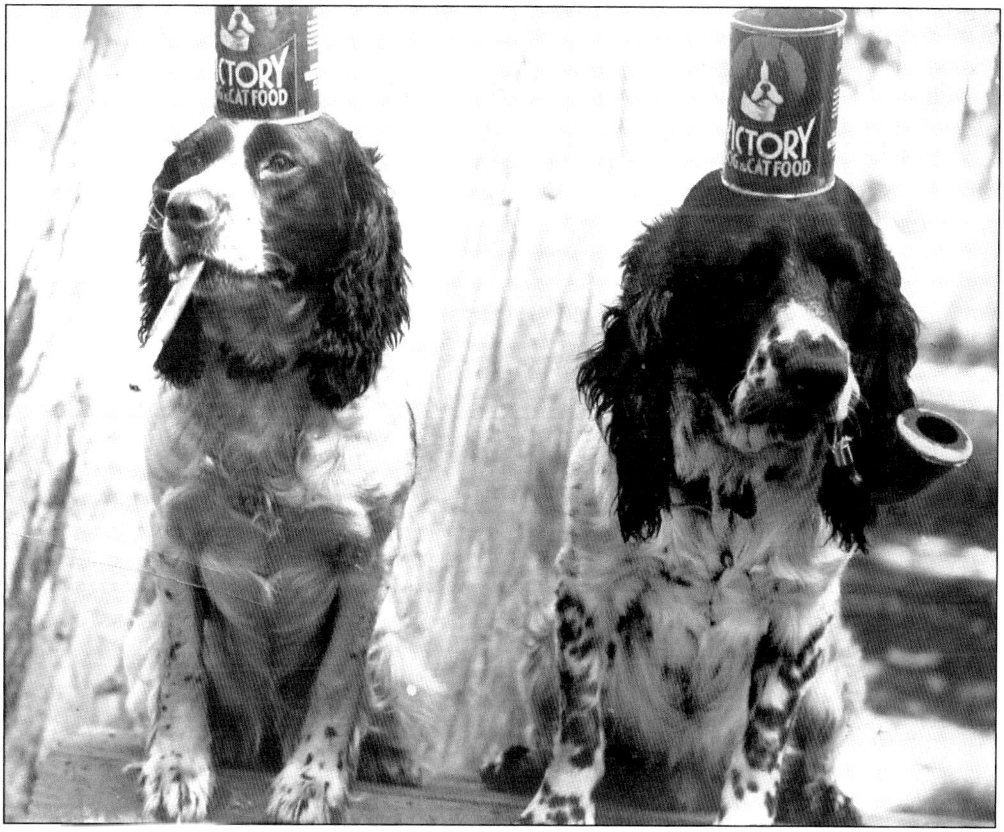

Leslie "Doug" Mitchell taught his dogs to balance cans on their heads and to "smoke" cigars. The reverse side of Doug's business card read, "I have 18 years experience in training and am capable of training all kinds of quail dogs. Spoiled dogs a specialty. Price, per season of two months, $25 and $50."

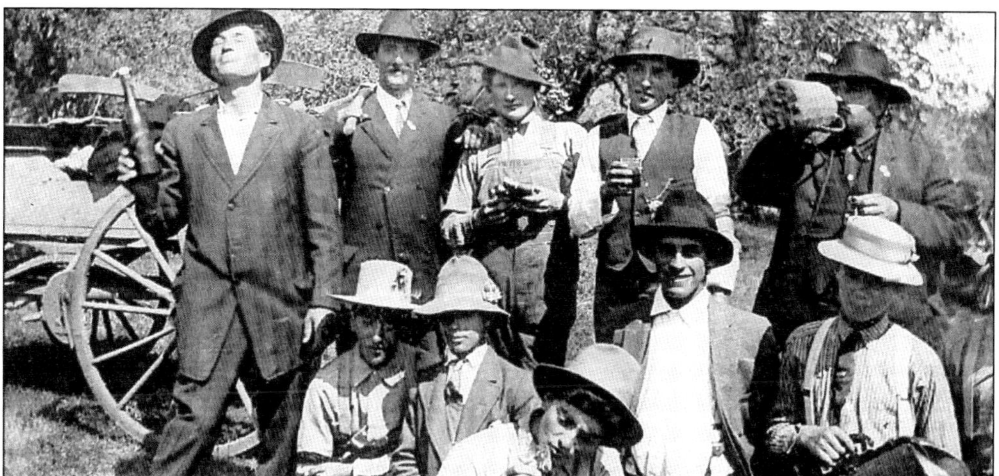

In the 1920s, these characters had a fine time at Mitchell Canyon Park. Pictured here, from left to right, are (first row) unidentified, unidentified, Tony Joaquin, Ben Correa Azevedo, and unidentified; (second row) Tony Gomez, Manuel Joaquin, and three unidentified men.

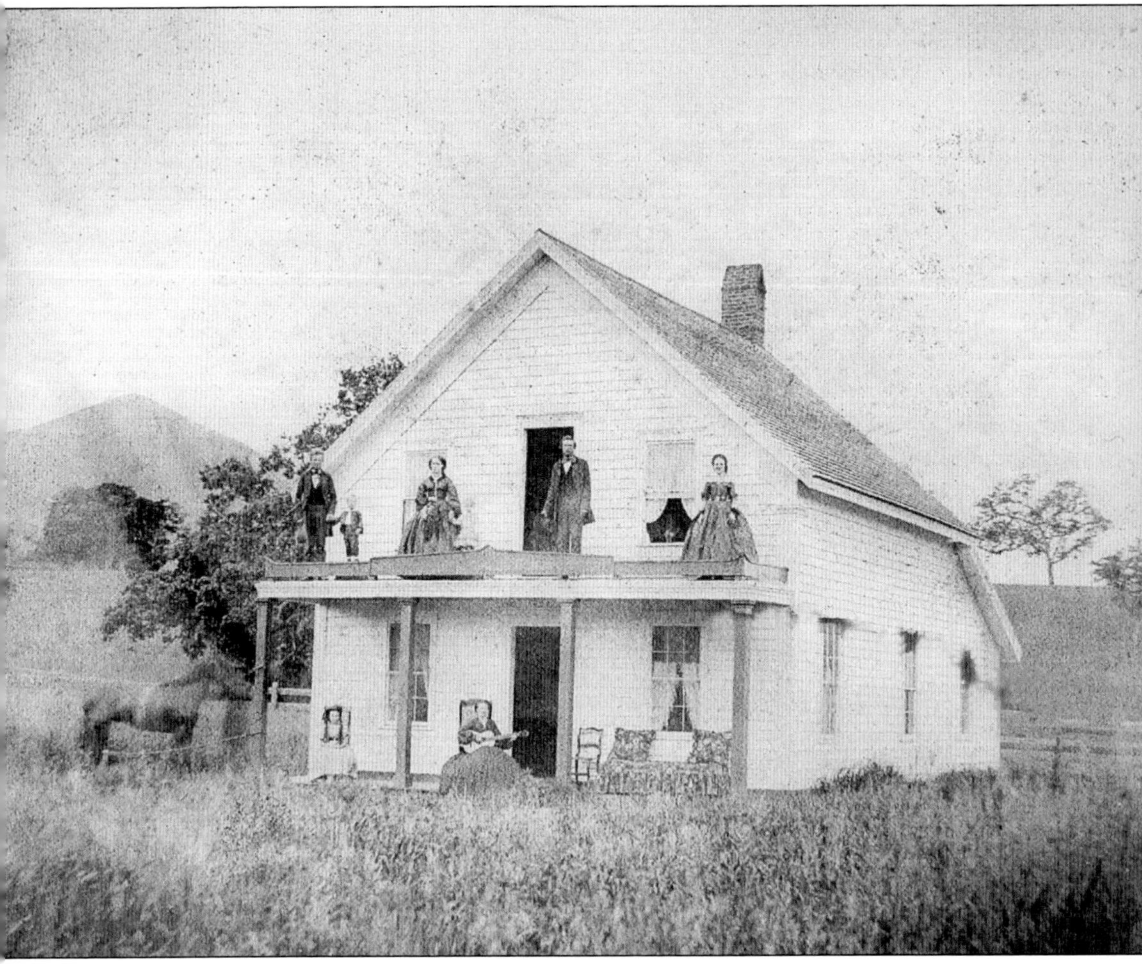

The members of the Graves family and Mrs. Stranahan pose in their best clothes. Note the indoor furniture on the porch and a horse tied up in this early photograph.

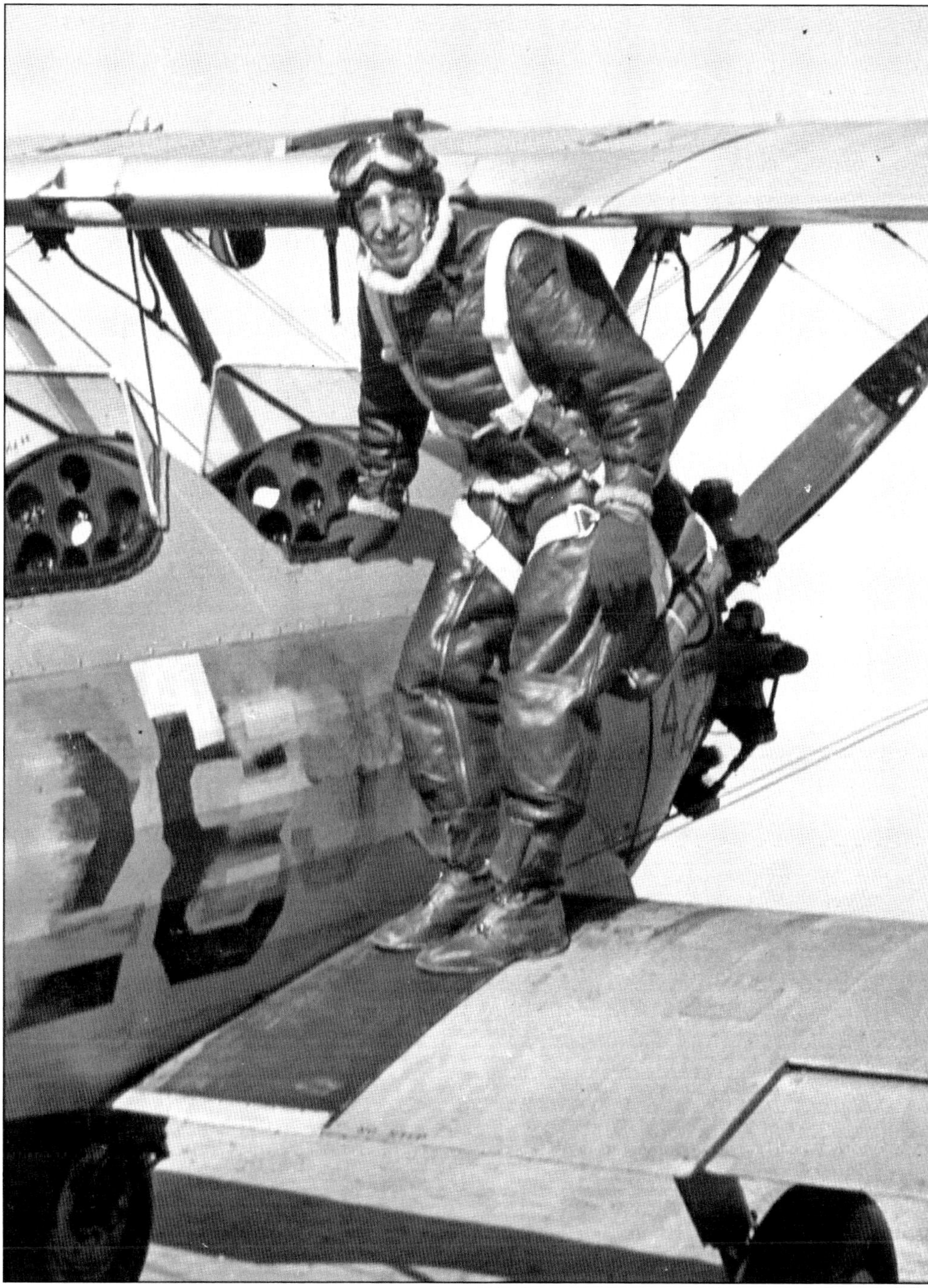

Andy Berendsen was noted for flying his Stearman airplane. In June 1948, he was performing stunts for members of the Martinez Gun Club, who were picnicking in Clayton, when the plane crashed in the Clayton hills. Andy was killed, and his nephew Andy Bloching, was seriously injured but survived. This photograph was taken just before his last flight.

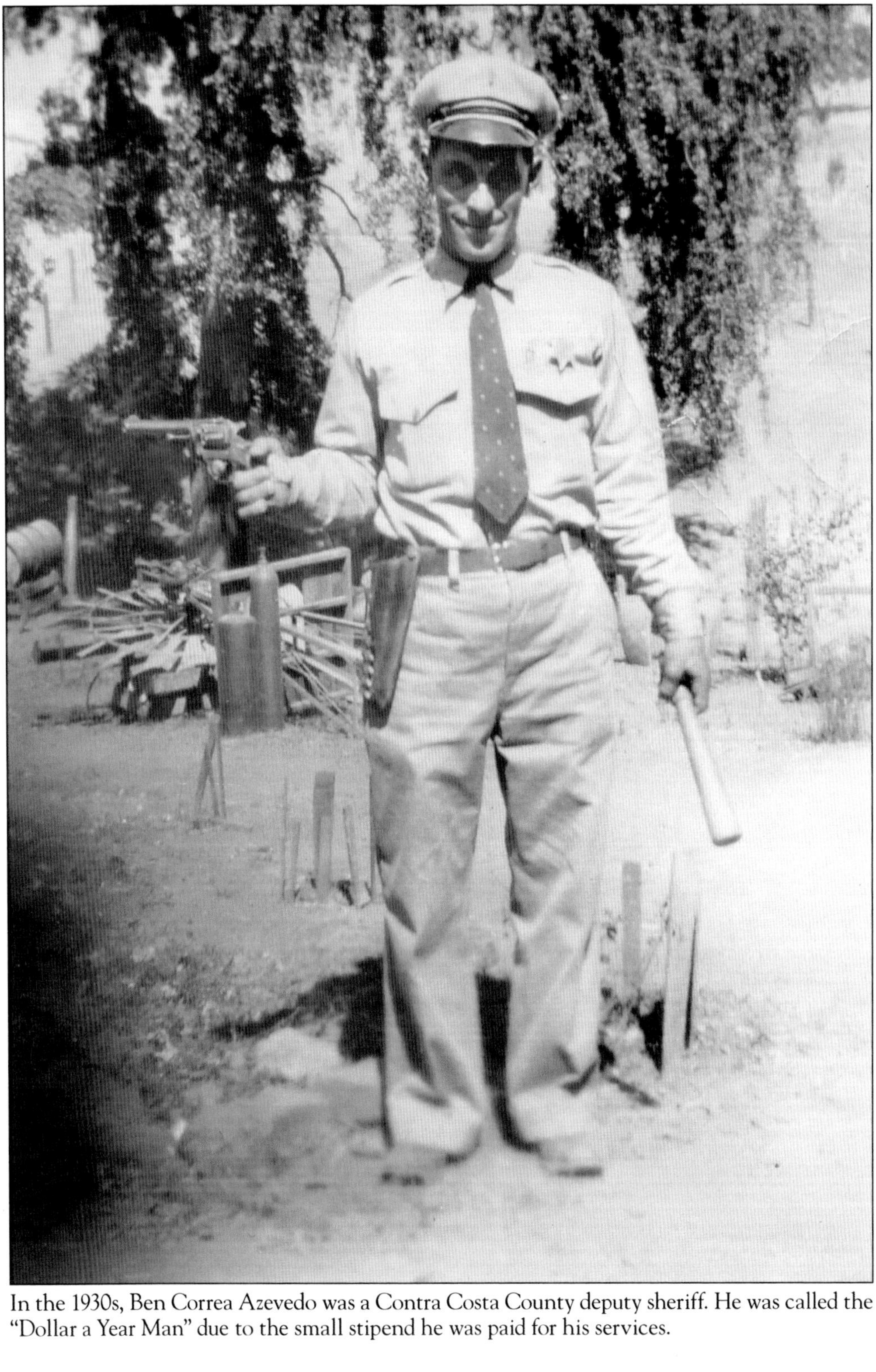

In the 1930s, Ben Correa Azevedo was a Contra Costa County deputy sheriff. He was called the "Dollar a Year Man" due to the small stipend he was paid for his services.